Prisons 2000

An International Perspective on the Current State and Future of Imprisonment

Edited by

Roger Matthews
Reader in Criminology and Sociology
Middlesex University

and

Peter Francis
Director of the Centre for
Criminal Justice Studies, and
Lecturer in Criminology
University of Northumbria at Newcastle

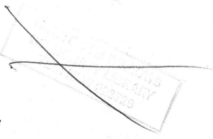

First published in Great Britain 1996 by
MACMILLAN PRESS LTD
Houndmills, Basingstoke, Hampshire RG21 6XS
and London
Companies and representatives
throughout the world

A catalogue record for this book is available
from the British Library.

ISBN 0–333–64479–4 hardcover
ISBN 0–333–64480–8 paperback

First published in the United States of America 1996 by
ST. MARTIN'S PRESS, INC.,
Scholarly and Reference Division,
175 Fifth Avenue,
New York, N.Y. 10010

ISBN 0–312–16096–8

Library of Congress Cataloging-in-Publication Data
available from Library of Congress

10   9   8   7   6   5   4   3   2   1
05   04   03   02   01   00   99   98   97   96

Printed and bound in Great Britain by
Antony Rowe Ltd, Chippenham, Wiltshire

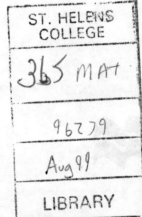

Contents

vi   *Contents*

Notes on the Contributors

Katerina Angelopoulou is a doctoral candidate in criminology and is associated with the Centre for Penal and Criminological Research (CPCR), at the University of Athens. She is currently working in the Department of Penal Sciences at the University of Athens, where her main interest lies in criminology and human rights abuses, especially the violent behaviour of state officials.

Kristel Beyens holds degrees in sociology and criminology and works as a researcher at the Free University of Brussels. Her research focuses on penal matters such as prison overcrowding and the privatization of prisons. She has published two books (in Dutch) and a number of articles in collaboration with Sonja Snacken. Currently she is preparing a PhD on sentencing policy.

Pat Carlen is Professor and Head of the Department of Criminology at Keele University. She was a founder member of Women in Prison and has published numerous books, five of them on women, crime and imprisonment.

Francis T. Cullen is Distinguished Research Professor in the Department of Criminal Justice at the University of Cincinnati, where he also holds a joint appointment in sociology. He is author of *Rethinking Crime and Deviance Theory* (1984), co-author (with K. Gilbert) of *Reaffirming Rehabilitation* (1982), (with W. J. Maakestad and G. Cavender) of *Corporate Crime Under Attack* (1987), (with J. R. Lilly and R. A. Ball) of *Criminological Theory* (1995) and (with G. Sykes) of *Criminology* (1992), and co-editor (with V. S. Burton) of *Contemporary Criminological Theory* (1994). He has served as President of the Academy of Criminal Justice Sciences and as editor of *Justice Quarterly* and the *Journal of Crime and Justice*.

Claude Faugeron is a sociologist and a Research Director at the Centre National de la Recherche Scientifique (CNRS). She has directed the Institut de Recherche Sociologique sur les Sociétés Contemporaines (IRESCO) and the Centre de Recherches sur le Droit et les Institutions

Notes on the Contributors

Pénales (CESDIP). Her main publications include *La Justice et son Public: Les Représentations Sociales du Système Pénal* (1978) and *Les Forces Cachées de la Justice: La Crise de la Justice Pénale* (1980). Claude Faugeron has been involved in the development of prison policies and prison administration and teaches at the Ecole des Hautes Etudes en Sciences Sociales.

Marian FitzGerald is a Principal Research Officer in the Home Office Research and Statistics Directorate, where she has special responsibility for work on 'race relations'/'race' equality issues generally and for criminal justice research related to this. She previously worked as a freelance researcher. Her publications have covered 'race' and politics, 'race relations' policies in local government and racial harassment as well as 'race' and criminal justice issues. She is the author of *'Ethnic Minorities and the Criminal Justice System* (1993)', which was published by the Royal Commission on Criminal Justice.

Peter Francis is a Lecturer in Criminology in the School of Social, Political and Economic Sciences and Director of the Centre for Criminal Justice Studies at the University of Northumbria. He is currently involved in research evaluating a project developing mediation services for prisoners and co-ordinating a two-year research project looking at young people, drug use and crime in north-east England.

Roy D. King is Professor and Director of the Centre for Comparative Criminology and Criminal Justice at the University of Wales, Bangor. Educated at the Universities of Leicester, Cambridge and the London School of Economics, he has held research fellowships at the Medical Research Council, the University of London Institute of Education and Yale Law School and teaching positions at the University of Southampton and the University of Wisconsin, Madison. He has written a number of books including: *A Taste of Prison* (with Rod Morgan, 1976), *Albany: Birth of a Prison - End of an Era* (with Kenneth W. Elliott, 1978), *The Future of the Prison System* (with Rod Morgan, 1980), *Prisons in Context* (with Mike Maguire, eds, 1994) and *The State of Our Prisons* (with Kathleen McDermott, 1995). He has also written numerous articles and contributions to books and is presently engaged in writing a book on the Russian system of corrective labour.

Nikos Koulouris is a doctoral candidate in criminology. He is associated with the Centre for Penal and Criminological Research (CPCR), and a member of the Laboratory of Criminological Sciences at the University of Thrace. His main interests lie in theoretical criminology and prison reform.

Peter Marshall is a Senior Research Officer in the Home Office Research and Statistics Directorate. His research interests include corrections, recidivism and effectiveness of treatment interventions with offenders, particularly sexual offenders.

Roger Matthews is a Reader in Criminology and Sociology in the Department of Sociology and Social Policy at Middlesex University. He has edited several books including *Informal Justice?* (1988), *Privatizing Criminal Justice* (1989) and (with J. Young) *Issues in Realist Criminology* (1992).

Alexander S. Mikhlin is Professor of Law and Honoured Scientist of the Russian Federation. He is now the Chief Researcher at the Research Institute of the Russian Federation (formerly of the Soviet Union) where he has worked for the last three decades. His principal fields of interest are in criminal and correctional law and he is the author of more than 300 publications including some fifty books and occasional papers, several of which have been published in the West. His most recent publications include commentaries on the Criminal Code and the Correctional Code of the Russian Federation.

Wayne Morrison teaches criminology and jurisprudence in the Faculty of Law at Queen Mary and Westfield College, London. His research interests are in the areas of legal theory and criminology and he is currently working on a book on jurisprudence in the changing contexts of modernity, and has recently written an undergraduate text in criminology for law students entitled *Theoretical Criminology: From Modernity to Post-Modernism* (1995).

Monika Platek is an Assistant Professor in the Faculty of Law at Warsaw University. She studied at the University of Oslo and became involved in comparative criminal justice and European parliamentary systems, and more recently she has been Visiting Professor at the University of Chicago (1992–94).

Margaret Shaw is an Assistant Professor in the Department of Sociology and Anthropology at Concordia University, Montreal, and a Research Associate at the Simone de Beauvoir Institute. She has worked as a criminologist and social policy adviser since 1964, first in the Home Office Research and Planning Unit in England, and since 1986 in Canada as an independent research consultant. She has a particular interest in women in conflict with the law, and has undertaken a number of studies of women's imprisonment in Canada for the federal and provincial governments.

Sonja Snacken holds degrees in law and criminology and is Professor of Criminology, Penology and the Sociology of Law at the Free University of Brussels. She has published books on sentencing, prison overcrowding and privatization of prisons in Dutch and a number of articles in French and English on the Belgian prison system, prisoners' rights, pre-trial detention, short- and long-term prisoners and other penal matters.

Richard Sparks teaches criminology at Keele University, having previously worked at the Open University and the University of Cambridge. He has written on a number of aspects of prisons and penal policy including: regimes in long-term prisons; prison disorders; international comparisons in prison populations; and the politics of prison privatization. He is co-editor (with John Muncie) of *Imprisonment: European Perspectives* (1991) and co-author (with Keith Bottomley and Alison Liebling) of *An Evaluation of Barlinnie and Shotts Units* (1994) and (with Tony Bottoms and Will Hay) of *Prisons and the Problem of Order* (1996). He is also the author of *Television and the Drama of Crime* (1992).

Calliope Spinellis is Professor of Criminology and Penology at the University of Athens Law School and Director of the Centre for Penal and Criminological Research at the same university. Professor Calliope Spinellis holds a Doctor of Comparative Law degree from the University of Chicago Law School and a postdoctoral degree from the Law School of the University of Athens, Greece. She has served on a number of law-drafting committees of the Greek Ministry of Justice and is the author of a number of books and articles, including *Crime and Criminology in Greece* (1983), *Custodial and Non-Custodial Sanctions in the Greek*

Penal Code and in Practice (1988), *Human Rights in Greek Prisons* (1993) and a technical report to the Council of Europe, *Ethnic Groups in Greek Prisons and their Human Rights* (1994).

Jody L. Sundt is a doctoral candidate in the Department of Criminal Justice at the University of Cincinnati. She has written on penal policy, and her current research interests include corrections, criminology and gender studies.

Chris Tchaikovsky is Director of Women in Prison, a charity she founded in 1983 together with Pat Carlen and which has the specific aim of working for women prisoners. In addition to delivering many lectures on the meaning of imprisonment from a decarcerationist perspective, she is the author of a number of articles and reports on women's imprisonment.

Stephen Tumim became a circuit judge in 1978 and was HM Chief Inspector of Prisons for England and Wales between 1978 and 1995. Educated at St Bede's School, Oxford, St Edward's School, Oxford (open scholar), and Worcester College, Oxford (open scholar), he was called to the bar, Middle Temple, 1955. Since this time he has chaired a number of committees and societies. Judge Tumim has written two books – *Great Legal Disasters* (1983) and *Great Legal Fiascos* (1985) –along with a number of occasional reviews and commentaries.

Patricia Van Voorhis is an Associate Professor of Criminal Justice at the University of Cincinnati, with an additional appointment in the Center for Women's Studies. She is the author of *Psychological Classification of the Adult Male Inmate* (1994), and co-author (with D. Lester and M. Braswell) of *Correctional Counselling* (1992). In addition, she has authored numerous articles in such journals as *Justice Quarterly*, *Criminology*, *The Prison Journal*, *Criminal Justice and Behaviour*, *Federal Probation* and the *Journal of Research in Crime and Delinquency*.

Acknowledgements

The idea for this volume developed out of a conference we organized at the University of Leicester during the spring of 1994. Our sincere thanks go to all those involved in supporting and assisting with the presentation of this conference, especially John Benyon, Francis White and Julie Trickey, as well as to the four hundred delegates who travelled from over thirty countries world-wide to participate.

Some of the papers which were initially presented at that conference have been revised – extensively in some cases – for this volume. Others were specially commissioned. Our deep thanks go to all those who agreed to contribute and to Annabelle Buckley at Macmillan for her support and encouragement. Last, but by no means least, our thanks to Heidi Robinson for preparing the final manuscript.

London and Newcastle   ROGER MATTHEWS
                                                                    PETER FRANCIS

Towards 2000: An Introduction
Roger Matthews and Peter Francis

As we approach the new millennium it is an appropriate time to look back over recent developments and to consider future options. Anticipating the future is an uncertain but nevertheless necessary activity, since the direction and pace of change is never inevitable but rather a consequence of choices and decisions which we make now. In respect to imprisonment a reappraisal of possible future options seems to be particularly appropriate since even over the last decade the nature of imprisonment appears to have undergone a relatively radical transformation in terms of its functions, organization, and the size and make-up of prison populations.

In this volume an international group of authors provide an evaluation of the changing role of imprisonment in contemporary society and explore the possibilities for penal reform. In the course of their exploration, and working from a number of perspectives, they tackle a variety of critical issues currently associated with the use of imprisonment.

One recurring issue which policymakers and penologists have discussed at length in recent years is whether the increased use of imprisonment can reduce the level of crime. In a number of countries, including Britain and America, the response to this question has been that 'getting tough' on crime means 'getting tough' on offenders. Consequently, it is argued that sending more people to prison for longer periods in increasingly harsh regimes will deter prospective offenders and take those who have been convicted off the street. This approach, recently dubbed the 'punishment paradigm', has become increasingly popular (Cullen and Wright, 1995). The prison building programmes which have occurred in a number of western countries and the growing emphasis upon military style regimes are testimony to this development as are the numerous examples of increasing incarceration rates across the globe.

Justification for proceeding in this direction has been provided by the premature rejection of the rehabilitative ideal during the 1970s and the cynicism that was expressed by a number of influential commentators regarding the possibilities of developing effective 'alternatives' to custody. The combination of these two developments, together with the accompanying pessimism concerning the possibility and desirability of reducing the numbers of people in prison, has resulted in an increased reliance upon incarceration and the transformation, in some cases, of

1

prisons into 'warehouses', and 'penal dustbins'. The ultimate attraction of the 'punishment paradigm' to its advocates has been its self-justifying character. On the one hand, if crime rates fall it can be claimed that this is a consequence of 'get tough' methods. On the other, if crime rates increase the intractability of the crime rate is taken not as evidence of the limits of harsh punishment but the need for more punitive measures (Clear, 1994).

The relationship between crime and imprisonment is, however, more complex than these accounts suggest (Box, 1987). The determinants of crime levels go far beyond prevailing systems of punishment, while the selection and deployment of methods of punishment are in turn conditioned by a number of socio-economic and cultural conditions as recent historical analysis has shown (Foucault, 1977; Ignatieff, 1978). Thus whilst the general mood of punitiveness remains on the ascendancy internationally, and prison populations continue to increase in many countries, the 'punishment paradigm' is coming under attack from a number of critics (Irwin and Austin, 1994). This is due partly to the lack of any clear demonstrable evidence of the deterrent effects of more severe forms of punishment on the one hand, and the limits of incapacitation to affect the crime rate and improve public safety on the other.

For example, the numbers of people who would need to be incarcerated in order to make any real impact upon levels of offending is daunting. In America it has been estimated that because of the difficulties of prediction the level of incarceration would have to increase dramatically in order to effect even a small decrease in offending levels (Currie, 1985). In view of this, as Elliott Currie has argued, it would seem to make more sense to try to rehabilitate persistent offenders and thereby reduce crime, rather than merely pursue a policy of incapacitation.

> The point is obvious. If we can predict criminality through characteristics that are amenable to change, there is no *logical* reason why we should lock up certain individuals on the basis of these characteristics rather than trying to change them. (Currie, 1985: 97)

The soaring costs of incarceration and the growing recognition of the dangerous and alienating effects which warehousing can produce, not only on prisoners, but on their families and dependents, has forced policy makers to reconsider the role of imprisonment and to explore new avenues.

The 'punishment paradigm' has also been questioned by those who reject the 'nothing works' assertion in favour of arguments supporting the view that useful and constructive programmes have been developed in prisons in recent years (Palmer, 1992). A growing body of literature suggests that prison itself is a debilitating experience for many prisoners and that doing nothing for offenders who are incarcerated will in many cases mean that they will leave prison more marginalised and more committed to offending than they were when they entered the prison system. Particularly in relation to groups like sex offenders and those convicted of violent crimes, neglect and isolation in prison tends to reinforce earlier behavioural patterns. At the same time innovative and imaginative interventions which have been directed at these 'intractable' offenders have indicated positive results (Sampson, 1994).

The volume opens with a post-Woolf assessment of imprisonment and the prison system of England and Wales by Judge Stephen Tumim, who suggests that prisons if properly organized, can make a positive contribution to society and that constructive rehabilitative work can be developed within them. On the basis of his considerable experience as Her Majesty's Chief Inspector of Prisons he argues for the development of regimes which allow prisoners to engage in paid productive work and which respond to and cater for the needs of different types of prisoners.

There are no universal penal policies which can be applied to the prison population as a whole. It is necessary, Judge Tumim argues, to begin from an understanding of the roles of different types of penal establishments and the nature of the resources which are available. From this starting point it is possible to develop realistic policies which can promote healthier prison regimes and which can involve a closer working relationship with community representatives. This closer working relationship between the prison and the community, he suggests, can help to reduce the alienating effects of imprisonment thereby encouraging prisoners to lead a less anti-social existence on leaving prison.

Thus Judge Tumim argues for the re-establishment of rehabilitation as one of the primary objectives of penal policy and questions the assertion made by the British Home Secretary, Michael Howard, that 'prison works'. Indeed, Judge Tumim calls for the development of prison regimes which while maintaining personal security are able to develop the skills and the self-confidence which will enable prisoners to address the reasons for their offending and the personal and social problems which they may experience both inside and outside prison.

It is ironic that when Michael Howard claimed 'prison works' he used America as his primary point of reference. As Francis Cullen, Patricia Van Voorhis and Jody Sundt suggest in their chapter the American prison system is currently in the throes of a deep and multi-layered crisis. This crisis or rather crises, they argue, goes far beyond the problems associated with overcrowding and deteriorating conditions. With over 1.5 million men and women in state, federal and local prisons in 1994, and with an incarceration rate over 500 per 100 000 in certain states such as Texas, the apparently relentless increases in the prison population are disturbing.

Like Judge Tumim, Cullen, Van Voorhis and Sundt are also critical of the adoption of incapacitation strategies and argue instead for the reaffirmation of rehabilitation. Drawing upon the experiences of 'what works' in prisons to reduce recidivism they suggest an alternative strategy centred around the development of treatment programmes designed to reduce the commitment to offending and enhance individual competencies.

As America and Britain continue to role back welfare provision, the question arises of what effect these socio-economic changes will have on the nature of imprisonment. Monika Platek, looking at this issue from the perspective of post-revolutionary Poland, raises the question of whether it is possible for Poland to achieve the levels of production and consumption which are enjoyed in many advanced western societies without at the same time embracing their penal policies. Taking Norway as an example of an advanced western society which offers a relatively humane approach combined with the parsimonious use of imprisonment, she asks if it is possible to combine an American-style economy giving a high level of national wealth with a reasonably humane prison system.

Platek's contribution raises the question of how the role of imprisonment has altered historically and how its operation is influenced by changing economic, political and cultural circumstances. A related question arises concerning the role of the prison in periods of recession and growing unemployment. Richard Sparks' contribution addresses this issue and examines the extent to which the recent emphasis upon penal austerity involves a reassertion of the principle of 'less eligibility'. Despite the progressive reforms which have been promoted over the last century, the principle of 'less eligibility', which Rusche and Kirchheimer (1969) identified as a fundamental constraint on the improvement of prison conditions, has continued, Sparks argues, as a 'suppressed but constraining presence in penal discourse and practice'. Echoing the concerns expressed by Platek, Sparks' contribution explores the parameters and determinants of penal reform, and in particular the ways in which the rhetoric of greater austerity interconnects with the problems of legitimacy which have resurfaced in recent years.

The changing role of imprisonment during the current period of post-modernity and post-industrialization is the focus of Wayne Morrison's chapter. Morrison is concerned with analyzing the historic relationship between modernity with its emphasis upon the promotion of rights and justice and of social progress through the application of science and the emergence of the modern prison. How is the prison implicated in the dialectic of freedom and repression, and of liberty and discipline? Following through this analysis Morrison goes on to ask the critical question of what role prisons play in the era of post-modernity.

From a slightly different vantage point Claude Faugeron also examines the changing functions of imprisonment in the current period. She argues that the prison is increasingly concerned with the discipline of a distinctly different population than its nineteenth-century counterpart. It is her contention that the use of custody in the present period is changing significantly and that this involves a changing relationship between the four fundamental functions of penal confinement – the custodial function, the restorative function, the controlling function and the maintenance function. Taking health and labour as points of reference Faugeron traces through the changing relationships between these core functions in recent years.

A continuing theme which runs through most of the papers in this volume is the changing composition of prison populations. Judge Tumim acknowledges 'the diversity of prisoners in terms of their social political and economic make up coupled with the issues of race and gender', while Wayne Morrison and Claude Faugeron draw attention to the changing nature of the 'problem populations' from which prisoners are drawn.

A central issue in this discussion, particularly in America, has been the disproportionate number of inmates who are drawn from minority groups. Recent research indicates that the chances of a black male experiencing imprisonment in America is six or seven times that of his white counterpart (Tonry, 1995). This widely circulated statistic has raised the issue of whether this disproportionality is a consequence of different levels and patterns of offending or whether it is the result of racist bias exercised by the police and other criminal justice agencies.

In their contribution, Marian FitzGerald and Peter Marshall address these issues within the British context. Drawing on three data sources – the National Prison Survey, material from the 1991 census, and data based on the new classification adopted by the prison service in 1992 – they examine the racial disparities in incarceration rates in Britain. It is their contention after reviewing the available literature, that the socio-economic versus discrimination debate rests upon – if not a false dichotomy – at least a strongly overstated dichotomization sustainable only on the basis of a very crude understanding of both the processes of discrimination and the links between crime and socio-economic factors. The importance of their analysis is that it attempts to avoid some of the limitations of Alfred Blumstein's 'racial disproportionality thesis' which suggests that ethnic differences in official data simply reflect actual ethnic differences in rates and patterns of offending (Blumstein, 1993).

The changing ethnic composition in prisons has also become a cause of some concern in Europe as the number of foreign prisoners locked up in European prisons increases yearly, with over thirty per cent of prisoners in some European countries being made up of non-nationals (Matthews, 1994). The extent of this development, which appears to be a function of changing mobility patterns throughout Europe, has resulted in what has been referred to as a dual system of incarceration; one for nationals and one for foreigners (Tomasevski, 1994).

Drawing on research conducted in Greece during the early 1990s, Calliope Spinellis, Katerina Angelopoulou and Nikos Koulouris examine the specific problems which arise not only for the prisoners but also for prison administrators as a result of the growing number of foreigners imprisoned in Greece each year. In many respects being a foreign prisoner is a 'second sentence' since those involved tend to experience a number of disadvantages associated with their alien status. Spinellis, Angelopoulou and Koulouris further examine the degree to which existing national and international legislation is able to safeguard the rights of foreign prisoners and ensure that they receive equitable and humane treatment.

Another area of growing concern is the imprisonment of women. Although the actual numbers of women incarcerated remains relatively low, the lack of attention given to the needs of female prisoners and the punitive disciplinary regimes which have been developed for women in some countries have attracted a substantial amount of critical commentary (Carlen, 1990; Eaton, 1993). Feminists have challenged the androcentric nature of imprisonment and in some countries begun to campaign for penal reforms to improve the nature of women's imprisonment. In a number of countries, including Britain, America, Australia and Canada, feminists have influenced penal policies and have lobbied for new programmes for women in prison.

Margaret Shaw in her contribution suggests 'that nowhere else has feminism made such marked inroads into official discourse than in Canada. Not only has there been a number of changes in the way women are perceived in society ... [but] ... ongoing policies and programmes relating to women offenders both inside and outside, and which are feminist in their conception, have also been established'. In reviewing legislative changes and policy documents she examines the principles which have informed the development of 'women centred' proposals for penal reform. These include: empowerment, the provision of meaningful choices, treating women with respect and dignity, providing a physically and emotionally supportive environment, and the sharing of responsibility for women's welfare between institutional staff, community members, and the women themselves. She then proceeds to evaluate the various interventions which have occurred in Canada in recent years, assesses the degree to which these principles have been implemented and examines their impact.

In a similar vein Pat Carlen and Chris Tchaikovsky raise further considerations in relation to the reform of women's imprisonment, specifically detailing some of the changes in the nature of womens imprisonment in Britain and the difficulties confronting prison reformers in general in increasing 'public awareness of the pains of women in penal custody' and of improving conditions. In opposition to the pessimists who argue that nothing can be done or that reforms will inevitably be incorporated into the 'repressive apparatus of the state', Pat Carlen and Chris Tchaikovsky argue from a 'utopian–realist' position that there have been significant reforms in recent years although many initiatives remain experimental and are often short lived.

Women in Prison and other campaigning groups have worked with prison administrators to improve services for hundreds of women and although these 'gains' may appear modest they are gains which can be built upon. In a climate of increasing punitiveness and increasing inequalities of wealth and income which have fallen most heavily on women over the last two decades, Carlen and Tchaikovsky maintain that those who are interested in promoting social justice must simultaneously address both the social inequalities which in future are likely to increase the number of women jailed, and the tendency in this context for the custodial conditions for women to deteriorate. Against the background of these changing material conditions the authors argue for the need to vigorously pursue realistic campaigning strategies while developing utopian theorizing, involving in this case the formation of a strategy for the abolition of women's imprisonment.

In assessing the possibilities of penal reform, one area which has received limited attention to date, is the changes which have taken place in Eastern Europe following the collapse of communist Russia. Comparatively little is known about the size, shape and structure of the Russian penal system, and of the conditions and regimes under which Russian prisoners live. Alexander Mikhlin and Roy King describe the appalling conditions which have been prevalent in Russia in the post-war period and the reforms which are currently under way to improve penal establishments in terms of administration, structure and purpose.

Following *Perestroika* there have been amnesties, the introduction of rehabilitation measures, the reduction in the length of sentences for some offences, increased visiting time and the recognition of certain prisoners' rights. However, given the rapid social changes which have taken place in recent years and the rising crime rates coupled with a failing economy there are signs that there will be a re-expansion of the prison population combined with a reduction in prison standards. With an estimated population of 760 000 inmates, and an increase of about 4000 prisoners per month, maintaining prison standards and safeguarding prisoners rights will undoubtedly come under increasing pressure in the near future.

One response to growing prison populations in a number of western countries has been the privatization of prisons. Privatization can take a number of different forms, but the most widely advocated and developed form in advanced western countries has been the shift towards the private management of institutions which were once run by the state (Matthews, 1989).

In assessing the spread of privatization Kristel Beyens and Sonja Snacken review the conditions and the rationales which lay behind this development. They show that the reasons for shifting towards the private management of prisons vary between countries. In America privatization has been justified in terms of rising prison populations and deteriorating prison conditions, while in Britain and Australia the introduction of privately owned prisons has been largely achieved through the lobbying of certain influential companies. It was evident in Britain, for example, that even when the prison population decreased towards the end of the 1980s and while certain newly built prisons stood half-empty there was still a call for the privatization of prisons. Interestingly, however, privatization has been less in evidence in western Europe. The French prison authorities toyed with the idea of privatization but like a number of their neighbours felt that the problems of legitimacy, responsibility and accountability were such that privatization of prisons was not a viable option.

In general, the contributions to this volume provide a unique set of international perspectives on recent and possible future developments in imprisonment. Although they employ a variety of perspectives they are unified in their scepticism about the value and effectiveness of the 'punitive paradigm' and are sensitive to the dangers of developing draconian systems of punishment. They also remain distanced from what Feeley and Simon (1994) have recently presented as the 'new penology' based on risk analysis with the objective of managing aggregates rather than changing individuals. This form of actuarial analysis aims at creating a more cost-effective system through the manipulation of 'inputs' and 'outputs' rather than by reducing recidivism. It is a form of administrative penology whose prime objective is cutting costs. It tends to promote the substitution of technology for people and has a close affinity with the private management of prisons.

By contrast, the articles in this collection gravitate towards what Cullen and Wright (1995) refer to as the 'progressive paradigm'. This focuses on issues related to the achievement of social justice and the safeguarding of prisoners' rights. It helps prisoners to take responsibility for their offending and to develop the skills and competencies which they will need to live 'a good and useful life'. The 'progressive paradigm' is also concerned with the standards in prisons, equitable and humane treatment for prisoners and the rejection of discriminatory practices.

From a perspective which analyses imprisonment in relation to the wider socio-economic community in which it operates, the 'progressive paradigm' expresses a commitment to reform. In opposition to the liberal pessimists who claim that reform is inevitably self-defeating or that it is preferable to do 'less good' rather than 'more harm', the progressive recognizes both the uncertainty and the necessity of reform. 'Non-intervention' is not a position of neutrality. Rather it is a position which accepts existing conditions and existing policies.

Thus, as we approach the twenty-first century we are faced with three broad choices with regards the future of imprisonment. First, the 'punishment paradigm' with its emphasis upon increased use of prisons and greater penal austerity on the premise that the combination of incapacitation and the deterrent functions of imprisonment will reduce crime and increase public safety. Secondly, there is the 'administrative paradigm' which is based on risk analysis and which claims to be a cost-effective way of managing aggregate populations through a greater reliance on technology.

The third option is the 'progressive paradigm' which is concerned with maintaining custodial standards and recognizing the needs of different types of offenders. At the same time it is concerned with the defence of prisoners' rights, attacking discriminatory policies and where possible re-establishing the links between prisons and the wider community. This involves developing prison regimes which promote meaningful opportunities for prisoners to improve themselves and to confront their anti-social behaviour. The decisions we make about these three alternatives are important. They will have a profound effect upon the future level of community safety and upon our attitudes not only to those who are incarcerated but also to ourselves.

References

Blumstein, A. (1993) 'Racial Disproportionality of US Prison Populations Revisited', *University of Colorado Law Review*, 64: 743–60.

Box, S. (1987) *Recession, Crime and Punishment*. (London: Macmillan).

Carlen, P. (1990) *Alternatives to Women's Imprisonment* (Milton Keynes: Open University Press).

Clear, T. (1994) *Harm in American Penology: Offenders, Victims and Their Communities* (Albany: SUNY Press).

Cullen, F. and Wright, J. (1995) 'The Future of Corrections', forthcoming in B. Maguire and P. Radosh (eds), *The Past, Present, and Future of American Criminal Justice* (New York: General Hall).

Currie, E. (1985) *Confronting Crime: An American Challenge* (New York: Pantheon).

Eaton, M. (1993) *Women After Prison* (Milton Keynes: Open University Press).

Feeley, M. M. and Simon, J. (1994) 'Actuarial Justice: The Emerging New Criminal Law' in D. Nelken (ed.) *The Futures of Criminology* (London: Sage) 173–201.

Foucault, M. (1977) *Discipline and Punish: The Birth of the Prison* (London: Allen Lane).

Irwin, J. and Austin, J. (1994) *It's About Time: America's Prison Binge* (Belmont, CA: Wadsworth).

Ignatieff, M. (1978) *A Just Measure of Pain*. (London: Macmillan).

Matthews, R. (1989) *Privatizing Criminal Justice* (London: Sage).

Matthews, R. (1994) *Prisoners Abroad: An Evaluation of the Role of the Consular Services* (Centre for Criminology, Middlesex University).

Palmer, T. (1992) *The Re-Emergence of Correctional Intervention* (London: Sage).

Rusche, G. and Kirchheimer, O. (1969) *Punishment and Social Structure* (New York: Columbia University Press).

Sampson, A. (1994) *Acts of Abuse: Sex Offenders and The Criminal Justice System* (London: Routledge).

Tomasevski, K. (1994) *Foreigners in Prison* (Helsinki: European Institute for Crime Prevention and Control).

Tonry, M. (1995) *Malign Neglect: Race, Crime and Punishment in America* (Oxford University Press).

1 The State of the Prisons
Stephen Tumim

As I walk along the landings of Her Majesty's Prisons I find myself addressing a number of basic questions. These include: what are prisons for?; what type of people go to prison?; and what impact does imprisonment have upon crime? The difficulty lies less in answering questions like these, but in framing and arranging them in the correct order. Additionally, in addressing such questions it is important to avoid the traps into which the current 'law and order' debate seems to have become enmeshed, driven as it is by prejudice and rhetoric and by what people expect and want to find rather than what is experienced.

WHAT ARE PRISONS FOR?

The short and admirable Prison Service *Statement of Purpose* hung prominently in every British prison provides a useful guide to the aims of imprisonment.

> Her Majesty's Prison Service serves the public by keeping in custody those committed by the Courts. Our duty is to look after them with humanity and help them lead law-abiding and useful lives in custody and after release.

I know no instruction with a more memorable and sharp message, and I regard it as a pity that recently the Prison Service has decided to wrap it up in the flannel of such sloppy words as 'purpose', 'vision', 'goals' and 'values', and other vapid, interchangeable and politically correct words and phrases. It is noteworthy that in the *Statement of Purpose* there is no mention of punishment and treatment. Punishment for prisoners is the deprivation of liberty imposed by the courts. Punishment is not the business of the prison service. Similarly, individuals who are sick and in need of treatment should be in hospital and not in prison. Prisoners, however, must be helped to take responsibility for their own lives.

What can be said of prisons, and this is appropriate for the majority of prisoners, is that they should be run as pre-release centres. From the moment the convicted prisoner goes to prison he or she should be actively helped to lead a law-abiding and useful life. The *Statement of Purpose* is not a bad text for an Inspector to apply. The bad prison is where the prisoner is in his or her cell and on his or her bed at midday. The good prison is one where the tests are not of niceness or nastiness, but the extent to which prisoners come to take part in law-abiding and useful occupations. The *Statement of Purpose* clearly puts the case against merely warehousing prisoners. The good prison is one which offers security, humane care and a reasonable level of sanitation. We have the guidelines, including the government's White Paper *Custody, Care and Justice* (Home Office, 1991), to increase the number of such prisons. Any delay in the improvement of prisons, as we recorded in the Woolf Report (1991), is more the result of a failure of attitude, than a shortage of money.

Clearly, no one wants prisons which are individually and socially damaging. When I first became HM Chief Inspector of Prisons approximately half the prison population in England and Wales were kept in overcrowded conditions often with no basic sanitary amenities. However, more recently, the prison system of England and Wales has become just about fully sanitized – significantly ahead of the date projected by the Prison Service. Given that the problems of overcrowding and sanitation have been for the most part addressed, it is necessary to confront the more difficult and controversial questions which concern the provision of humane treatment in prisons and the kind of life prisoners should lead while they are in custody

There are two standard responses to such questions. Penal reformers, on the one hand, emphasize rehabilitation, although in general they do not view the prison as a suitable place for its provision. Consequently, the emphasis in recent years has been on reducing the use of imprisonment or on finding alternatives. The libertarians, on the other hand, emphasize the need to do less harm. The outcome of these opposing views has been the suggestion that prisons are simply bad news and ultimately unable to do any good. As a result the positive work of the prison service and prison officers has gone largely unrecognized.

I would like to endorse the use of non-custodial sanctions, and would like to see prisons used as sparingly as possible. However, there remains a need to work with offenders in prison, although the type of work conducted will depend in part on the type of prisoners involved, since those who are given custodial sentences fall into several types. Remand prisoners represent a growing proportion of the custodial population, although approximately fifty per cent of these prisoners do not receive custodial sentences when their cases are decided. The majority of convicted prisoners receive sentences of less than four years which means that they will serve up to two years in prison.

The length of time which different categories of prisoner serve in prison is important in addressing the question of what can be done. It is also important in assessing and responding to different prisoners' needs. Regimes should be adapted to the type of prisoners held. Short-sentence prisoners, for example, should go to prisons where the regime is predominantly concerned with preparation for release. This means that prisons should be developing education and training as well addressing offending behaviour. Such prisons need the support of the outside community. Prison governors need to develop contacts with community groups, in order to make sure that community services operate within the prison. In doing this it will make it much less possible to single out prisoners as having special privileges, but rather it will ensure that the prison operates like any community. In my opinion it is undesirable for the community to isolate short-term prisoners. It is much better to integrate them while you still have custody over them, and to actively promote the links which prisoners will need on release. For long-term prisoners, the quality of life in custody is important. It is necessary to consider what productive work can be done in prison, for which prisoners can be properly paid and out of which they can make payments in support of their families and victims. Community participation in thinking through such possibilities is important; while an understanding of what is going on behind the walls is essential to any successful work with offenders.

It is my personal view that the organization of the Prison Service requires a form of management which recognizes the diversity of the prison population. In accordance with the recommendations of the Woolf Report (1991), which was prepared by Lord Justice Woolf and myself, prisons should be grouped coherently in regime terms so that, as far as possible, prisoners of all types are housed as closely as possible to what they would call home. Governors and staff would have to work within the clusters to build regimes which are appropriate to the different types of offender housed. Take two examples.

A person remanded in custody for the first time. This is someone whose life has been totally and harshly disrupted at every level. Employment, family and local networks are all at a distance and all are vulnerable. A person entering a remand unit should enter a regime which is consistent with the objective that while in custody the remanded person is assisted in keeping all possible contacts open. Additionally, it should aim to allow the kind of facilities which promote the maintenance of health and sanity. One in two of those held in remand will walk free from the trial court. At this point they might have cause to be thankful that such a system was in place.

Secondly, a person who receives a short sentence. The allocation unit at the remand prison (a different department) would direct such a prisoner to a prison specializing in such sentences. The regime would be based on the simple truth that there is not much time before release, and that there is a great deal to be done. The regime would in effect be one big pre-release course and would involve the outside community. Non-custodial and custodial agencies, whether criminal justice, educational or employment related, would thus be encouraged to have dealings with the prison.

Viewed this way, I believe I am charting a way forward for a new type of prison system. A new era of thinking about custody is necessary if we are to move away from the polarized debates about its limits.

WHO GOES TO PRISON?

The majority of people incarcerated in prison are under the age of thirty. Most have failed, or have been failed by school and have weak, if any family links. Often they are drawn from impoverished inner city areas. The effects of poor social and economic conditions was highlighted well by Cardinal Manning some time ago when he wrote:

> Those who live among statistics, and have seldom, if ever, lived among the poor, little know how poverty brings temptation, and temptation both vice and crime ... It would be an affectation of scepticism to say that this close relation is not by way of cause and effect. (Cited by Radzinowicz and Hood, 1986: 69)

There are other prisoners, however, who cannot be simply described as having lost their way with school and family. There are, for example, a significant number of violent offenders in prison, many of whom are held for long periods and under conditions of humane containment.

The diversity of prisoners in terms of their social, political and economic make up, coupled with the issues of race and gender pose numerous problems. For example, although the number of women in prison is relatively small, the low numbers make it more difficult to secure a place within reasonable distance of family and friends – the most dangerous and difficult women prisoners are held in one of the most remote English prisons, Durham. However, the issue of distance does not only relate to women in prison. Many offenders are often held in institutions which are a considerable distance from their families and friends. And prison location is only one problem. There are many more. Prison size can also be problematic.

Juvenile Institutions are often too big. Feltham, for example, holds nearly 800 teenagers. Very few staff are trained to deal specifically with teenagers, and often Young Offenders Institutions are insufficiently distinguished, save by name, from the ordinary prison. The job of helping the criminal teenager lead a law-abiding and useful life after release is an exceedingly demanding one, and there are far too many establishments in which the young are warehoused and discharged without the skills or the self-respect which they need. Consequently, the recidivist rates remain in the region of 80 per cent. Institutions which produce this result are clearly not working.

With regards to remand prisoners, it is difficult to encourage activities amongst those who remain unconvicted. This was witnessed, for example, at the Wolds Prison in which the available facilities were underused by prisoners who prefered to loiter. Probably a secure bail hostel is a better model for remand prisoners than existing remand prisons. There is no reason why a well-organized hostel should not be able to encourage an active life amongst prisoners. Some consideration should also be given to the issue of whether remand prisoners could not be brought more speedily to trial. I frequently meet remand prisoners who have been held in custody for over a year.

Mental illness is another problem. There are a number of mentally ill prisoners who need psychiatric treatment. Although it has been found that the numbers of mentally ill persons moving from hospitals to prisons is not as high as might have been expected, there are a disturbing number of people in prison who need expert psychiatric help. In a number of cases these inmates need special attention which prison doctors are ill equipped to provide. Either prison doctors must be trained to deal with these problems or the people concerned should be removed to specialist hospitals where they can receive the appropriate treatment.

From the examples above, it can be seen that different categories of prisoner create different problems and challenges for the prison service. If the aim is to encourage prisoners to lead law-abiding and useful lives on release the type of prison regime available for each type of prisoner will have to be adapted to the different sets of needs and the levels of risk. Where the aim of imprisonment is to reduce crime, more general considerations come into play.

IMPRISONMENT AND CRIME REDUCTION

Achieving a clear purpose for the prison system in relation to crime reduction is difficult in that there is currently a lack of clarity about the role of imprisonment. As David Faulkner, the former Deputy Secretary at the Home Office, wrote in the press:

> The Prison Service is unclear whether it is meant to implement the programme set out in the Woolf Report and the Government's own White Paper, or to concentrate on containing a much enlarged prison population and on developing more austere regimes. (Faulkner, 1993)

In a similar vein, Professor Eric Caines – the architect of *Fresh Start* – wrote even more gloomily in another newspaper article:

> Everything is short-term, without any understanding that services such as prisons and police ... cannot operate effectively if what they are required to do, and how they are required to do it, can be changed almost overnight ... What we have to settle for are services which, if not wholly second-rate, are much less effective than they ought to be. (Caines, 1993)

Given such confusion, it may appear impossible to run an effective prison system where the sentimental questions of how nice or nasty it is have faded away and ceased to be relevant, where the prisoner is actively employed and able to develop skills and self-respect.

However, it *is* possible, and a key aspect of this process is the provision of appropriate educational programmes. It is therefore necessary to examine the type of education provided in prisons and ensure that the curriculum is suitable for different categories of prisoner. Too often it is designed on the basis of what teachers or a tiny minority of prisoners want. It is no use teaching 'Management Studies' to boys of seventeen years of age who may be streetwise but can barely read. They need to learn to use their hands and their imagination. Education should include art therapy, in particular the provision of 'enabling space', where amid the ceaseless clank of prison sounds, the prisoner can learn to develop creative possibilities. It should include the type of teaching, whether in cell or classroom, which makes it possible for the prisoner to receive the social and moral education from which he or she can gain self-respect. It should include higher education, although provision here is less of a problem. Correspondence courses can be made available. However, as we are aware, it is often not easy to persuade the adult uneducated to go to school or attend lessons. School is an unhappy memory for many inmates and for this reason we should consider re-naming the classes – words like 'tutorial' and 'study period' – may ease the problem. (It is not unlike re-naming those who teach Judges their business the Judicial Studies Board.)

In addition, inmates could benefit from social education. Many prisoners are ignorant about matters of hygiene, and need instruction about drink, drugs (including tobacco) and HIV/AIDS. They need to learn to address their offending behaviour. They also need to learn to control their anger, and to understand the gravity of their crimes as well as the suffering experienced by their victims. They need to learn the practice of work. They need a social education which for many others began with their parents and in nursery schools. Building family links, in the broader sense, is part of social education and part of the support system which may enable ex-prisoners to resist the temptation to re-offend. Thus maintaining and strengthening family links while in prison should be encouraged. When the prisoner is discharged he or she will need all the help they can get. The probation service alone cannot produce law abiding ex-prisoners.

Prison must also be perceived as a place of robust activity if the crime rate is to be reduced. Prisoners need to be encouraged to develop skills and to engage in productive work. There is little point in learning a skill you may have no opportunity to practise. The industrial prison is one where work comes first. Education and sport are available only at the end of a working day. The outside company employs the prisoners to make goods. The company pays the industrial wage and provides materials and machinery. The Prison Service, who supervise the work, take a cut, and the prisoners are paid wages in accordance with how hard and skilfully they work. The prisoners pay tax and insurance on their earnings, and their net earnings are divided, after discussion with prison officials, between their families and their own savings. Instead of 'private cash' in small amounts being paid to prisoners by their families, the money goes the other way. Relations are improved between prisoners and family. Dependency on social security payments for family members may be reduced. The prisoner leaves prison with substantial savings, working skills, and the habit of work. All this happens in Germany and in other European countries. It works to the advantage of everybody, although better in a period of fairly full employment and with the agreement of the unions.

In England it has been tested out at Coldingley, although here it has failed. Failure in this case was due to the restriction of prisoners to pocket-money. They were paid only a few pounds a week. They are not allowed to earn anything approaching full wages. Prisoners unfortunately will not work hard eight hours a day in order to repay their moral debt to society. If you walk into a workshop in any English prison, heads turn and the mood is one of apathy. If you go into a German prison where prisoners are employed at acceptable wages – lower in fact than the full industrial wage – you will find an efficient factory, where contract terms have to be met. I do not believe that this is solely a result of differences of temperament between the English and Germans, although this may play its part. If an industrial prison is to work, the prisoners will need to be paid as workers or given some other compensation, such as a substantial shortening of sentence. It is my belief that prisons can make a positive contribution to society and that rehabilitative work can be done within them. While it is undoubtedly the case that the prison service deals with some of the most difficult members of the community it should be remembered that the vast majority of offenders are young, under educated and persistent minor offenders. For the vast majority of those prisoners prison should be about preparation for release. What happens after prison is not only important to the prisoner but it is also of great significance to the rest of us. Most prisoners are not incarcerated for very long, but what occurs during this period in relation to education, training and work can have considerable implications for how these people behave when they are released.

CONCLUSION: THE WAY FORWARD

Punishment for prisoners I believe is not the business of the prison service but of the courts. This is really another way of putting that celebrated maxim of Sir Alexander Paterson – *Prisons are as punishment, not for punishment.* Sentencers have to consider the need for punishment, public protection, deterrence, and compensation. The prison service, on the other hand, has the job of providing security, humanity and help. Thus, courts commit offenders to custody for crimes deemed serious enough to warrant loss of liberty. Provided that basic standards are maintained in prison, is it not enough for fair-minded people to consider that society has problems enough within its law-abiding population, without having to consider prisoners further? Problems of unemployment, education, health and welfare are complex enough when considered in relation to the majority of the population who do not break the law. Prison is expensive and there is a significant belief that little works anyway. So, some ask, why do we not concentrate our energies on those areas of social life where there is some chance of success? This issue has been a feature of prison debate for many years with discussion tending to fall into traditional well-worn opposing trenches. On the one side some have argued that the health of society can to some extent be measured by the way prisoners are treated within it. Underlying this approach is the belief that criminal activity arises not only through individual malevolence, but also as a result of the social environ-

ment. Criminal behaviour emerges as a result of joint failures
vidual and the society of which he or she is a part. As a resu
must take some responsibility for crime, and at least make the
rehabilitate offenders.

On the other side, there are those who emphasize that individuals are responsible for their actions. Social need and individual misfortune do not alter the basic premise. The argument is that for most people real freedom of action results when such a system works well. The downside is that, when adversity strikes, the wind blows colder. On a radio programme, the Director of the Adam Smith Institute was asked his attitude towards reports that a number of people in newly privatized businesses had been driven to suicide by the resulting stresses. He replied, honestly enough, that this may be a feature of radical social change, however regrettable, but that it was not sufficient to make such problems reason to change the policy. On such a view, the life chances for people in prison will be very much a matter for themselves. As an imprisoned person you will serve your time and make of the experience what you will. Rehabilitation is your own responsibility.

The phrase 'prison works' can have different meanings for different groups. For the prison reformer prison works if it does something useful with the prisoner. For the libertarian, it works to the extent that it removes the offender from society for a specified time, so that the rest of us can have respite from the offending behaviour. On becoming Her Majesty's Chief Inspector of Prisons, I was able to have a constructive dialogue with both these groups. Both groups believe that it is bad policy to make prisoners worse. It is obvious why a prison reformer might say so. The libertarian argument would agree that to oppress prisoners would be to store up trouble when the time comes for release. The argument centres on how much assistance you give to a prisoner, on the assumption that he or she has been fairly treated while in custody.

One way of reducing the debilitating effects of imprisonment, it was suggested by Lord Justice Woolf (1991) was to reduce the distance between the prisoner and the wider community. Thus, Lord Woolf argued that as far as possible prisoners should be held in prisons which are as close geographically to the prisoners' family and friends as possible. On this premise he argued for the introduction of local 'community prisons'. Community prisons are an important proposal but one which suffers a number of shortcomings. As mentioned already, even if those institutions were satisfactory on other counts, it is physically impossible for prisons to fulfil the local commitment for large areas of the country, because prisons do not exist in all centres of the population. There is another objection.

Community prisons on this model could help maintain links between the individual prisoner and his or her family, and provide assistance in resettlement at the time of release. If what happens after prison is important from a wider point of view, in that successful release benefits the community as well as the prisoner, the place of the prison in the community has to be more fundamentally re-evaluated than Woolf describes. Prisons have traditionally been largely separate from the wider community. Prisoners are removed to them and life in custody is conducted away from the public view. Instead of this, I think that it is the prison itself which should be seen as part of the community in which it is placed and some kind of relationship should be established between the two.

The Report of Lord Justice Woolf, however, remains an important point of reference, especially as the underlying message is that what is required in the current period are changes in attitude rather than in resources. His findings undermine the belief that if you make prisons bad enough, people will not commit crimes, and show it to be historically untrue. What happens to people in prison is important both for individuals and for the community. What happens after prison is equally important. We cannot address these issues without the help and the support of the communities in which prisons exist. Until we explore this relation, the real reasons for the rising levels of crime and the use of custody will also remain unaddressed. This will be bad news for us all.

References

Caines, E. (1993) 'No Gain without Pain: Short-Term Solutions to Long-Term Problems Are Bound to come Unstuck', *The Times*, 16 December.

Faulkner, D. (1993) *The Guardian*, 11 November.

Home Office (1991) *Custody, Care and Justice: The Way Ahead for the Prison Service in England and Wales*, Cmnd 1647 (London: HMSO).

Radzinowicz, L. and Hood, R. (1986) *History of English Criminal Law*, vol 5 (London: Stevens and Sons).

Woolf Report (1991) *Prison Disturbances April 1990: Report of an Inquiry by the Rt Hon. Lord Justice Woolf (Parts I and II) and His Honour Judge Stephen Tumim (Part II)*, Cmnd 1456 (London: HMSO).

2 Prisons in Crisis: The American Experience

Francis T. Cullen, Patricia Van Voorhis and Jody L. Sundt

INTRODUCTION

Over the past two decades, an increasingly lengthy roster of commentators has characterized prisons in the United States as being in 'crisis' (see, for example, Blumstein, 1989; Colvin, 1992; Cullen and Gilbert, 1982; Gottfredson and McConville, 1987; Selke, 1993; Sherman and Hawkins, 1981; Simon, 1993). The term has been invoked to describe virtually every aspect of the American correctional system, but two uses have been most prominent and will occupy our attention here.[1] Most obvious and most often, commentators speak of the 'crowding crisis' – how escalating inmate populations tax system resources and create an unrelenting administrative nightmare. Less clearly articulated but perhaps more fundamental, there is a sense that the very purpose or 'conscience' (Rothman, 1980) of the correctional enterprise is up for grabs or, still worse, undergoing a disquieting transformation.

This chapter attempts to recount the 'American experience'.[2] This task merits pursuit, because so much policy discourse and penal practice is framed by considerations of crowding and by prevailing correctional consciences (or ideologies). The limits of our contribution, however, should be immediately confessed. It takes a good measure of hubris to suggest that the 'American experience' with imprisonment can be boiled down to a discussion of two forms of crises. Prisons in the United States are part of an unwieldy, decentralized system that has an enormous amount of 'within group' variation (Zimring and Hawkins, 1991). Accordingly, the reader should beware that in our attempt to convey essential features of the current state of United States imprisonment, our analysis cannot escape the limits of reductionism.

Similarly, our very choice to focus on 'crisis' constructs only one reality – albeit a salient one of American prisons. In fact, Sherman and Hawkins (1981: 3–8) warn that when it comes to prisons, Americans are prone to adopt a 'crisis mentality'; perhaps our vision is narrowed by this cultural lens.[3] In any case, the rhetoric of crisis can mask the reality that most

21

United States prisons grind along each day without the spectre of inmate insurgency looming immediately beneath the surface, and that some prisons are orderly, clean, justly administered, and reasonably attentive to inmate needs (DiIulio, 1987; Wright, 1994; but see Colvin, 1992; Irwin, 1980; Jacobs, 1977).

This much admitted, we reiterate that the two crises identified - crowding and conscience - are integral to any understanding of American correctional policy and practice, and to any understanding of how politicians, the public, and criminologists think about prisons. We begin, then, with an assessment of the crowding crisis, focusing in particular on its scale, sources and solutions. We then turn to the interrelated crisis of conscience. We point to the growing appeal of 'caging criminals' as a guiding correctional ideology, but then argue – contrary to a fair number of our American colleagues – that rehabilitation retains public and scientific support that make reports of its demise premature.

THE CROWDING CRISIS: THE SCALE OF IMPRISONMENT

'Overcrowded conditions in our prisons have become a national crisis.' This quote, one might assume, is taken from a recent news report or criminological journal. In fact, the remark was voiced in 1978 by Strom Thurmond, the arch-conservative United States Senator (quoted in Sherman and Hawkins, 1981: 3). Even though more dramatic increases lay on the horizon, by that time the intractable rise in prison populations had become unmistakable. In the space of a decade, Thurmond and his fellow Americans had seen the number of inmates in state and federal prisons jump by over 100 000 – from 187 914 in 1968 to 294 396 in 1978 – with most of that increase coming in the last half of the decade (Maguire and Pastore, 1994: 600).

Looking to trends earlier in the century provides a context for understanding why the boom in prison populations would have seemed so alarming in the late 1970s. Between 1925 and 1974, the incarceration rate had averaged between 107 and 108 per 100 000 citizens (Maguire and Pastore, 1994: 600) and the number of inmates 'grew at a fairly consistent and negligible rate, averaging perhaps 3 per cent–5 per cent, and reflecting little more than the growth in the general population' (Office of Criminal Justice Services, 1995: 72). Between 1961 and 1972, moreover, the in-carceration rate had dropped from 119 to 93. Criminologists witnessing these trends proposed theories of the 'stability of punishment' (Blumstein and Cohen, 1973; see also Blumstein, 1995) and predicted that 'decarceration' would be a permanent feature of United States corrections (Scull, 1977; see also Miller, 1991). By 1978, however, talk of the crowding crisis was rampant: the incarceration rate per 100 000 had increased to 133, and by the decades end the size of the prison population had broken the previously unimaginable barrier of 300 000 inmates (Maguire and Pastore, 1994: 600).

The concern about crowding produced much public and criminological commentary (see, for example, Gottfredson and McConville, 1987; National Institute of Corrections, 1985; *New York University Review of Law and Social Change*, 1983–1984), but this discourse did little to slow the pace of the prison population boom. Between 1980 and 1990, the number of state and federal inmates had more than doubled to over 700 000, and in 1994 this population surpassed the one million mark (Maguire and Pastore, 1994: 600; Office of Criminal Justice Services, 1995: 72). The incarceration rate per 100 000, which in 1980 was 138, today stands at 370 (Camp and Camp, 1994: 7). Even these figures, however, underestimate the full scale of imprisonment in the United States, for they do not include offenders in county, city, and other local jails. When all forms of adult imprisonment are computed, the United States incarceration rate is 519, with over 1.3 million Americans behind bars on any given day (Mauer, 1994).

Virtually all informed observers forecast that the United States scale of imprisonment will continue to grow in the foreseeable future (see, for example, Blumstein, 1995; DiIulio, 1991). The prison system in the State of Ohio provides an example of what most jurisdictions can anticipate. In 1975, the state incarcerated less than 10 000 offenders; by 1994, this figure had quadrupled to 40 784. The Ohio Criminal Sentencing Commission, however, projects that the inmate population will exceed 50 000 in the first year of the next century and will reach nearly 55 000 by the year 2003 (Office of Criminal Justice Services, 1995: 73).

In and of themselves, numbers of inmates do not constitute a crisis. But it is clear that jurisdictions have had enormous difficulty coping with the unrelenting demand to house more and more offenders. Between 1988 and 1993, over 300 new prisons were constructed (bringing the nation's total to over 1400). In 1993 alone, 48 institutions with nearly 43 000 beds were built, at a cost of over \$47 000 per bed. More than 86 000 beds are now being added, with another 115 000 in the planning stages (Camp and Camp, 1994: 33–50). Estimates place the total cost of imprisoning offenders in the United States at \$26.8 billion (Mauer, 1994: 6).

Despite this attempt to meet the demand for space, the average state prison system operates at 112.3 per cent of its 'related' population capacity (Camp and Camp, 1994: 35). Furthermore, in 24 states, prisons are under court orders placing caps on the number of inmates that correctional facilities can house (Camp and Camp, 1994: 6). 'Prison crowding', concludes a Bureau of Justice Statistics report, 'is a major issue in nearly every state' (Zawitz, 1988: 108). Not surprisingly, correctional administrators regularly define crowding as the most pressing problem they face (Grieser, 1988; Guynes, 1988).

These broad trends again can be illustrated in more detail by examining corrections in the State of Ohio. Despite 'the State's most aggressive prison building programme ever', reports Ohio's Office of Criminal Justice Services (1995: 74–5), the prison system remains at 180 per cent of its rated capacity, with crowding 'a problem in virtually every Ohio prison'. Between 1983 and 1993, the corrections department's budget jumped from $144 million to over $519 million, making it the forth largest governmental expenditure behind Medicaid, welfare, and education (Associated Press, 1994; Schwaner, 1994). In contrast to fiscal limits, if not cut-backs, in nearly all other areas of governmental expenditures, the prison budget is estimated to rise as much as 30 per cent in 1995 (Associated Press, 1994).[4]

The crowding crisis reaches to the local level as well. A 1993 survey of Ohio's 76 counties found that 29 were using waiting lists for offenders who had been sentenced to jail but could not yet be institutionalized due to a lack of bed space. Remarkably, the survey revealed that over 26 000 offenders – twice the existing jail population in the state – were waiting to serve their sentences, many of whom would not report to the county jail for 'months, or even years, after their convictions' (Office of Criminal Justice Services, 1995: 75).[5] This last observation points to a broader concern: the crowding crisis affects not only institutional corrections but also community corrections. Between 1980 and 1990, the population of offenders under community supervision grew at rates equal to, if not greater than, the prison population. Thus, during this period, offenders on probation increased 139 per cent (from 1.1 million to 2.7 million), and offenders on parole increased 141 per cent (from 220 438 to 531 407) (Irwin and Austin, 1994: 4).

In short, the crowding crisis pervades virtually all components (community, institutional) and levels (federal, state, local) of America's correctional system. This hard reality places limits on the extent to which the system can be manoeuvred to relieve crowding. As DiIulio (1991: 3) cautions, 'over the next two decades there will be no escape from increasing numbers of citizens in prison, in jail, on probation, and on parole'.

VARIATION IN THE SCALE OF IMPRISONMENT

As noted above, the United States prison system cannot be reduced to a single 'American experience' without overlooking the diversity within the system. We do not have the space to sketch the full mosaic of American corrections, but two salient variations in imprisonment warrant attention.

First, it is often reported that the United States rivals Russia for the world's highest rate of incarceration (Mauer, 1994), but this fact masks the wide variation in the use of imprisonment across states and Washington, D.C. – so much so that Zimring and Hawkins (1991: 137) suggest that it might be more appropriate to speak of prisons in 'fifty-one different countries'. In 1994, for example, the incarceration rate per 100 000 ranged from a high of 539 for Texas to a low of 80 for North Dakota; nearly a sevenfold difference; Washington, D.C. surpassed all jurisdictions with the disquieting rate of 1426 (Camp and Camp, 1994: 7–8). Despite this persistent state-level variation in prison use, Zimring and Hawkins (1991: 155) conclude that state incarceration rates are converging 'toward a single national trend': regardless of jurisdiction, an increasing scale of imprisonment over the last two decades. This convergence is significant, because the decentralized nature of American criminal justice means that 'imprisonment policy decisions are made by state and local governments' (Zimring and Hawkins, 1991: 220).

Second and more disturbing, the use of imprisonment varies greatly for African-American and white citizens. Although blacks comprise only 12 per cent of the nation's population, they make up almost half (48 per cent) of the prison and jail inmates (Tonry, 1994: 97). Data from 1992–3 indicate that the incarceration rate for African-Americans is more than six times that for whites: 1947 to 306 per 100 000 (Mauer, 1994: 6). When the statistics are disaggregated by age and gender, the picture is even bleaker. In 1990, Tonry estimates (1995: 130), 'something like 1 in 12 black men aged eighteen to fifty-four was in jail or prison'. The number of 'young African-Americans' under correctional supervision, add Irwin and Austin (1994: 5), 'is greater than the total number of African-American men enrolled in college'.

Although not fully discounting the continuing presence of discrimination in the criminal justice system, most American criminologists conclude that the bulk of the racial disparity in incarceration rates reflects the nation's racial disparity in crime rates, especially the differential involvement of blacks in violent offences that are most likely to be sanctioned with imprisonment (Blumstein, 1982; Currie, 1985; DiIulio, 1994b; Langan, 1994; Tonry, 1995). Disparities in crime and corrections are thus most accurately seen as a reflection of underlying racial inequities in society – that is, social injustice reproduces itself within the prison system (Currie, 1985; Tonry, 1995; see also Hacker, 1992). Moreover, Tonry (1994) notes, the racial gap in incarceration is not a case of American exceptionalism. Given that the black–white ratio in imprisonment in Australia, Canada and the United Kingdom is strikingly similar to that in the United States, he suggests that it may be 'a general problem in English speaking white-dominated countries that minority citizens are locked up grossly out of proportion to their numbers in the general population' (Tonry, 1994: 106; see also FitzGerald and Marshall in this volume).

These considerations may provide a context for understanding variations in the use of imprisonment, but they do not obviate the continuing salience of race in American corrections. In fact, the black–white gap in incarceration has worsened markedly in the past decade (Tonry, 1994; 1995). Admissions to state and federal prisons furnish a revealing indicator of this deepening racial cleavage. In 1986, 53 per cent of prison admissions were white and 46 per cent black, but by 1989 the figures had flip-flopped and 53 per cent of the admissions were African-American (Tonry, 1994: 100).

America's 'War on Drugs', claim commentators, is largely responsible for this recent jump in minority imprisonment (Hagan, 1994: 157; Tonry, 1995: 81–123). Data from North Carolina are instructive. Between 1970 and 1980, the black–white ratio in prison admissions held fairly constant (between two and three to one). The white rate of admissions remained steady in the following decade, but the black rate doubled (making the ratio almost five to one). What accounted for this disproportionate increase? To a large extent, it appears, drug arrests. Between 1984 and 1989, drug arrests for whites increased 36 per cent, but 183 per cent for African-Americans. A similar pattern emerged in Pennsylvania. During the decade of the eighties: prison commitments for drugs increased 477 per cent for white males but an astounding 1613 per cent for black males (Tonry, 1994: 110–11).

A benign explanation exists for the disproportionate use of imprisonment for African-Americans involved with illegal substances. In this view, the crack-down on drugs represents a much overdue investment by the government in inner-city neighbourhoods (see DiIulio, 1994b). Responding to the will of these impoverished residents, the state is attempting to restore community order by deterring open-air drug trafficking, closing down 'crack houses', and placing drug pushers and users in jail. Whites escape similar legal scrutiny because their drug involvement is less visible. Police officials frequently claim, Gordon observes, that; 'It is a lot easier to bring in the dealer who is operating from a phone booth on a ghetto street corner than one who completes his transactions in his suburban study or college dorm or Wall Street Office' (Gordon, 1994: 158).

A less sanguine view, however, is possible. In this scenario, the War on Drugs is seen as a crass attempt to purchase the votes of affluent white Americans. Young, inner-city, minority males are singled out for repression because they lack political capital and because they can be portrayed as a 'dangerous class' ruthlessly pushing drugs on kids and killing their competitors in the drug trade (Gordon, 1994). This symbolic crusade, which experience shows has virtually no meaningful effect on drug markets and consumption, reassures anxious suburban residents that 'something is being done about the crime problem' and obscures the need for more fundamental structural transformations in underclass communities. As a result: politicians gain votes without having to address the enduring 'malign neglect' of minorities (see Currie, 1993; Tonry, 1995).

Specific drug policies – whether their intent is benign or malign – can also produce glaring racial disparities in punishment. Most salient, penalties for 'crack' cocaine are far harsher than for 'powder' cocaine. Sentencing guidelines for Minnesota, for example, instruct judges to assign the presumptive sentence of four years in prison for possession of three grams of crack cocaine and probation for possession of the same amount of powder cocaine. The racial dimension of these laws only becomes apparent when it is realised that the 'drug of choice' for blacks is crack and for whites is powder. Data from Minnesota reveal, for example, that African-Americans comprised over 95 per cent of those charged under the more punitive crack cocaine law while whites comprised almost 80 per cent of those charged under the more lenient powder cocaine law (Tonry, 1995: 188–9). Similarly, within the federal correctional system, research at the end of 1993 showed that 'on average prison sentences for blacks were 41 per cent longer than for whites and that the different penalties for crack and powder cocaine were the major reason for that difference' (Tonry, 1995: 189).

Thus far, we have focused on variations in the use of incarceration within the United States. Before proceeding, however, we will consider another form of variation: How does the scale of imprisonment in the United States compare to that of other advanced industrial democracies? American liberal commentators, including many criminologists, commonly assert that the United States is a 'punitive society', with Russia (and, until recently, South Africa) as its only rival for leadership in putting its citizens behind bars (see for example, Currie, 1985; Irwin and Austin, 1994; Mauer, 1994; Wicker, 1991). And on the surface this claim seems irrefutable. According to Mauer (1994) among 52 nation's studied in 1992–3 only Russia's incarceration rate per 100 000 exceeded the United States rate (558 to 519). He also notes that the United States uses incarceration 'generally 5–8 times the rate of most industrialised nations'.

Citing per capital incarceration rates, however, can be misleading. These data cannot disentangle whether the United States high use of imprisonment is due to greater punitiveness or merely to the fact that America has a larger and more serious crime problem. As Lynch (1995) points out, judging the merits of these competing interpretations requires information on how much punishment, on average, those arrested for each type of crime (say, murder) receive within each nation. Such cross-cultural comparisons are fraught with difficulties – given, for example, that nation's differ in their laws, correctional systems, and methods for collecting crime and criminal justice statistics – but Lynch (1995) makes a rigorous attempt to compare incarceration rates among the United States, Australia, Canada, England and Wales, and West Germany. His analysis suggests that blanket statements about America's punitiveness are difficult to substantiate.

The United States clearly hands out longer sentences than the other advanced industrial democracies in his sample, reports Lynch, but do American offenders actually serve more time in prison? Here the results become more complex. It appears that for homicide and serious violent offences, the time served in prison is similar between the United States and the other nation's. For property and drug offences, however, the United States is more punitive in its use of imprisonment (Lynch, 1995). Accordingly, the larger scale of the United States prison population is partially a function of the nation's 'high levels of lethal violence ... At the same time', Lynch concludes, 'reasonably large reductions in the prison population could be achieved by reducing the use of incarceration and the length of time served for property crime (and possibly drug offences) to the level of nation's like England and Canada' (Lynch, 1995: 37).

SOURCES OF THE SCALE OF IMPRISONMENT

There is no dispute that the scale of the United States prison system experienced a precipitous growth over the past two decades that has left America's prisons with a seemingly intractable crowding crisis, but the sources of this prison population boom are less well understood. After more than two hundred pages of careful analysis in *The Scale of Imprisonment*, for example, Zimring and Hawkins (1991) could do no more than conclude their 'inquiry with significant questions whose answers are shrouded in mystery':

> Are the forces that determine the scale of imprisonment the same as those that explain cross-sectional differences in the use of imprisonment? Why do large numbers of political entities exercising independent powers tend to move in the same direction at the same time? Are there cycles analogous to the business cycle or the demographic cycle that underlie or influence fluctuations in rates of imprisonment? And if so, why? (1991: 215–16)

The best we can offer, therefore, are informed guesses as to why America's inmate population increased so dramatically in recent times. Four factors deserve consideration: crime rates, the impact of age on imprisonment, the prolonged campaign to 'get tough' with crime, and the declaration in the 1980s of the 'War on Drugs' (see Blumstein, 1995).

First, America's large prison population clearly reflects the nation's high rates of serious crime (Lynch, 1995). Crime and punishment, however, do not exist in a finely calibrated close relationship, in which an increment in the crime rate produces a commensurate increment in the number of prison inmates. Instead, it appears that crime and punishment are loosely coupled, and that fluctuations in offence rates and incarceration rates, both across states and across time, are 'largely independent' of one another (Zimring and Hawkins, 1991). Blumstein's (1995) analysis is instructive. He notes that FBI data reveal that between the mid-1970s and the first part of the 1990s, the crime rates for murder, robbery, and burglary 'did not increase dramatically', thus 'making it very unlikely that the growth in prison population was a consequence of growing crime rates' (Blumstein, 1995: 391).

Second, as those familiar with criminology know, a 'baby boom' will produce increases in crime rates fifteen to twenty years later, because involvement in street crimes peaks in people's late teens and early twenties. Less well known, however, is that a baby boom's effects on prison admissions occur about a decade later than its effects on offence rates; the peak age for imprisonment is in the late twenties. The delay between peak crime ages and peak imprisonment ages is because few juvenile offenders are sent to adult prisons and because incarceration is reserved primarily for 'career criminals' who have had time to demonstrate to the courts that they are recidivists (Blumstein, 1995).

In the United States, high birth rates following World War Two and the 1960s, which bulged the number of crime-prone youths, exacerbated the nation's crime problem into the late 1970s. By the early 1980s, the declining youth of the age structure helped to restrain crime rates. Due to the lagged effect of age on peak imprisonment rates, however, large baby boom cohorts continued to boost the numbers of offenders eligible for incarceration. 'As a result', concludes Blumstein (1995), 'prison populations were expected to increase over the 1980s as the bulge of the baby boom (with a peak at about the 1960 cohort) continued to flow through the high imprisonment ages' (Blumstein, 1995: 395).

Third, for two decades, the United States has been in the midst of an inexhaustible campaign to 'get tough' with crime (Clear, 1994; Cullen and Gilbert, 1982; Currie, 1985; Forer, 1994; Gordon, 1994). Indeed, it is difficult to find any elected official – Democrat or Republican, legislator or judge – who has not jumped on to the punishment bandwagon. The result has been an array of policies – from mandatory minimum prison sentences, to restrictions on parole release, to 'three strikes and you're out' laws requiring life imprisonment for a third felony – aimed at putting more offenders in prison and for lengthier stays (Skolnick, 1994).

Demonstrating a precise link between specific 'get tough' policies and prison crowding is often difficult. Even so, this punishment campaign has moved beyond rhetoric to influence sentencing practices (Cohen and Canela-Cacho, 1994). 'Sentences in the United States became generally tougher during the 1980s', reports Forst 'the ratio of imprisonment to [FBI] index crimes more than doubled during the 1970s and 1980s ... Imprisonments have increased for violent crimes as well: the average prison time served per violent crime roughly *tripled* from 1975 to 1989 (Forst, 1995: 380; emphasis in original). Indeed, Langan (1991) contends that higher imprisonment rates are due primarily to increases in the likelihood that, first, crimes result in felony convictions and secondly, that such convictions are sanctioned with a prison term – accounted for over half the rise in prison population growth between 1974 and 1986 (see also Farrington and Langan, 1992).

Fourth, in the 1980s, especially during the administration of President Bush, the United Stated declared a 'War on Drugs'. The central thrust of this attack was to use the criminal law to punish, rather than to treat, offenders (Currie, 1993; Gordon, 1994; Zimring and Hawkins, 1994). Commentators question whether the drug war is winnable, but one of its consequences has been to bring more drug criminals within the walls of the nation's prisons. The 'War on Drugs' contribution to the crowding crisis can be seen by tracing over time the proportion of the prison population comprised of drug offenders. In 1983, only 10 per cent of the jail population were sentenced for drug offences, but by 1989 this figure had more than doubled. In 1979, drug offenders were 6.4 per cent of the state prison population, and stood only at 8.6 per cent in 1986; by 1994, however, the proportion of drug offenders in state facilities had jumped to about 25 per cent. In 1980, drug offenders were 24.9 per cent of the federal inmate population; a decade later the figure had increased to over 50 per cent and by 1994 to over 60 per cent (Blumstein, 1995; Bureau of Justice Statistics, 1992). Zimring and Hawkins (1994) point out the shocking fact that 'more persons were in prison for *all* offences in California at the end of 1979' (Zimring and Hawkins, 1994: 399; emphasis in original). And one study estimates that 44 per cent of the increase in prison populations between 1986 and 1991 could be attributed to the boom in the number of offenders imprisoned for drug offences (Blumstein, 1995).

SOLUTIONS TO THE SCALE OF IMPRISONMENT

Discussions on prison crowding usually are initiated on the premise that this crisis, now more than two decades old, can be solved. In theory, of course, solutions do exist, and many insightful commentators have talked about alleviating crowding pressures through alternatives to incarceration, revising sentencing structures, placing caps on populations, early release procedures for inmates, and the like (see, for example, Gottfredson and McConville, 1987; National Institute of Corrections, 1985; *New York University Review of Law and Social Change*, 1983–1984). Some successes in using these policies have been achieved, but they have been overwhelmed by the unrelenting flow of offenders into the correctional system. History gives some comfort that things do change, and thus it would be short-sighted to assume that prison crowding will be a permanent fixture of American corrections. But as we move towards the year 2000, theories of reducing the crowding crisis remain mainly academic exercises with little prospect of substantively affecting the extent of the crisis.

Whatever the underlying sources fuelling this crowding crisis, escaping its grip is constrained by the existing political climate. With 'getting tough on crime' seen as a prerequisite for re-election, virtually all American politicians enthusiastically voice their desire to send more offenders to prison for longer periods, a goal (as we have noted) they appear to be achieving. As part of this agenda, they pass law after law not only mandating prison terms but also restricting the discretion of corrections officials to release offenders from prison (for example by eliminating parole release, placing restrictions on 'good time', giving life sentences to habitual felons). In contrast, ideas on reducing prison crowding – such as the avenues criminologists theorize about – are judged too dangerous, because their endorsement would expose elected officials to charges of being 'soft on crime'. As a result, politically viable options for reducing prison crowding are in short supply. A fundamental contradiction thus challenges attempts in the United States to relieve prison crowding: how to have fewer people in prison, when sending more people to prison seems a political necessity. In this context, three 'politically correct' options (see Wright, 1995) present themselves: create more capacity to house inmates; punish offenders outside prison; and crisis management.

Creating Capacity

An obvious strategy for resolving this contradiction is to build the space needed to house all those the government wishes to incarcerate. We have earlier reviewed the massive prison building campaign under way across America (about 50 new facilities a year), and it appears that state budgets will continue to allocate monies for the construction of new facilities. States also have searched for ways to meet the demand for bed space more cheaply by hiring private companies to build and run correctional institutions (see Christie, 1993; Lilly, 1992). For-profit companies operate over 40 secure adult facilities (Welch, 1990), while a number of jurisdictions contract with private vendors for services such as food and medical care (Camp and Camp, 1994). Commentators might debate whether, in certain historical eras, prison construction might be able to meet the demand to house inmates. Regardless, in this period states have not succeeded in building their way out of the crowding crisis or in using privatization to avoid budget woes (Blumstein, 1995). Despite constant prison construction, crowding persists and America's scale of imprisonment shows no sign of abating.

Elected officials are facing difficult political choices. As the cost of corrections escalates, the United States has ostensibly moved into a post-welfare state period in which pressures to limit taxes will be immense – especially for politicians who campaigned against 'tax and spend liberals'. How will they be able to pay for rising prison expenditures in a time of shrinking governmental resources? One option is to cannibalize other state services. 'In California,' reports Gottfredson, 'state spending for corrections increased 25 per cent from fiscal 1990–91 through 1993–94 (to $3.3 billion), while funds for higher education declined by 25 per cent (to $4.4 billion) (1995: B1). But this strategy has limits: electoral constituencies, such as college students, will exert pressure if their interests are sufficiently violated. Inevitably – and despite all the rhetoric – the pressure emerges to consider less expensive community-based alternatives to incarceration.

Intermediate Punishments

Again, however, traditional community-based corrections cannot be easily advocated as a reasonable alternative to imprisonment, at least not by 'get tough' legislators who have vilified liberals for 'setting offenders free to victimize again'. The alternative to prison must save money but not appear to be soft on crime. And over the past decade, such a 'politically correct' option has emerged: punishing offenders in the community.

These attempts to 'get tough' in the community usually are called 'intermediate punishments', because they stand between prison, costly and crowded, and 'mere' probation, a sanction equated with 'no punishment at all'. Their distinctive feature is that they are directed at closely monitoring offenders. Thus, they seek to displace the traditional social welfare function of 'corrections' by transforming probation (and parole) officers from helping into policing agents. In America, the most popular means of achieving this surveillance, which often are used in some sort of combination, have been intensive supervision programmes, home confinement and electronic monitoring, drug testing, day reporting centres, and 'boot camps' (Byrne, Lurigio and Petersilia, 1992; McCarthy, 1987; Morris and Tonry, 1990).[6]

The cost savings from intermediate punishments are supposedly two-fold. First, as with all community-based programmes, they potentially divert offenders from prison. Second, monitoring increases the certainty that misbehaviours will be detected, and if so, that offenders will have their community sentence revoked and will be sent to prison. Advocates assume that faced with this heightened threat of punishment, offenders will be deterred from waywardness while in the community. Assessments of intermediate punishments suggest, however, that they are not panaceas for the prison crowding crisis. They have proven to be more expensive than portrayed, and their effectiveness in reducing recidivism beyond traditional community corrections has yet to be demonstrated. Further, the scale of the typical programme is too small to make much of a dent in the mammoth crowding crisis that most states and local jurisdictions face (Byrne and Pattavina, 1992; Clear and Braga, 1995; Cullen, Wright and Applegate, in press; Gendreau, Cullen and Bonta, 1994; Petersilia and Turner, 1993).

Two other problems limit the ability of intermediate punishments to solve the crowding crisis. First, like all community corrections programmes, they are susceptible to 'net widening': rather than use intermediate punishments to divert offenders from prison, which would save money and save space, judges tend to use them to exert more control over offenders who otherwise would have received probation. Second, intermediate punishments are vulnerable to the special, unforeseen problem of working too well: the more closely offenders are watched in the community, the more they will be found to have violated the conditions of their probation or parole sentence (Petersilia and Turner, 1993). This reality creates an unresolvable dilemma. If corrections officials do not respond when offenders violate programme rules (for example leave their house, use drugs), then the deterrent powers of monitoring are weakened; but if officials do respond to such 'technical violations', programme costs rise (for example arresting offenders, court time for revocation hearings) and increasing numbers of offenders are imprisoned. In short, the choice is between robbing the programme of its integrity or achieving programme integrity at the price of failing to achieve the original goal of reducing costs and reducing prison populations (see, for example, Goldkamp and Jones, 1992; Jones and Goldkamp, 1993).

Crisis Management

In effect, then, there is no coherent, politically viable solution to the crowding crisis on the horizon. The pressure to increase imprisonment seems constant; the political courage to deal with prison crowding seems scarce. In this situation, politicians will continue to pass policies that purchase votes and to pass the buck to corrections officials to deal with the effects of these policies. 'It is relatively easy', warns Blumstein (1995: 403), 'for a state ... to close its eyes to the potential impacts of overcrowding and to hold its breath hoping that no disasters follow and that the courts keep their hands off'. In the short-term, corrections officials are left to perform emergency relief. As the inmate population rises, they find legal loopholes to release inmates early, convert gymnasiums into inmate dormitories, turn single cells into double cells, erect tents to shelter offenders, and use busses to shuffle inmates from institution to institution. The long-term effects of this crisis management, however, may prove profound and disquieting. The constancy of the crisis, we anticipate, will foster goal displacement – a situation in which larger social purposes of corrections become irrelevant to the need to manage system inputs and outputs.

In this scenario, which commentators suggest already is well under way, correctional officials will adapt to organizational pressures by de-emphasizing the delivery of human services and by seeking more efficient ways to allocate bed space. This approach to correctional management will see offenders not as individuals in whom investments are made to effect their normalization, but as cogs in a well-oiled production line. In its worst form, corrections will become 'a kind of waste management function' in which underclass males, disproportionately African-American, are processed inexpensively and without much thought to their improvement and return to society (Feeley and Simon, 1992, 1994; Simon, 1993).

At this juncture, the 'crowding crisis' intersects with the broader 'crisis in conscience' in American corrections. As prison crowding fosters pressures to rationalize corrections to the point of forgetting the humanity of the people involved, the very purpose of the correctional enterprise is called into question. Countervailing moral or ideological forces, which might resist or shape these changes, have seemingly lost their power. In a very real way, the conscience that will guide the future of the American prison seems up for grabs.

CRISIS IN CONSCIENCE

For the first seventy years of this century, the rehabilitative ideal dominated American correctional thinking. To be sure, this ideal was rarely achieved, and in many cases served to justify inhumane penal practices (Platt, 1969; Rothman, 1980). None the less, a general consensus prevailed among policy elites and criminologists that punishment was an ineffective, uncivilized relic of the past and that progressive corrections should seek the individualized treatment of offenders. In the social turbulence of the late 1960s and early 1970s, however, the hegemony of the rehabilitative ideal was shattered (Cullen and Gilbert, 1982). Many commentators mistakenly assume that the attack on rehabilitation has achieved its demise, but this is not the case (a point we return to below). However, this onslaught, massive and many-sided, did send treatment into retreat.

Conservatives politicized the 'crime issue', and caricatured efforts at reforming offenders as a liberal masquerade to be soft with predators. More consequential, liberals, the traditional defenders of rehabilitation, joined the anti-treatment crusade. Suspicious of state power, they grew critical of the wide discretionary powers the rehabilitative ideal granted to criminal justice officials. They argued that officials frequently used these powers not for individualized treatment but to coerce inmate conformity and to send minorities disproportionately to prison. The final blow they levelled was that treatment programmes were ineffective; in fact, 'nothing works' became a slogan that could finish off any opponent (see Martinson, 1974; also Cullen and Gendreau, 1989).

The ensuing two decades have witnessed the ongoing quest to establish a coherent conscience or ideology to guide American corrections. We realize, of course, that much of our previous discussion suggests that this 'crisis in conscience' is all but settled. The 'get tough crowd' seemingly has set an agenda wildly popular with the American public: reduce crime by caging as many offenders as possible (see Zimring and Hawkins, 1995). The willingness of large proportions of the American electorate to support 'three strikes and you're out' laws is strong evidence favouring this conclusion.

The dominance of this idea, however, is far from complete. As the popularity of 'get tough' rhetoric abounds, commentators are prone to overlook the degree to which social welfare sentiments have permeated American thinking about corrections. Opinion polls, including those conducted in 1994, show that the American public opposes the mere warehousing of offenders, and that a strong majority sees rehabilitation as an important goal of imprisonment (Johnson, 1994; Maguire and Pastore, 1994; see also Cullen, Skovron, Scott and Burton, 1990; Thomson and Ragona, 1987). Research also reveals that correctional officials and line staff resist having their work reduced exclusively to the custodianship of society's dregs; they retain a belief in treatment and see human services as integral to their daily tasks (Cullen, Latessa, Burton and Lombardo, 1983; Cullen, Lutze, Link and Wolfe, 1989; DiIulio, 1991; Johnson, 1987).

Most salient, the ascendancy of the idea that incapacitation – 'caging criminals' – is a solution to the crime problem will mean that its credibility will be under continuing scrutiny. This conscience will confront the difficult reality that its pursuit will exacerbate the crowding crisis, and thus will create financial and administrative nightmares for correctional and state officials. Moreover, claims that massive doses of imprisonment can reduce offence rates will be challenged by liberal interest groups. In particular, American criminologists can be counted on to persist in their critique of the unrealistic promises of 'get tough' crime policies (see, for example, Clear, 1994; Currie, 1985; Gordon, 1991; Irwin and Austin, 1994; Selke, 1993; Zimring and Hawkins, 1995).

We do not wish to be naive and underestimate the power of the 'get tough' conscience; virtually all elected officials publicly embrace this ideology, and law after law seeks to fulfil its mission of enlarging prison populations. Still, we contend that the hegemony of 'get tough, imprison them all' thinking is far from complete. Indeed, as United States prisons move towards the year 2000, we expect the 'great American prison debate' to heat up and for space to exist for the reaffirmation of the rehabilitative ideal.

THE GREAT AMERICAN PRISON DEBATE

Twenty-five years ago, American criminologists were engaged in an internecine battle over the rehabilitative ideal. Traditional rehabilitationists were under siege from advocates of the 'justice model', who wished to constrain criminal justice officials' discretion, increase equity in decision making, and reduce the length of sentences (see Cullen and Gilbert, 1982). Today, however, criminologists fight less within the group and see a common enemy in the popular mentality that the United States can punish its way out of the crime problem.

Conveying the many strands of this critique would require a book-length manuscript, but we can identify a powerful metaphor – the *punishment experiment* – that criminologists have used, and will continue to use, in their debate with those who see prisons as panaceas for crime (see, for example, Clear, 1994; Cullen and Wright, in press; Currie, 1985; Zimring and Hawkins, 1994). In this view, the past two decades can be conceptualized as a natural experiment in which the ability of prisons to reduce crime has been amply tested. Despite four-to-five-fold increases in prison populations during this time, the crime rate has not decreased. This stubborn reality, they observe, is proof of the limits inherent in a punitive approach to crime control. The power of this metaphor is that it merges notions of science with common sense. On one hand, the language of an 'experiment' suggests that a scientific litmus test has been conducted that has 'proven' the failure of prisons to make society safer. On the other hand, the metaphor appeals to common sense, for how could prisons be effective if their enormous expansion left crime rates unchanged?[7]

American advocates of prison expansion, however, also invoke common sense: How can crime not be saved if criminals are no longer running free in the community? Indeed, the special appeal of caging criminals over other correctional alternatives is the certainty of protection it ostensibly provides. Imprisonment '*controls* rather than *influences* the behaviours of potential offenders', observe Zimring and Hawkins. 'The risk of a drug test or a large monetary fine may persuade some potential offenders to forgo criminal opportunities, but a functioning system of restraint provides assurance that potential offenders cannot commit crimes even if they want to' (Zimring and Hawkins, 1995: 157; emphasis in original). The attractiveness of current 'three strikes and you're out' laws is precisely this promise to prevent offenders from ever victimizing again.

Criminologists defending the use of prisons are in the minority, but they furnish the intellectual foundation for building more correctional facilities (see, for example, DiIulio, 1994a, 1994b, 1994c; Logan and DiIulio, 1992;

Wilson, 1975; Wright, 1994). While liberal criminologists emphasize the uncertain relationship between incarceration rates and crime rates, these researchers often draw their data from a criminological source of relatively recent origin: the inmate self-report study (see Visher, 1986). In this technique, prison inmates are asked to report on the number of crimes they committed in the year before their current prison term. Once the average number of offences committed per offender is determined, the 'crime savings' from incarceration is easily computed: simply multiply this mean number of offences by the number of inmates behind bars (DiIulio and Piehl, 1991).

This approach was initially popularized by Zedlewski (1987), who claimed that inmate self-reports showed that, while free in the community, offenders averaged 187 crimes annually. Using estimates that the average cost per crime to victims was $2300, he argued further that society saved $430 000 for each year an offender was incarcerated (187 × $2300) – a figure that far outstripped the $25 000 yearly cost of imprisoning the offender. In short, prisons were not a drain on the public treasury as liberals had long argued, but rather were a shrewd policy investment.

Zimring and Hawkins (1988, see also 1995) subjected Zedlewski's analysis to a withering critique. Their most devastating point is that given the figure of 187 crimes annually and the enormous rise in the number of offenders imprisoned since the 1970s, the United States crime rate should have dipped below zero from incapacitation effects alone. Their critique, however, has not stopped Zedlewski's analysis from assuming the status of criminological truth in public policy circles. Writing in the *New York Times*, for example, United States Senator Phil Gramm (1993), who is often mentioned as a leading candidate for the 1996 Republican Presidential nomination, confidently proclaimed that 'the active street criminal imposes a financial cost of $430,000 a year on the general public ... by Washington standards (or anybody's, for that matter), spending $30,000 a year [the cost of incarceration] to save $430,000 a year is a brilliant allocation of resources'.

The actual amount of crime saved through America's two-decade experiment with incapacitation is open to question, with estimates running from near zero to less than 10 per cent to upwards of 30 per cent (see, for example, Cohen and Canelo-Cacho, 1994; Petersilia, 1992; Visher, 1987; Zimring and Hawkins, 1995). Analyses claiming savings in crime, however, are based on two often-hidden assumptions that bias the case in favour of imprisonment.

First, these analyses compare offences prevented during incarceration with how many crimes offenders would have committed if they had been subjected to no control whatsoever. Clearly, there are non-incarcerative alternatives to 'letting predators run free in society'. What if offenders had been given intensive rehabilitation in the community? Indeed, evidence suggests that greater savings in crime might well be achieved through this option than through placing offenders in prison (Gendreau, et al., 1994; see also Petersilia and Turner, 1986). Second, these analyses overlook the 'opportunity costs' inherent in the expansive use of imprisonment. Thus, they do not assess now much crime might have been saved had the money allocated for prison construction and administration been used instead to fund crime prevention programmes, such as interventions with families of at-risk children (see, for example, Currie, 1985; Rivara and Farrington, in press).

We expect that prisons will continue to be the source of a 'great debate' within the United States. Those who present prisons as panaceas for the crime problem have had the upper-hand in the exchange and, in an entrenched 'get tough' era, seemingly will hold the advantage for the foreseeable future. As noted, however, prison advocates are likely to confront the uncomfortable reality that prisons are crowded and in crisis, difficult to pay for in a time of shrinking government revenues, and capable of reducing crime rates only at the margins. In this context, the liberal critique that prisons are a 'failed experiment' is likely to earn increasing credibility and to play a larger role in shaping penal policy. Whether this occurs sooner or much later, however, remains to be seen.

The more significant challenge for prison detractors will be to move beyond the critic's role to advancing a coherent correctional agenda that offers a positive, defensible alternative to caging criminals as the only means to reduce offender recidivism. The most promising approach, we contend, is to reaffirm rehabilitation as the guiding conscience of American corrections.

REAFFIRMING REHABILITATION

Admittedly, many American progressives, including many criminologists, still harbour suspicions about the coercive aspects of the rehabilitative ideal. The realities of the past two decades, however, offer incontrovertible evidence that the abandonment of treatment has not resulted in prisons that are more just or more effective in reducing recidivism. Liberal prescriptions for corrections – do justice for offenders, shorten prison terms – have fallen on deaf ears and now represent a bankrupt correctional conscience (Cullen and Gilbert, 1982; Currie, 1985; Griset, 1991).

Space limitations prevent our presenting a full-blown case for reaffirming rehabilitation (see Cullen and Gendreau, 1989; Cullen and Gilbert, 1982; Cullen and Wright, in press; Palmer, 1992; Rotman, 1990), but two considerations deserve attention. First, as noted above, survey research reveals that support for treatment remains high among the public and correctional workers. Second, amidst the debate over prisons and punishment, a cadre of researchers has conducted studies which, taken together, show that 'rehabilitation works' and is a promising alternative to the current generation of 'get tough' correctional practices. We briefly summarise these important developments, focusing in particular on the growing knowledge on 'what works' to reduce recidivism, on offender classification systems, and on levels of programme effectiveness.

PRINCIPLES OF EFFECTIVE CORRECTIONAL INTERVENTION: WHAT WORKS?

One of the most valuable contributions to our understanding of what works in correctional interventions comes from a series of reviews of numerous treatment programme evaluations. Some of these are extensive traditional literature reviews (see, for example, Cullen, et al., in press; Gendreau and Ross, 1987; Palmer, 1975, 1992), while others are more sophisticated empirical meta-analyses of the size of programme effects (see, for example, Andrews, Zinger, Bonta, Hoge, Gendreau and Cullen, 1990; Garrett, 1985; Lipsey, 1992; Whitehead and Lab, 1989).

Together, these reviews converge to identify the treatment modalities most likely to produce optimal success. These modalities include: behavioural, cognitive behaviour, life skills, and modelling (social learning) approaches; family intervention; and some multi-modal approaches. Equally important is the emerging picture of the types of interventions that are likely to be wasted efforts, such as individual and group therapy/counselling (particularly insight-oriented approaches), medical model approaches, probation and parole enhancements, confrontation (deterrence/shock) strategies, delinquency prevention (area wide strategies), diversion, and the newest generation of intermediate sanctions (primarily when they fail to include a treatment component) (see, for example, Andrews, Zinger, Bonta, Hoge, Gendreau, and Cullen, 1990; Cullen, et al., in press; Gendreau, in press; Palmer, 1992). The consensus achieved across studies adds strong credibility to their utility.

The meta-analyses and literature reviews also show us that treatment modality is not the only factor associated with programme success. Indeed, a host of programmatic factors also differentiate successful programmes from unsuccessful ones. These include such programme practices as: allocating more intensive treatments to high-risk offenders,[8] providing aftercare services, matching offenders to appropriate treatments, employing a structured programme manual, using authority in a sensitive and constructive manner, and targeting 'criminogenic needs' rather than factors that are not associated with crime. The reviews also recommend such programme qualities as high staff motivation and appropriate training and clinical supervision of staff (see Andrews and Bonta, 1994; Andrews and Kiessling, 1980; Gendreau, in press; Cullen and Gendreau, 1989; Gendreau, et al., 1994; and Palmer, 1992).

IMPROVEMENTS IN CORRECTIONAL CLASSIFICATION

Several of the principles set forth depend on the ability to classify offenders accurately (for example, determining risk levels and criminogenic needs, matching offenders with appropriate treatments). Research, which began in the 1960s with parolees (Gottfredson, Kelley and Lane, 1963; Gottfredson, Wilkins and Hoffman, 1978) and later advanced to probationers (Baird, Heinz and Bemus, 1979) and to incarcerates (Kane and Saylor, 1983; National Institute of Corrections, 1982), has identified several consistent predictors of new infractions. These studies and others led to the development of risk-assessment instruments that have greatly assisted the task of directing correctional resources to the most serious offenders and away from less serious ones.

Despite these advances, classification practices frequently have not been adequately researched. Current practices are flawed by the failure to validate instruments (Wright, Clear and Dickson, 1984; Van Voorhis, 1987, 1994a) and by a tendency to use less than ideal criterion variables (Jones, in press; Van Voorhis, 1994a).[9] Risk-assessment and classification strategies also are not used to their fullest potential. In particular, when employed exclusively for security purposes (for example, who is safe to release in the community), the potential for risk-assessment technology to assist in achieving treatment goals is overlooked (Andrews and Bonta, 1994; Gendreau and Ross, 1987; Van Voorhis, 1992, 1994a).

The research identifies several directions that could aid correctional treatment efforts. First, such common risk-assessment factors as 'age at first arrest', 'prior revocations', and 'number of prior offences' fail to direct offenders or their treatment practitioners to meaningful treatment targets, because these are variables that cannot change; as such, they are called 'static' predictors (Gendreau and Roass, 1987; Andrews, Bonta, and Hoge, 1990). Instead, scholars suggest consideration of a number of 'dynamic risk predictors' – such as criminal values, antisocial peers, and personality – that offenders can alter while under correctional supervision (Andrews, 1982; Andrews and Bonta, 1994; Andrews, Bonta, and Hoge, 1990; Gendreau and Ross, 1987; Van Voorhis, 1994a). In fact, if a programme brings about changes on these dynamic variables (for the better or the worse), they might also address a security function, because changes on dynamic risk factors are highly predictive of future criminal behaviours (Andrews and Bonta, 1994).

A second direction taken by current classification research rests on a body of studies pertinent to psychological and personality-based classification systems. These classify offenders according to developmental stages (Harvey, Hunt and Schroder, 1961; Kohlberg, Colby, Gibbs, Speicher-Dubin and Candee, 1978; Reitsma-Street, 1984; Warren, 1983) or according to personality (Jesness and Wedge, 1983; Megargee and Bohn, 1979; Quay, 1983; Warren, 1983). The utility of these classification typologies is to direct practitioners not only to important dynamic risk factors but also to the most responsive and amenable treatment options. While earlier research faults these psychological systems as too cumbersome for use in correctional settings, more recent research by Van Voorhis (1994a) suggests that less complex systems are as adequate as their complicated counterparts. This study also offers strong support to the construct validity of the personality-based systems.

Personality classification models and dynamic risk-assessment models have not only pointed us to the importance of addressing offenders' 'criminogenic needs' during treatment, they have also shown us that correctional outcomes are differential; what works with one type of offender may be a dismal failure for a different type of offender (Andrews, Zinger, Bonta, Hoge, Gendreau and Cullen, 1990; Palmer, 1978; Warren, et al., 1966). Unfortunately, this lesson typically is ignored by American correctional agencies. Misleading evaluation results can emerge when treatment effects are masked. Agencies often report one summary recidivism figure for the entire treatment group; accordingly, they ignore the possibility that the results of successful subgroups are cancelled by those for unsuccessful groups (Palmer, 1978).

HOW WELL DO EFFECTIVE PROGRAMMES WORK?

In addition to directing us to the most effective treatment strategies and principles, the meta-analyses and the narrative reviews illuminate how successful we might expect our best treatment programmes to be. These results are regularly ignored by critics of treatment, including, of course, advocates of punishing offenders more harshly.

The most common way to assess treatment effectiveness is to examine recidivism across all studies (rather than to dissect a sample of studies to discern why some programmes are particularly successful). Using this analytical technique, recent researchers report that in the studies sampled, treatment groups achieved more favourable reductions in recidivism than control groups, 64 per cent, (Lipsey, 1992) and 47 per cent (Whitehead and Lab, 1989) of the time. When the average savings in recidivism is computed across all studies, Lipsey (1992) reports a mean reduction of 10 per cent. If this figure is calculated only for the subset of programmes that has achieved positive outcomes, reductions in recidivism (over those for the control group) climb to approximately 20 per cent (Palmer, 1992). Most instructive, when researchers separate out those programmes that follow treatment principles shown to be effective (see 'what works' above), reductions in recidivism approach, if not exceed, 50 per cent (Andrews, Zinger, Bonta, Hoge, Gendreau and Cullen, 1990; Gendreau, et al., 1994).

Treatment scholars have expressed frustration over the failure to translate the research on effective programming and classification into practice. Additional research reports that when asked where their idea for a particular intervention originated, most programme personnel failed to indicate a link to the knowledge base of our discipline (Gendreau, 1994). Thus, most strategies known to work are not currently in practice, and much of what is currently in practice did not emanate from the knowledge base on how best to achieve effective correctional treatment.

None the less, the growing research on rehabilitation is developing an empirical basis for arguing that the knowledge exists to reduce recidivism through treatment interventions. Even if more conservative estimates for treatment effectiveness are used (say, 10 to 20 per cent reductions in recidivism), the cost savings achieved from the reduced use of prison space is impressive (Gendreau and Ross, 1987). Further, whatever its shortcomings, the case is growing increasingly strong that rehabilitation decreases recidivism more than any competing correctional practices, including incapacitation (Cohen, 1983; Greenwood, 1994, Visher, 1987) and punishment-oriented programmes (Andrews and Bonta, 1994; Gendreau and Little, 1993).

CONCLUSION: THE AMERICAN PRISON IN CONTEXT

The future of the American prison will be shaped by the crisis of crowding and conscience. As the year 2000 approaches, policymakers will be confronted with the practical problem of finding room for the escalating inmate population and with the ideological problem of what purpose, beyond caging criminals, American corrections should serve. In the time immediately ahead, it seems safe to forecast more of the same: more crowding and more punitive policies. In the longer term, the campaign to 'get tough' may be frustrated by the sheer costs inherent in imprisonment and by the limited ability of punitive policies to reduce America's crime rates. If so, space may emerge for second thoughts, and thus for considering the growing evidence on the effectiveness of correctional rehabilitation.

We suspect, however, that the American prison will also reflect – perhaps more fundamentally – larger decisions on what kind of society America will be. At present, it appears that the United States is being transformed into a post-welfare state in which at-risk individuals will be left to fend for themselves and in which wide racial and class inequalities will be attributed to individual failings (see, for example, Herrnstein and Murray, 1994). If this is America's future, we can expect prisons to degenerate more fully into warehouses whose only function is to contain, not improve, the nation's dangerous classes.

At the risk of being accused of unwarranted optimism, we are hopeful that policymakers and citizens will see the folly in this bleak path. It is possible, of course, that elected officials, now comfortable in purchasing votes with promises of 'locking 'em all up', will not change course until major social upheaval shakes them to their senses – until the Los Angeles riots are writ large. If so, the United States will pay a high and tragic price before its harsh social and penal policies are reconsidered.

But another possibility remains. Despite the sharp tilt to the right in American politics, it is far from clear that Americans are prepared to roll back the welfare state and the safety-nets it offers. In particular, there are increasingly loud warnings that investments must be made with at-risk citizens – for example, that too many of the nation's children are in jeopardy, and that displaced workers in post-industrial America cannot simply be left to fend for themselves (see, for example, Currie, 1985). If this call for social investment is heard and perhaps generalized, it may force a reconsideration of the wisdom of simply neglecting America's vulnerable populations. In this context, the possibility may emerge to redirect correctional policy – to see prisons not as cages to be crammed full but as institutions with the dual responsibility to restrain the truly dangerous and to reform those who will soon be among us.

Notes

1. For example, commentators suggest that a number of factors have made the maintenance of order more difficult in American prisons, thus producing a crisis in control (Colvin, 1992; Irwin, 1980; Jacobs, 1977).

2. Due to limited horizons or perhaps to cultural arrogance, United States writers commonly use the term 'American' as a synonym for 'United States'. For convenience, we do the same here, but we do so in full recognition that other nation's in the western hemisphere have equal claim to 'American'.

3. Sherman and Hawkins (1981: 3) also quote Frank Kermode as saying, 'To be in the midst of a ... crisis is what we all want, for it makes us more interesting.' Whether this is a typical American trait (which we share) we will leave to the reader to decide.

4. Readers familiar with United States criminology will know that most writings on state-level corrections focus on California, the state with the largest population and largest prison system, with almost 115 000 inmates (see, for example, Irwin and Austin, 1994; Petersilia, 1992; Zimring and Hawkins, 1994). We chose to use examples from Ohio in part because it is our home state. We also wished to show, however, that correctional trends are not idiosyncratic to the most unusual state, California, but penetrate to the heartland of the United States.

5. In the United States, county and other local jails typically are used to detain the accused who are awaiting trial and when offenders are sentenced to a term of less than one year's incarceration. When sentences exceed a year, offenders are assigned to a state prison. Federal prisons are used when offenders are convicted of violating federal statutes.

6. 'Boot camps' expose offenders to the rigours of military discipline (that is, 'basic training') during a limited prison sentence (about four months). They differ from traditional intermediate punishments in two ways. First, they are not community-based. Second, the criminological theory underlying boot camps is not deterrence through supervision, but rather the notion that military training can instil discipline, which in turn will prevent recidivism. Boot camps are classified as an intermediate punishment, however, because they are punitively oriented and are designed to be an alternative to traditional, lengthier prison sentences.

7. Of course, the issue is more complicated than common sense would dictate, although that may not matter in the debating arena. A perceptive critic would note that an adequate outcome measure for assessing the punishment experience would not be gross changes in offence rates, but rather how much crime was saved through higher levels of incarceration than would have been the case had prison populations remained at 1970 levels.

8. This is not solely because high-risk offenders have more room for improvement, but also because low-risk offenders do worse in the intensive treatments than in less restrictive settings (Andrews and Bonta, 1994).

9. According to Jones (in press), many risk-assessment instruments predict less serious infractions; as a result, they may be inflating correctional

populations with inmates who commit rule infractions but may not be dangerous to society.

References

Andrews, D. A. (1982) *The Level of Supervision Inventory (LSI): The First Follow-Up* (Toronto: Ontario Ministry of Correctional Services).

Andrews, D. A. and Bonta, J. (1994) *The Psychology of Criminal Conduct* (Cincinnati: Anderson).

Andrews, D. A.; Bonta, J.; and Hoge, R. D. (1990) 'Classification for Effective Rehabilitation: Rediscovering Psychology', *Criminal Justice and Behaviour*, 17: 19–52.

Andrews, D. A. and Kiessling, J. J. (1980) 'Program Structure and Effective Correctional Practices: A Summary of the CAVIC Research', in R. Ross and P. Gendreau (eds), *Effective Correctional Treatment* (Toronto: Buttersworth): 441–63.

Andrews, D. A.; Zinger, Ivan; Hoge, R. D.; Bonta, J.; Gendreau, P.; and Cullen, F. T. (1990) 'Does Correctional Treatment Work? A Clinically-Relevant and Psychologically-Informed Meta Analysis', *Criminology*, 28: 369–404.

Associated Press (1994) 'Prison Budget to Rise', *Cincinnati Post* (November 21): F7.

Baird, C.; Heinz, R.; and Bemus, B. (1979) *The Wisconsin Case Classification/ Staff Deployment Project*, Project Report No. 14 (Madison, WI: Department of Health and Social Services, Division of Corrections).

Blumstein, A. (1982) 'On the Racial Disproportionality of United States' Prison Populations, *Journal of Criminal Law and Criminology*, 73: 1259–81.

Blumstein, A. (1989) 'American Prisons in a Time of Crisis', L. Goodstein and D. L. MacKenzie (eds), *The American Prison: Issues in Research and Policy* (New York: Plenum): 13–22.

Blumstein, A. (1995) 'Prisons', in J. Q. Wilson and J. Petersilia (eds), *Crime* (San Francisco: ICS Press): 387–419.

Blumstein, A. and Cohen, J. (1973) 'A Theory of the Stability of Punishment', *Journal of Criminal Law and Criminology*, 64: 198–206.

Bureau of Justice Statistics (1992) *Drugs, Crime, and the Justice System: A National Report* (Washington, D.C.: Bureau of Justice Statistics).

Byrne, J. M.; Lurigio, A. J.; and Petersilia, J. (eds) (1992) *Smart Sentencing: The Emergence of Intermediate Sanctions* (Newbury Park, CA: Sage).

Byrne, J. M. and Pattavina, A. (1992) 'The Effectiveness Issue: Assessing What Works in the Adult Community Corrections System', in J. M. Byrne, A. J. Lurigio, and J. Petersilia (eds), *Smart Sentencing: The Emergence of Intermediate Sanctions* (Newbury Park, CA: Sage): 281–303.

Camp, G. M. and Camp, C. G. (1994) *The Corrections Yearbook 1994: Adult Corrections* (South Salem, N.Y.: Criminal Justice Institute).

Christie, N. (1993) *Crime Control as Industry: Towards GULAGS, Western Style?* (New York: Routledge).

Clear, T. R. (1994) *Harm in American Penology: Offenders, Victims and Their Communities* (Albany: SUNY Press).

Clear, T. R. and Braga, A. A. (1995) 'Community Corrections', in J. Q. Wilson and J. Petersilia (eds), *Crime* (San Francisco: ICS Press): 421–44.

Cohen, J. (1983) 'Incapacitation as a Strategy for Crime Control: Possibilities and Pitfalls', in M. Tonry and N. Morris (eds), *Crime and Justice: An Annual Review of Research*, vol. 5 (Chicago, University of Chicago Press): 1–84.

Cohen, J. and Canelo-Cacho, J. A. (1994) 'Incarceration and Violent Crime: 1965–1988', in A. J. Reiss, Jr. and J. A. Roth (eds), *Understanding and Preventing Violence: Consequences and Control*, vol. 4 (Washington, D.C.: National Academy Press).

Colvin, M. (1992) *The Penitentiary in Crisis: From Accommodation to Riot in New Mexico* (Albany: SUNY Press).

Cullen, F. T. and Gendreau, P. (1989) 'The Effectiveness of Correctional Rehabilitation: Reconsidering the "Nothing Works" Debate', in L. Goodstein and D. L. MacKenzie (eds), *The American Prison: Issues in Research and Policy* (New York: Plenum): 23–44.

Cullen, F. T. and Gilbert, K. E. (1982) *Reaffirming Rehabilitation* (Cincinnati: Anderson).

Cullen, F. T.; Latessa, E. J.; Burton, V. S., Jr.; and Lombardo, L. X. (1993) 'The Correctional Orientation of Prison Wardens: Is the Rehabilitative Ideal Supported?' *Criminology*, 31: 69–92.

Cullen, F. T.; Lutze, F. E.; Link, B. G.; and Wolfe, N. T. (1989) 'The Correctional Orientation of Prison Guards: Do Officers Support Rehabilitation?' *Federal Probation*, 53: 33–42.

Cullen, F. T.; Skovron, S. E.; Scott, J. E.; and Burton, V. S., Jr. (1990) 'Public Support for Correctional Rehabilitation: The Tenacity of the Rehabilitative Ideal', *Criminal Justice and Behaviour*, 17 (1990) 6–18.

Cullen, F. T. and Wright, J. P. (in press) 'The Future of Corrections', in B. Maguire and P. Radosh (eds), *The Past, Present, and Future of American Criminal Justice* (New York: General Hall).

Cullen, F. T.; Wright, J. P.; and Applegate, B. K. (in press) 'Control in the Community: The Limits of Reform?' in A. T. Harland (ed.), *Choosing Correctional Interventions that Work: Defining the Demand and Evaluating the Supply* (Newbury Park, CA: Sage).

Currie, E. (1985) *Confronting Crime: An American Challenge* (New York: Pantheon).

Currie, E. (1993) *Reckoning: Drugs, the Cities, and the American Future* (New York: Hill and Wang).

DiIulio, J. J., Jr. (1987) *Governing Prisons: A Comparative Study of Correctional Management* (New York: The Free Press).

DiIulio, J. J., Jr. (1991) *No Escape: The Future of American Corrections* (New York: Basic Books).

DiIulio, J. J., Jr. (1994a) 'Instant Replay: Three Strikes Was the Right Call', *American Prospect*, 18 (Summer): 12–15.

DiIulio, J. J., Jr. (1994b) 'The Question of Black Crime', *Public Interest*, 117 (Fall): 3–32.

DiIulio, J. J., Jr. (1994c) 'A Philadelphia Crime Story, *Wall Street Journal* (October 26): A21.

DiIulio, J. J., Jr. and Piehl, A. M. (1991) 'Does Prison Pay? The Stormy National Debate Over the Cost-Effectiveness of Imprisonment', *Brookings Review*, 9 (Fall): 28–35.

Farrington, D. P. and Langan, P. A. (1992) 'Changes in Crime and Punishment in England and America in the 1980s', *Justice Quarterly*, 9: 5–31.

Feeley, M. M. and Simon, J. (1992) 'The New Penology: Notes on the Emerging Strategy of Corrections and Its Implications', *Criminology*, 30: 449–74.

Feeley, M. M. and Simon, J. (1994) 'Actuarial Justice: The Emerging New Criminal Law', in D. Nelken (ed.), *The Futures of Criminology* (London: Sage): 173–201.

Forer, L. G. (1994) *A Rage to Punish: The Unintended Consequences of Mandatory Sentencing* (New York: W. W. Norton).

Forst, B. (1995) 'Prosecution and Sentencing', in J. Q. Wilson and J. Petersilia (eds), *Crime* (San Francisco: ICS Press): 363–86.

Garrett, C. J. (1985) 'Effects of Residential Treatment on Adjudicated Delinquents', *Journal of Research in Crime and Delinquency*, 22: 287–308.

Gendreau, P. (1994) 'Community Corrections in the US: A Decade of Punishing Stupidly', presentation to the annual meeting of the Academy of Criminal Justice Sciences (March), Chicago, IL.

Gendreau, P. (in press) 'The Principles of Effective Intervention with Offenders', in A. T. Harland (ed.), *Choosing Correctional Interventions That Work: Defining the Demand and Evaluating the Supply* (Newbury Park, CA: Sage).

Gendreau, P.; Cullen, F. T.; and Bonta, J. (1994) 'Intensive Rehabilitation Supervision: The Next Generation in Community Corrections?', *Federal Probation*, 58 (No. 1): 72–8.

Gendreau, P. and Little, T. (1993) 'A Meta-Analysis of the Effectiveness of Sanctions on Offender Recidivism', unpublished manuscript, Department of Psychology, University of New Brunswick–Saint John.

Gendreau, P. and Ross, R. R. (1987) 'Revivification of Rehabilitation: Evidence from the 1980s', *Justice Quartely*, 4: 349–407.

Goldkamp, J. S. and Jones, P. R. (1992) 'Pretrial Drug-Testing Experiments in Milwaukee and Prince Georges County: The Context of Implementation', *Journal of Research in Crime and Delinquency*, 29: 430–65.

Gordon, D. R. (1991) *The Justice Juggernaut: Fighting Street Crime, Controlling Citizens* (New Brunswick: Rutgers University Press).

Gordon, D. R. (1994) *The Return of the Dangerous Classes: Drug Prohibition and Policy Politics* (New York: W. W. Norton).

Gottfredson, D. M.; Kelley, B.; and Lane, L. (1963) *Association Analysis in a Prison Sample and Prediction of Parole Performance* (Vacaville, CA: Institute for the Study of Crime and Delinquency).

Gottfredson, D. M.; Wilkins, L.; and Hoffman, P. (1978) *Guidelines for Parole and Sentencing: A Policy Control Model* (Lexington, MA: Lexington Books).

Gottfredson, S. D. (1995) 'Fighting Crime at the Expense of College', *Chronicle of Higher Education* (20 January): B1–B2.

Gottfredson, S. D. and McConville, S. (eds) (1987) *America's Correctional Crisis: Prison Populations and Public Policy* (New York: Greenwood).

Gramm, P. (1993) 'Drugs, Crime and Punishment: Don't Let Judges Set Crooks Free', *New York Times* (8 July): A19.

Greenwood, P. W. (1994) 'Estimating the Effects of Three Strikes and You're Out Sentencing Laws on Crime Rates and Costs', presentation to the annual meeting of the American Society of Criminology (November), Miami, FL.

Grieser, R. C. (1988) *Wardens and State Corrections Commissioners Offer Their Views in National Assessment* (Washington, D.C.: National Institute of Justice).

Griset, P. L. (1991) *Determinate Sentencing: The Promise and the Reality of Retributive Justice* (Albany: SUNY Press).

Guynes, R. (1988) *Nation's Jail Managers Assess Their Problems* (Washington, D.C., National Institute of Justice).

Hacker, A. (1992) *Two Nation's: Black and White, Separate, Hostile, and Unequal* (New York: Charles Scribners Sons).

Hagan, J. (1994) *Crime and Disrepute* (Thousand Oaks, CA: Pine Force).

Harvey, O.; Hunt, D.; and Schroder, H. (1961) *Conceptual Systems and Personality Organisation* (New York: John Wiley).

Herrnstein, R. J. and Murray, C. (1994) *The Bell Curve: Intelligence and Class Structure in American Life* (New York: Free Press).

Irwin, J. (1980) *Prisons in Turmoil* (Boston: Little, Brown).

Irwin, J. and Austin, J. (1994) *It's About Time: America's Prison Binge* (Belmont, CA: Wadsworth).

Jacobs, J. B. (1977) *Stateville: The Penitentiary in Mass Society* (Chicago: University of Chicago Press).

Jesness, C.F. and Wedge, R. (1983) *Classifying Offenders: The Jesness Inventory Classification System* (Sacramento: California Youth Authority).

Johnson, B. (1994) 'To Rehabilitate or Punish: Results of a Public Opinion Poll', *American Jails*, 8 (November–December): 41–5.

Johnson, R. (1987) *Hard Time: Understanding and Reforming the Prison* (Monterey, CA: Brooks/Cole).

Jones, P. R. (in press) 'Risk Prediction in Criminal Justice, in A. T. Harland (ed), *Choosing Correctional Interventions That Work: Defining the Demand and Evaluating the Supply* (Newbury Park, CA: Sage).

Jones, P. R. and Goldkamp, J. S. (1993) 'Implementing Pretrial Drug-Testing Programs in Two Experimental Sites: Some Deterrence and Jail Bed Implications', *Prison Journal* 73: 199–219.

Kane, T. and Saylor, W. (1983) *Security Designation/Custody Classification of Inmates* (unpublished manuscript, Washington, D.C.: Department of Justice).

Kohlberg, L.; Colby, A.; Gibbs, J.; Speicher-Dubin, B.; and Candee, D. (1978) *Standard Scoring Manual* (Cambridge: Harvard University Press).

Langan, P. A. (1991) 'America's Soaring Prison Population', *Science*, 251: 1568–73.

Langan, P. A. (1994) 'No Racism in the Justice System', *Public Interest*, 117 (Fall): 48–51.

Lilly, J. R. (1992) 'Selling Justice: Electronic Monitoring and the Security Industry', *Justice Quarterly*, 9: 493–503.

Lipsey, M. W. (1992) 'Juvenile Delinquency Treatment: A Meta-Analytic Inquiry into the Variability of Effects', in T. D. Cook, H. Cooper, D. S. Cordray, H. Hartmann, L. V. Hedges, R. J. Light, T. A. Louis, and F. Mosteller (eds), *Meta-Analysis for Explanation* (New York: Russell Sage Foundation): 83–127.

Logan, C. H. and DiIulio, J. J., Jr. (1992) 'Ten Myths About Crime and Prisons', *Wisconsin Interest*, 1: 21–35.

Lynch, J. (1995) 'Crime in International Perspective', in J. Q. Wilson and J. Petersilia (eds), *Crime* (San Francisco: ICS Press): 11–38.

McCarthy, B. (ed.) (1987) *Intermediate Punishments: Intensive Supervision, Home Confinement and Electronic Confinement* (Monsey, N.Y.: Willow Tree Press).

McCorkle, R. C. (1993) 'Punish and Rehabilitate? Public Attitudes Toward Six Common Crimes', *Crime and Delinquency*, 39: 240–52.

Maguire, K. and Pastore, A. L. (eds), *Sourcebook of Criminal Justice Statistics –1993* (Washington, D.C.: Bureau of Justice Statistics).

Mauer, M. (1994) *Americans Behind Bars: The International Use of Incarceration, 1992–1993* (Washington, D.C.: Sentencing Project).

Martinson, R. (1974) 'What Works? – Questions and Answers About Prison Reform', *Public Interest*, 35 (Spring): 22–54.

Megargee, E. I. and Bohn, M. J., Jr. (1979) *Classifying Criminal Offenders: A New System Based on the MMPI* (Beverly Hills, CA: Sage).

Miller, J. G. (1991) *Last One Over the Wall: The Massachusetts Experiment in Closing Reform Schools* (Columbus: Ohio State University Press).

Morris, N. and Tonry, M. (1990) *Between Prison and Probation: Intermediate Punishments in a Rational Sentencing System* (New York: Oxford University Press).

National Institute of Corrections (1982) *Classification: Principles, Models, and Guidelines* (Washington, D.C.: US Department of Justice).

National Institute of Corrections (ed.) (1985) 'Our Crowded Prisons', *Annals of the American Academy of Political and Social Science*, 478: 9–182.

New York University Review of Law and Social Change (1983–1984) 'Colloquium: The Prison Crowding Crisis', 12: 1–356.

Office of Criminal Justice Services (1995) *The State of Crime and Criminal Justice in Ohio* (Columbus: Office of Criminal Justice Services).

Palmer, T. (1975) 'Martinson Revisited', *Journal of Research in Crime and Delinquency*, 12: 133–52.

Palmer, T. (1978) *Corrections Intervention and Research: Current Issues and Future Prospects* (Lexington, MA: Lexington Books).

Palmer, T. (1992) *The Re-Emergence of Correctional Intervention* (Newbury Park, CA: Sage).

Petersilia, J. (1992) 'California's Prison Policy: Causes, Costs, and Consequences', *Prison Journal*, 72: 8–36.

Petersilia, J. and Turner, S. (1993) 'Intensive Probation and Parole', in M. Tonry (ed.), *Crime and Justice: A Review of Research*, vol. 17 (Chicago: University of Chicago Press): 281–335.

Petersilia, J. and Turner, S., with the assistance of Peterson, J. (1986) *Prison versus Probation in California: Implications for Crime and Offender Recidivism* (Santa Monica, CA: RAND).

Platt, A. M. (1969) *The Child Savers: The Invention of Delinquency* (Chicago: University of Chicago Press).

Quay, H. C. (1983) *Technical Manual for the Behavioral Classifications System for Adult Offenders* (Washington, D.C.: Department of Justice).

Reitsma-Street, M. (1984) 'Differential Treatment of Young Offenders: A Review of the Conceptual Level Matching Model', *Canadian Journal of Criminology*, 26: 199–212.

Rivara, F. P. and Farrington, D. P. (in press) 'Prevention of Violence: Role of the Pediatrician', *Archives of Pediatrics and Adolescent Medicine* .

Rothman, D. J. (1980) *Conscience and Convenience: The Asylum and Its Alternatives in Progressive America* (Boston: Little, Brown).

Rotman, E. (1990) *Beyond Punishment: A New View on the Rehabilitation of Criminal Offenders* (New York: Greenwood).

Schwaner, S. (1994) 'Percent of Prison Population Violent Offenders and Budget Expenditures' (Ohio Department of Rehabilitation and Correction, personal communication).

Scull, A. (1977) *Decarceration: Community Treatment and the Deviant – A Radical View* (Englewood Cliffs, N.J.: Prentice-Hall).

Selke, W. L. (1993) *Prisons in Crisis* (Bloomington: Indiana University Press).

Sherman, M. and Hawkins, G. (1981) *Imprisonment in America: Choosing the Future* (Chicago: University of Chicago Press).

Simon, J. (1993) *Poor Discipline: Parole and the Social Control of the Underclass, 1890–1990* (Chicago: University of Chicago Press).

Skolnick, J. H. (1994) 'Wild Pitch: "Three Strikes, You're Out" and Other Bad Calls on Crime', *American Prospect*, 18 (Spring): 30–7.

Thomson, D. R. and Ragona, A. J. (1987) 'Popular Moderation Versus Governmental Authoritarianism: An Interactionist View of Public Sentiments Toward Criminal Sanctions', *Crime and Delinquency*, 33: 337–57.

Tonry, M. (1994) 'Racial Disproportion in US Prisons', *British Journal of Criminology*, 34: 97–115.

Tonry, M. (1995) *Malign Neglect: Race, Crime, and Punishment in America* (New York: Oxford University Press).

Van Voorhis, P. (1987) 'Correctional Effectiveness: The High Cost of Ignoring Success', *Federal Probation*, 51 (no. 1): 56–62.

Van Voorhis, P. (1992) 'An Overview of Offender Classification Systems', in D. Lester, M. Braswell and P. Van Voorhis (eds), *Correctional Counseling*, 2nd edn (Cincinnati: Anderson): 73–94.

Van Voorhis, P. (1994a) *Psychological Classification of the Adult, Male Prison Inmate* (Albany, N.Y.: SUNY Press).

Van Voorhis, P. (1994b) 'A Multiple Indicators Approach to Understanding Prison Adjustment', *Justice Quarterly*, 11: 679–709.

Visher, C. A. (1986) 'The Rand Inmate Survey: A Reanalysis', in A. Blumstein, J. Cohen, J. A. Roth and C. A. Visher, *Criminal Careers and 'Career Criminals'*, vol. 2 (Washington, D.C.: National Academy Press): 161–211.

Visher, C. A. (1987) 'Incapacitation and Crime Control: Does a "Lock 'Em Up" Strategy Reduce Crime?' *Justice Quartely*, 4: 513–43.

Warren, M. (1983) 'Applications of Interpersonal Maturity Theory to Offender Populations', in W. S. Laufer and J. M. Day (eds), *Personality Theory, Moral Development, and Criminal Behavior* (Lexington, MA: Lexington Books): 23–50.

Warren, M. and the Staff of the Community Treatment Project (1966) *Interpersonal Maturity Level Classification: Diagnosis and Treatment of Low, Middle, and High Maturity Delinquents* (Sacramento, CA: California Youth Authority).

Welch, R. (1990) 'Private Prisons – Profitable and Growing', *Corrections Compendium*, 15 (April): 1, 5–8, 16.

Whitehead, J. T. and Lab, S. P. (1989) 'A Meta-Analysis of Juvenile Correctional Treatment', *Journal of Research in Crime and Delinquency*, 26: 276–95.

Wicker, T. (1991) 'The Punitive Society', *New York Times* (12 January).

Wilson, J. Q. (1975) *Thinking About Crime* (New York: Random House).

Wright, J. P. (1995) 'Not Liberals' Fault', *Johnson City Press* (27 January): A4.

Wright, K. N. (1994) *Effective Prison Leadership* (Binghamton, N.Y.: William Neil).

Wright, K. N.; Clear, T. R.; and Dickson, P. (1984) 'Universal Application of Probation Risk-Assessment Instruments: A Critique', *Criminology*, 22: 113–34.

Wright, R. A. (1994) *In Defense of Prisons* (Westport, CT: Greenwood).

Zawitz, M. W. (ed.) (1988) *Report to the Nation on Crime and Justice*, 2nd edn (Washington, D.C.: Bureau of Justice Statistics).

Zedlewski, E. W. (1987) *Research in Brief: Making Confinement Decisions* (Washington, D.C.: National Institute of Justice).

Zimring, F. and Hawkins, G. (1988) 'The New Mathematics of Imprisonment', *Crime and Delinquency*, 34: 425–36.

Zimring, F. and Hawkins, G. (1991) *The Scale of Imprisonment* (Chicago: University of Chicago Press).

Zimring, F. and Hawkins, G. (1994) 'The Growth of Imprisonment in California, *British Journal of Criminology*, 34: 83–96.

Zimring, F. and Hawkins, G. (1995) *Incapacitation: Penal Confinement and the Restraint of Crime* (New York: Oxford University Press).

3 We Never Promised Them a Rose Garden

Monika Platek[1]

INTRODUCTION

As we approach the year 2000 and look back over 200 years of penal reform we are forced to admit that the fundamental problems of imprisonment are much the same today as they were in the past. It is time, therefore, to enquire whether we have been asking the wrong question. When thinking of penal reform we have concentrated on changing the prison itself. We have been preoccupied with asking the question of what is wrong with the prison system instead of asking the critical question of how society produces a system of punishment which relies so heavily on a system of imprisonment, which itself exhibits so many problems. It is well known that prison mirrors society and that systems of punishment reflect the level of evolution and maturation (Foucault, 1977; Rusche and Kirchheimer, 1969). By investigating this two-way process we are able to move beyond the usual concentration on the internal operation of prisons and formulate a broader perspective that can incorporate the wider social processes that shape, and that are shaped by imprisonment.

In this chapter I want to explore the reciprocal relationship between prison and society through an examination of the situation in America, Norway and Poland. America is a country with a notoriously high rate of imprisonment, while Norway is renowned for its relatively low rate of imprisonment. Poland has been selected as an example of a society which is undergoing rapid changes both politically and economically and which is also experiencing interesting fluctuations in the use and level of imprisonment. The differences between these countries are considered to be sufficient to illustrate some important aspects of the relationship between social and economic configurations, the organization of criminal and penal policy and the distribution of social and individual freedoms.

It is not my intention to elaborate a comprehensive philosophy of imprisonment. However, it is important to make some reference to the key roles assigned to the prison. Prisons are designed primarily to eliminate wrongdoers from the open society in order to free us from crime and the fear of crime. This is what we want. We want to be free from crime and to be safe. Prisons are meant to reduce crime. Therefore, in order to be safe and free, we build more prisons. We build institutions with high walls, razor wire and armed towers. And yet, paradoxically, in the process of removing the menace of crime we create institutions which affect the way we think and the way we talk. As outsiders we do not want to think of prison but are nevertheless strongly affected by it.

The issues of crime and the fear of crime are, however, posed differently in America, Norway and Poland. In America people ask: How can *I* avoid it? In Norway they ask: What can *we* do about it?; while in Poland they ask; *Who* is to blame for it? These differences illustrate the variance of social norms, in the respective approaches to social problems and to the question of punishment. Different attitudes to punishment and imprisonment have, in turn, different social effects.

Conducting comparative analysis is particularly difficult when the countries concerned are so diverse (King and Maguire, 1994; Selke, 1993). A simple statistical comparison between the respective social systems might tell us about numerical differences but the objective is to investigate the interrelation between crime, punishment and society. It may be that the differences between these countries are too vast to make comprehensive comparisons between their related prison systems. However, in this context it will be enough to draw out some general points of comparison. The aim is to learn something about both the successes and the failures of the systems of penality operating in each of these different social and economic contexts.

PRISON AND SOCIETY IN THREE COUNTRIES

America

The United States, with a population of over 250 million consistently breaks many records. One of its less glorious achievements lies in the area of incarceration. America currently leads the world with a rate of 455 persons per 100 000 of the population imprisoned. There are over a million people incarcerated in prisons and jails in the United States. Between 1980 and 1992, the number of Americans behind bars increased by almost 160 per cent (Edna McConnel Clark Foundation, 1993). The second highest rate of incarceration is in South Africa which had a rate of 311 inmates per 100 000 in 1992. A growing proportion of people in the United States are imprisoned for drug-related crimes. More prisoners are sent into American prisons each week than the existing cells can hold. In

1991, the increase in prisoners created a need for 1060 new prison beds nationwide each week. Overcrowded prisons and jails have become the norm. There are 51 separate state prison systems, most of which have witnessed increases in their prison population. As a result, 128 000 new prison beds were created in 1989 and an additional 69 487 between 1990 and 1991. During 1992, 41 new institutions were opened in 18 states (Platek, 1994a).

While writing about California, Zimring and Hawkins (1994) argue that the growth of imprisonment cannot be explained either by the increase in non-drug-related crimes, nor even by the determinate sentencing laws which were passed in 1977 and which required judges to apply exact terms when specific crimes occurred. Instead they assume, it was caused by a 'revolution of practice rather than theory'. Prison simply began to be used more often (Zimring and Hawkins, 1994: 94).

Poland

Poland, with a population of over 40 million has also broken a record. In the middle of 1989, Poland introduced revolutionary changes. These changes did not materialize overnight but were the culmination of years of slow but steady rejection of the previous system. In June 1989, the communist government was overtaken by the democratic opposition forces led by the trade union 'Solidarity'. Subsequently a non-communist government was established in Poland (Frankowski and Wasék, 1993).

At the beginning of 1989, the prison population was almost 100 000 with a rate of more than 200 per 100 000. The number at the end of the same year dropped below 40 000 (Platek, 1990; 1994), although after several months the number began to grow again, reaching 64 000 in 1993. In the meantime new directors of the central prison administration were appointed. They were selected for the first time from the civilian population and from university professors who were known for their critical writings and reform activities. A new Prison Law was introduced allowing prisoners to take legal action against the prison administration.

Norway

Norway is roughly equivalent in size to Poland but has only 4 million inhabitants. It has a long history of a rather stable and relatively low rate of imprisonment. There were some 1800 Norwegians in prison in 1981. This was approximately 44 per 100 000 of the population. This rate has remained fairly constant since the turn of the century (Christie, 1981). The number has however increased lately with the consequence that two inmates are placed in a cell originally designed for one. In September 1990, there were 2200 prisoners in Norway with a detention rate of 56 per 100 000 inhabitants (Council of Europe, 1992). This increase is partly due to growing anxiety about drugs which has fuelled demands for greater use of punishment. However, this more punitive approach has been perceived by many in Norway as a giant step backwards on the road toward the realization of a humane and rational criminal policy (Christie and Bruun, 1985; Larsson, 1991; Christie, 1987).

THE PRICE OF FREEDOM

All three countries are characterized as democratic regimes. Norway has the oldest and best-established democracy. American democracy is the best publicized; while Poland is building a new democracy after years of communist rule. All three declare the dominant role of the law, and equality of all before the law. In all three countries, however, the number of prisoners is growing, although at significantly different rates. Moreover, this process appears to have little to do with the number of registered crimes, and while there is evidence of a tougher approach to crime control there are substantial differences in how these policies have been implemented.

Both the United States and Norway operate with a 'just deserts' model of justice. Both are critical of disparities in sentencing and of indeterminate sentencing. In both countries there is a desire for more uniform forms of punishment, although these procedures have produced different consequences. The just deserts model has resulted in an increase in the use of long-term punishment in America but a decrease in Norway. As one writer recently put it: 'In the United States, harsh conditions of imprisonment are purposeful, and it is claimed that prison must be unpleasant in order to deter' (Selke, 1993: 59). Consequently in Norway, as well as in other Scandinavian countries, a just deserts policy has resulted in a more limited use of imprisonment. The difference of outcomes on this model appears to be a function of the value placed on individual freedom. Paradoxically, freedom is cheap in America and highly valued in Norway. What is lenient in the United Stated is considered harsh in Norway. Long-term imprisonment in Norway means sentences of more than three months, whereas three months in the United States is perceived as a trivial punishment.

Given the established standards of punishment in America and Norway, Poland sits somewhere in the middle of these two systems. Poland looks towards America for an economic model, or rather, an American style of life, and towards Norway for its criminal justice model. However, this raises the critical question of whether in Poland it possible to have an American-style economy and a Norwegian-style criminal justice system.

CRIME, IMPRISONMENT AND THE AMERICAN DREAM

Americans are consistently looking for 'quick fix' solutions to the crime problem. Time is money, and the average American has no time to wait for long explanations or time-consuming crime prevention programmes. In this context, the prison, which is already established and easy to use, seems to be the obvious answer. This attitude is now strongly embedded in American culture.

According to the 'American Dream' everyone has a chance, no matter where he or she comes from, to become a winner. It is not important how you play the game; it is whether you win or lose. This specific philosophy measures action by outcome only, and not by its quality. Personal worth is measured and evaluated by the financial outcome. At this point friends become competitors and rivals in the struggle to achieve social rewards, and ultimately, to validate personal worth (Merton, 1968).

Despite the universal component of the American Dream, the basic logic of this cultural ethos actually presupposes a high level of ine-quality. A competitive allocation of monetary rewards requires both winners and losers. Since the winners are the only ones who count there is little incentive for society to care for prisoners who have failed to achieve success. They are functional in terms of distinguishing between those who have succeeded and those who have failed. Prison walls provide a clear distinction between winners and losers, although they do not protect the former from the fear of crime. This fear in America has an important racial component, as does the criminal justice system which tries to reduce it.

Is it possible to realize the American Dream and simultaneously reduce the prison population? Steven Messner and Richard Rosenfeld, authors of *Crime and The American Dream* (1994), would probably answer no. They would argue that American attitudes towards prison and prisoners consti-tutes an intrinsic element of what is known as the 'American Dream'.

Currently in the United States it is the fear of crime rather than crime itself which seems to be fuelling the nation's increased incarceration rates. Despite the image of a ubiquitous increase in crime in America in recent years, auto thefts, for example, are less frequent in America than they are in Denmark (Selke, 1993: 54). Moreover, there are higher crime rates per 100 000 people in Sweden than in the United States.

In Norway and Sweden, fear of crime, even if present, hardly appears to influence criminal policy. How can we account for these differences? Crime, and the reaction to it, is not a product of mysterious forces. It is rather a response to prevailing socio-cultural conditions. Messner and Rosenfeld would argue that in the case of the United States the high level of violent crime as well as punitive sanctions are in the very nature of American society. They would argue that at all social levels, America is better organized for crime (Messner and Rosenfeld, 1994: 6).

But there is an important difference between the strong egalitarianism of Norway and the distinct individualism of America. The promised land of so many generations offers a dream that celebrates individualism. Norwegian egalitarianism protects the country from serious racial and ethnic conflicts. In contrast, American individualism creates racial issues, despite the legal regulations, and turns it into one of the most acute social problems.

INTO THE ROSE GARDEN?

It is a short step from the increased use of imprisonment to overcrowding and the decline of penal conditions. Recent developments in America indicate that these changing prison conditions are coming to be seen as positive rather than negative achievements. In a recent judgement, for example, Chief Justice Rehnquist stated that:

> There is nothing in the Constitution that says that 'rehabilitation' is the sole permissible goal of incarceration, and we have only recently stated that retribution is equally permissible ... In short, nobody promised them a rose garden; and I know of nothing in the Eighth Amendment [restriction against cruel and unusual punishment] which requires that they be housed in a manner most pleasing to them, or considered even the most knowledgeable penal authorities to be likely to avoid confrontations, psychological depression, and the like. They have been convicted of crime, and there is nothing in the Constitution which forbids their being penalised as a result of that conviction.[2]

In the name of the law, then, the Supreme Court of the United States has moved from the course of prison reform and declared that criminals should simply be punished. In making such a decision, the Supreme Court has sent out the important message that criminals alone are responsible for the crimes and that they alone should pay. The more, the better. This more punitive and less understanding response towards crime has vindicated the use of harsher and more debilitating methods in a number of new maximum security prisons. These institutions have been designed to instil terror and are often brutal and dangerous. In order to survive, prisoners become aggressive and indifferent toward others.

In Dwight, the State Prison for Women in Illinois, other processes are in operation. There are on the one hand serious criticisms directed towards some of the prison officers who, it is alleged, have smuggled drugs into prison, and traded them with the prisoners for sex. On the other hand, in the very same institution, is the 'Gateway' programme, which is designed to help drug-addicted and alcoholic prisoners regain their pride and confidence. This programme aims to help prisoners free themselves of addiction, and to gain professional skills. The prison staff, in fact, run several training and education programmes for inmates and attempt to create as relaxed and friendly an atmosphere as the crowded conditions allow. Most of the officers employed there are genuinely concerned about the present and future well being of the inmates.

Thus, despite the pronouncements of Chief Justice Rehnquist, there are attempts in prison, not to destroy, but to help inmates. In many cases prison staff do dedicate a great deal of time and effort and do perceive rehabilitation as a duty. In the majority of cases prison staff would prefer to have the opportunity to offer prisoners quality time in prison, but they have little influence on the way criminal policy is shaped (Rideau, 1994: 80)

THE AMERICAN PRISON BUSINESS

Nobody among America's decision-makers can claim ignorance. There are volumes of articles, reports, books, manuscripts and documents explaining the reasons for prison overcrowding as well as methods for avoiding it (Morris and Hawkins, 1970; Murton, 1976). This literature discusses everything from crime prevention through environmental design (Newman, 1973), to community projects (Felson, 1994; Morris 1974). Despite these developments the numbers of new prisons and number of people incarcerated is increasing.

Popular ignorance, genuine demands for crime control, and the actual presence of violent crime go well together. This combination of factors provides the basic ingredients for an extremely lucrative business associated with imprisonment. Imprisonment costs society a fortune, but it brings relatively few rewards. Despite this enormous expense it produces more harm than good. There are some investors and operators who are, nevertheless, eager to keep the business going (Christie 1993).

The development of mandatory minimum sentences has resulted in more prisoners serving longer sentences; while federal sentencing guidelines have reduced the use of parole, so some deserving inmates are no longer eligible for early release. Moreover, judges at both the state and federal level are barred from imposing lesser sentences regardless of mitigating circumstances. The result is an increasing prison population and an expanding prison industry. Once established there is a strong material interest in keeping this industry going (Christie, 1993). *Corrections Today* the glossy publication of the American Correctional Association, devotes many of its pages to this new prison industry. For example, in the annual security issue published in July 1993, which had the cover story 'Managing Death Row', there were 171 different products in the abbreviated product category index (Chambers, 1993). The so called 'war on crime' can also be viewed in the post-Cold War era as providing politicians with a new enemy.

And yet there are growing concerns that the process is, in fact, problematic. Surely, there is something wrong with society in which prison building becomes the only economic activity in certain parts of the country? The prison near Tamms, in Southern Illinois, is just one of several such examples. This institution which is Illinois' first supermaximum security prison resembles Pelican Bay State Prison's Security Housing Unit in California. It is designed to hold the 500 worst offenders in the corrections system under lock-down conditions. It will cost $60 million, employ 300 staff and have a $15 million operating budget and is perceived as an economic miracle to the Alexander County town with a population of 748 people. Nobody asked why the prison was the only available business, although many assumed that there was some relationship between the expansion of imprisonment and the level of personal safety.

HOMO HOMINI LUPUS, OR HOW TO BE SAFE IN AMERICA

On 11 November 1993, ABC News Primetime Live devoted an evening slot to the question of how to be safe in America. It was not very original. Like other programmes it reported in great detail killings, robberies and sensational beatings and offered a number of tips about how to avoid similar incidents happening to you. The message was that it is not difficult to avoid crimes like burglaries. It is enough to build walls around your community to keep the criminals out. On the other hand, it is more difficult to understand and to avoid violent crimes. Therefore, there is a need to be constantly prepared since the criminal can be anywhere, anytime, any place.

When you get into your car look around, be careful. The criminal might be right behind you. While driving your car keep the door locked and the window up. Rule number one – do not get out of the car especially when someone calls for help. Do not react. It might be a trap. Do not look conspicuous. Do not read the map. Do not look lost even if you are, and do not ask for help yourself if you do not want to become a victim. Invest in security devices: gas, guns, or at least a cellular phone. And most important – trust your instinct. Just before a crime occurs, the hair on the back of your neck stands up, and that is your warning. In the words of the programme presenter – that is 200 million years worth of evolution grabbing you by the neck and saying: 'Get out of here'.

The interesting aspect of these 'safety tips', and the attempts to inform the audience about how to avoid violent crime, is that they do not involve strategies to combat crime, but rather to block it out or escape from it. Such strategies are both products of and influences on American social relations. They reflect a tendency to reject the essence of social bonds – mutual sympathy, co-operation, trust and mutual support. The message is cut yourself off from crime, take care of your own personal safety and disregard the rest.

Despite the thousands of individuals behind bars, the number of violent crimes is increasing and offenders are not deterred by this policy. In fact, it is getting worse than one might imagine since the majority of crimes are apparently committed by juveniles. The official response to these developments is to get tough and to 'lock them up and throw away the key'. But youngsters in America do not always kill or steal. They are often the victims of crime as well. Children are taught not to talk to strangers, especially if he or she is older, looks nice and asks you for help. They are advised to scream and run away. Maybe we have good reason to teach children to mistrust elders rather than respect them as we used to do. We may feel it is necessary to teach them to be more assertive and more apprehensive. We should, however, be aware of the possible side effects of these preventative measures.

There is a growing fear and dread of strangers. People expect others to be evil. In such an atmosphere it is hard not only to solve, but even to identify the problem correctly. All that people are able to do is to think in terms of their own personal safety. The focus is on removing and displacing crime rather than on solving it. People try to escape from crime by retreating into the private realm. But is it really the best way to be safe in America?

In 1990, 194 people in Canada, 76 people in Australia, 90 people in Japan, 54 people in war-torn Northern Ireland and 13 035 people in the United States were killed by guns. In the first quarter of 1994 in Chicago with just over 2 million inhabitants, over 300 people were killed. That is double the rate for Poland and four times the rate for Norway. And yet the debate on how to be safe in America does not face the fact that placing people behind bars, scaring and making people mistrust each other, fragments and dissolves human relations, rather than promotes safety and freedom. Nevertheless, in this vision of fear and terror which is spread and reinforced by the media, one might easily forget that in the United States most people live in small and relatively peaceful communities. Far away from the turbulence of the city life many Americans experience relatively low levels of crime and victimization. However, they are subject to the same media messages and images.

Fear in America has its place, colour and racial component. And the overriding message is that people are not to be trusted. Each of us is a potential malefactor, or potential victim. Be aware of the danger. Be aware of a criminal lurking around the corner. Be prepared. Stay alert. Do not let sentimental feelings of friendship jeopardize your safety and ruin your life. And be sure to keep all those criminals behind bars. People in such a scenario become prisoners of fear. They can even become prisoners within their own homes.

This is not a parody. It is the actual message that American society gives out. The problems are not faced squarely. Instead the solution is to build more prisons and incarcerate more people. At the same time the money spent on prisons is taken from other social services. In Norway, by contrast, the situation seems to be significantly different. The issues of personal safety and of imprisonment are approached in a distinctly different way.

BEING SAFE – THE NORWEGIAN WAY

Norwegians like to ski, stay in close contact with nature, and feel free. They also feel strongly for their fellows and traditionally treat each other equally. The tough physical conditions of life have encouraged them to help each other, respect each other and co-operate with each other. In cases of conflict they seek harmony and mediation rather than aggression. They prize self-esteem and personal discipline. Simultaneously they tend to use external punishment and discipline with prudence and caution. These are some of the factors that makes investment in prisons less acceptable to Norwegians. Its cultural norms are not simply a function of its size and low population. It is crucial to see how their attitudes toward each other influence the way they approach the question of crime and its control.

It is not a coincidence that the leading figures in the European Abolition movement are from the Netherlands and Norway (see the work of Christie, 1981; Mathiesen, 1990; Hulsman, 1987; Bianchi, 1986; and Scheerer, 1986). Both countries have low imprisonment rates, relatively short-term sentences and prison conditions which are perceived by the rest of the world as being extremely good.

Norway has 2000 prisoners compared to America's 1.4 million and 40 people in prison per 100 000 citizens compared to 400 per 100 000 in the United States (Council of Europe, 1992). This gives the Norwegians space and time to think about the problems of imprisonment – space and time which Americans no longer seem to be able to afford. Norwegians are free from the pressure of dealing with a steady flow of inmates. This allows them time to consider the possibility that society could actually manage without prisons (Mathiesen, 1990: 136–68). And yet, because of this, one can feel safe in Norway because the streets belong to people, both during the day and at night. Norwegians, like Americans, cherish material success and yet manage to combine it with the other values so that money does not dominate everything.

Interestingly enough, the stories from the front pages of Norwegian newspapers and magazines involve murders, rape and robberies. In Norway, however, they are able to talk about one case for some time before a new one appears. In America a new sensational case emerges almost daily. The important difference is that in Norway the 'fight against crime' is felt to be a collective responsibility. Norwegians feel that they need to address these issues together since they share responsibility.

It should be noted that the number of crimes committed in Norway each year is not insignificant. The number of violent crimes, however, is substantially lower in Norway than in the United States. It is not only that guns are more readily available in America and that there are cultural and historical differences (Messner and Rosenfeld, 1994; Andenaes, 1974). It has actually got a great deal to do with the way society approaches the question of imprisonment.

BUSINESS AND NORWEGIAN CRIMINAL JUSTICE

Norway is rich. This does not mean, however, that Norwegians are willing to spend their money on prisons. They are even less interested in making money out of imprisonment. Norwegians are very aware that prison has a social as well as financial cost. Scandinavian prisons look, to many foreigners, like luxury hotels. They are aware that the high standards existing in Norwegian and other Scandinavian prisons reflects the high standard of living in the society in general. As Sveri (1975) has pointed out, a country without slums cannot let its prisoners live under slum conditions. Scandinavians know that their prisons are perceived as some of the best in the world, but appreciate that is due to the generally abominable conditions existing in most other countries.

Prosperity and the welfare system guarantees all citizens a certain degree of security from the 'cradle to grave'. But there is more to it than that. Norway reached the present level of imprisonment at the beginning of the century when the country was very poor (Christie, 1981: 33). Even in that period Norwegians were lenient. The basis of this leniency comes from a tradition of equality, a genuine respect for the law, and a sense of the collective responsibility. A strong egalitarianism and rationalism leaves little space for personal vengeance. It also makes people aware that today's decisions will have consequences for tomorrow. Thus, instead of prisons, it is considered preferable to invest in the labour market, in health, in education and in housing and welfare policies. No matter how guilty the felon is, it is hard to ignore the social forces which lie behind his or her actions. Nothing positive is achieved by denying this process. It will not make the social environment any safer. Developing a solution to these problems requires an understanding of the causes (Selke, 1993).

The terms of imprisonment are shorter in Norway than most other countries and the conditions of imprisonment are better. In Norway it is possible in prison to have a room of one's own, the chance to study, to work and to receive conjugal visits. Being a prisoner does not prevent a person from being a human being. The atmosphere is more relaxed in Norwegian institutions, and there is an understanding that deprivation of liberty is in itself a harsh punishment which does not require additional sanctions.

For Norwegian prisoners imprisonment is seen as punishment enough, although they stay in clean and well-equipped units. And yet Norwegians do understand that certain negative elements are endemic to imprisonment. Even in Norwegian prisons, the prisoners themselves give accounts about the monotony, about helplessness and hopelessness and about feeling repressed and restricted (Falck and Mathiesen, 1981).

Unlike the Americans who like 'quick fixes', even if it means a greater use of imprisonment, Norwegians do not want to place more people behind bars, or spend more money on prison construction. They prefer a long waiting period before those sentenced can serve their term. They are also reluctant to change prison conditions and to put two prisoners in a cell designed for one. Such a solution brings tension, decreases safety and creates a difficult environment for both inmates and staff. Although the formal goal of rehabilitation was abandoned a long time ago, the humanitarian ethos has remained. Therefore, the use of imprisonment in Norway, despite the growing demands to control drugs and get tough on crime, is still treated with scepticism.

Norwegians know that there is little difference in recidivism whether an offender is fined, put on probation, or placed in an open or a closed prison (Andenaes, 1975). This realistic approach encourages them to achieve their safety at the lowest possible expenditure in terms of money and human suffering (Christiansen, 1973), and it seems they are doing very well, particularly in comparison to the United States.

What can be learned from the situation in America and Norway? We are faced with the question of whether Poland can, in the post-revolutionary period, learn some lessons from established western capitalist countries about crime and punishment.

THE POLISH REVOLUTION

In 1989 Poland had more than 100 000 people behind bars. The prison population then dropped in 1990 to less than 40 000 inmates. How was this possible? What major changes occurred and how difficult was it? Actually, it was relatively simple. It was easy enough conditionally to release a number of prisoners and to use imprisonment with prudence. Imprisonment was used less often and for shorter periods than before. New legislation was introduced and new people were appointed. It really was that easy, once the social revolution had occurred.

The law and criminal justice policy in Poland had been based on Russian models. The communist system which was imposed on Poland gave Russia the authority to control many aspects of Poland's political, economic and social life. The jails and prisons were filled up with people who would not be perceived as criminals in the western sense of the word. People were sent to prison, for example, for being consistently late for work, or for stealing a bottle of milk or vodka. There were also many who fought against the Nazis in the Polish Underground Army and who survived the terror of the Second World War only to be persecuted, tortured and imprisoned by the new communist regime.

People felt safe in the streets but not safe in the country. They did not feel free and independent. Almost all, in fact were under strict state control. Therefore the question of how to be safe was transformed into: 'Who is to blame for crime in society?' The question was rather a rhetorical one. It was always obvious who was to blame. In this tightly controlled society there were a number of similarities between life outside and inside the prison. Prisons were run as a state business. They brought revenue to the state budget and were one of the few agencies that actually fulfilled state economic plans. People in prison provided a source or cheap labour.

The prison business has a number of different faces. In the United States it is profitable to build prisons and operate private prison industries. In Norway it is seen as prudent to limit the number of prisons. In communist Poland, the more prisoners there were, the better because they worked for free and brought profit to the state.

There are 240 penitentiary units in Poland, including 151 prisons. Most of these were built in the last century and none have been built since 1945. Some penal institutions are located in strongholds, army barracks or monasteries dating back to the times when Poland was under partition. Some of these buildings are even older than that. For example, there are two castles dating from the thirteenth and fourteenth centuries which are currently used as prisons (Platek, 1991).

Prisoners were sent to prison to work, no matter what other official reason was given. The Polish prison system had more than sixty independent production units which were both industrial and agricultural. Many auxiliary workshops and supplementary forms of employment were operated (manual work was performed in cells, and contracts were arranged with factories) (Beres and Burnetko, 1994). A characteristic feature of prison manufacture was its multi-faceted nature. Production which was organized in prison was also important for the national economy. The majority of enterprises usually had contracts with the key state enterprises. Prisoners were treated like slave workers. They had legal rights written into the Criminal Executive Code, but no procedural remedies to execute them. There were statutes outlining the prison rules, but since the system was almost cut off from the rest of society prisoners were actually totally dependent on the prison administrators and had little recource to legal rules. The conditions in prison were often appalling and little was done about it.

According to the statistics, one in every eight young men in the period prior to revolution experienced at least six months in prison. Despite having to work in prison, it does not mean, however, that prisoners were working effectively or gaining skills. In fact, the hard and often brutal prison conditions often encouraged them to develop anti-social rather than pro-social attitudes. With such an attitude towards work and, convinced that they were worthless, these young people were eventually returned to society. It is not hard to appreciate that such attitudes hardly facilitated social progress.

The Solidarity movement in 1980, mobilized and demanded changes in the prison system. Some years later the prison authority admitted that prisoners' production was not always cost-effective. Ironically, at that time, while still under Communist control, the first reforms were initiated in Polish prisons. It turned out to be cheaper to get rid of unproductive prisoners (mainly women) than to keep so many people in the prison system.

In 1987, there were still over 100 000 people imprisoned in Poland. In 1988 the number dropped to 67 824. In 1988 the report of a Human Rights Watch summarized the Polish situation as of 1987 as follows:

Prison conditions are dreadful. Many prisons are from the 19th century. There is not satisfactory plumbing ... sanitary facilities do not function ... The worst places are police lock-ups. The cells were filthy and overcrowded – up to 14 women in a cell about 13ft. by 16ft. There was no toilet, only a bucket, and no toilet paper ... The food was dreadful and the cells were infested with insects. No exercise was permitted.

Overcrowding is a severe problem throughout the Polish prison system – Poland's penal code imposes very long prison sentences and its prisoner to population ratio, between 280 and 320 per 100 000. It is one of the highest in Europe and North America ... Serious health problems are inevitable. Tuberculosis is common, as are herpes as well as other skin diseases and diseases of the back and spine because of lack of exercise. Most prisoners are only allowed a half-hour walk each day. Prison rules forbid lying in during the day.   (Human Rights Watch, 1988: 7–9)

These conditions, the Report noted, had direct effects upon the prisoners:

Among the most troublesome features of the Polish prison system is the enormous amount of brutality and other forms of physical abuse ... Prisoners have almost no recourse for relief ... The courts are not available. Prison rules setting out the rights and duties of prisoners are kept secret ... The lack of a meaningful remedy has produced a particularly bizarre form of protest, especially among younger and emotionally disturbed prisoners, self-mutilation. (Human Rights Watch, 1988: 29)

With the changing economy in the country, together with the changing political atmosphere, it was obvious that changes in the prison system had to follow, although when they came at the end of 1989 the country was in deep economic crisis. As a result, there was limited interest in keeping so many people behind bars, especially as it was cheaper to let them out and make them feed themselves. There was a genuine will to reform the prison system, but it had to be quick and comprehensive.

Polish people tend to ask who is to blame, rather than seeking ways of eradicating the problem or discussing what could be done about it. The reason for this is that for a long time they have been discouraged from using their own initiative by the powerful state apparatus. Today, almost five years after the peaceful revolution the question of crime, and the lack of safety remains the same: 'Who is to blame?' You do not change the system overnight by changing the name. The transformation takes time, and the process is often painful.

Traditionally, Polish courts and prisons were designed to intimidate society. Following the revolution new legislation is being developed, changes in the system of criminal classification have been introduced, the level of prison overcrowding has been reduced and there have been improvements in relation to the protection of human rights. At the same time, however, there are growing fears among the general public about crime, despite the fact that according to Interpol statistics Poland's reported crime rate is currently below that of other European countries such as France and Britain. People still want to 'get tough' on crime. Sanctions are especially harsh for repeat offenders, giving the Polish criminal justice system 'no other choice' but to send them to prison. However, the Polish ombudsman Ewa L. Ketowska and her present successor Tadeusz Zielinski have worked towards the liberalization of this outdated system.

In recent years prisoners have gained the right to seek court remedies to defend their rights. According to new prison law there should be three square metres of space for every male prisoner and four for every female. These norms are, however, being violated already. This prison population which stood at 40 000 in 1989 increased to over 63 000 in 1994. The system is prepared to accommodate a maximum of 62 000 prisoners. Poland is therefore facing overcrowding again. The major difference, however, between the current situation and the pre-revolutionary system is that this time prison officials together with 20 000 prison staff have expressed their disappointment and hold the state responsible for violating its own objectives. They are no longer prepared to remain silent and are often the first to demand changes. Since they are not alone it is possible that Polish society might realize that imprisonment is not the only option. In fact it is becoming clear to many that imprisonment creates offenders in addition to a range of other social problems.

SEARCHING FOR THE RIGHT ANSWER

The three countries discussed illustrate the many processes operating on different scales in many countries. A great deal of attention has been given to the United States because it graphically illustrates the dangers of using imprisonment as the main tool for fighting crime. Discussion has also focused on the situation in Norway and Poland where different approaches prevail. In these countries there has been an attempt to reduce the use of imprisonment rather than to use it as a panacea for all social problems.

Prison from its inception has created social problems. Moreover it has served as a warehouse in which everything which is considered difficult or dangerous is placed out of sight. This strategy has never worked very well. Even when prison has served this warehousing function, it still has negative effects on society. Little has changed since the days of Howard and Fry (Whitney, 1937; Rose, 1980). They, like their followers, concentrated on the internal reform of prisons. Experience has indicated, however, that this is the wrong priority. To be effective in reforming the prison the problem needs to be considered in a wider context. We can hardly succeed in reforming prisons without asking how society affects the prison and how the prison affects society. Grasping this reciprocal relationship is a necessary step in making policymakers more sensitive to the cause of prison reform. It is only in this way that we can achieve the changes which Howard and Fry were hoping for (Christie, 1981; Hulsman, 1987).

THE VICIOUS CIRCLE

Despite the vast sums of money spent on prison construction and administration, imprisonment has a limited effect on the level of crimes or the fear of crime. Imprisonment is one among several available sanctions provided by the law. Criminal law, however, even if designed to prevent and deter, is *always* used post factum. Each time we use it, it is invariably too late to stop a particular crime occurring. And each time we send someone to prison we have to admit that all of those who have previously been incarcerated did not prevent this crime from taking place. Moreover, the employment of the criminal law indicates the failure of all other social agencies. Criminal law is used as a last resort. In every case its application is not designed to help, or to change people, but rather to punish. Criminal law by its very nature has little creative ability and is largely negative and constraining.

Prisons belong to the criminal law. Like the criminal law, imprisonment is not designed to solve social problems. Rather, it can at best contain these problems and at worst it makes them worse. An increase in the prison population does not stop violence in the street, nor does it improve housing programmes, nor does it improve the quality of education in schools, nor does it decrease the level of fear among the general public.

The attempt to control crime through the use of imprisonment is a deeply flawed strategy and often results in prison overcrowding. Paradoxically, one probable consequence of prison overcrowding is to increase violence and disorder in these institutions. Prisoners at some point return to society equipped with their prison experiences (Bondenson, 1989).

Overcrowded prisons, therefore, create problems for the safety of inmates. In order to control the number of inmates, prison authorities are often forced to release certain prisoners early in order to allow for the influx of new inmates (Logan and DiIulio, 1993). As a result these 'dangerous' criminals are put back in the community. Overcrowded prisons promote brutality and this often spreads back on to the streets. As a consequence, the violence which society had hoped to eliminate in fact increases.

Prison is not a place to develop self-esteem. Prison, and particularly overcrowded prisons, destroy rather than build a positive self-identity. The more people experience imprisonment the greater the number of people in society with a low self-esteem. This negative self-image is often transmitted to the younger generations. The more widespread the prison experience the greater the number of people in society who have anti-social tendencies. Bad manners, like diseases, are widespread in prisons. In some countries disease is transmitted into society through the prison gate. Problems of hygiene, proper health care and nutrition are present in every prison. They become more evident in overcrowded institutions. Tuberculosis, hepatitis, HIV/AIDS, as well as psychological problems are becoming a feature of prison systems around the world. Within the prison system those suffering from these illness are often stigmatized and segregated.

The rate of crime in a country hardly determines the rate of imprisonment (Rothman, 1994; Platek, 1988). If incarceration is held up to be the solution then we have to expect more of these kinds of problems (Porowski, 1991; Rothman, 1971). The time, money and energy devoted to prison could be better spent on other social areas such as education, health care, housing projects or new jobs.

We are hardly in a position to spend an equal amount of money and energy on prisons and public schools. At some point we have to identify priorities. If prison is prioritized, education and health care will probably lose out. If prison is the first choice, many homeless and poor people may have to accept a prison cell rather than an apartment. New prisons and new jobs might seem to go together. This is, however, a short-sighted view. The expansion of prisons may indicate the failure to create jobs elsewhere. Moreover, something must be wrong in society if building a new prison is seen as the only way to develop the local economy. There is something genuinely perverse in a situation in which the prison becomes the main industry in a community (Goering, 1993). When a new prison becomes the ultimate source of local employment it is hard to escape the thought that we are developing a material interest in fostering rather than combating crime.

Notes

1. I would like to thank Lisa Frohman, of the University of Illinois at Chicago, for her help in the preparation of this paper.
2. *Atiyeh, Governor of Oregon, et al.* v. *Capps, et al.* 449 US1312 1981: 5–8

References

Andenaes, J. (1974) *Punishment and Deterrence* (Michigan: The University of Michigan Press).

Andenaes, J. (1975) 'General Prevention Revisited: Research and Policy Implications', in *The Journal of Criminal Law and Criminology,* vol. 66, no. 3.

Beres, W. and Burnetko, K. (1994) 'Night-stick and Narrow Doors. An Interview with Pawel Moczydlowski, Director of the Central Board Of Penal Institutions', in *The Warsaw Voice* (6 February).

Bianchi, H. (1986) 'Abolition: Assensus and Sanctuary', in H. Bianchi and R. V. Swaaningen (eds), *Abolitionism: Towards a Non-Repressive Approach to Crime* (Amsterdam: Free University Press).

Bondenson, U. V. (1989) Prisoner in Prison Societies (New Brunswick: Transaction Books).

Chambers, M. (1993) 'Sua Sponte', in *The National Law Journal,* October 25

Chapman, S. (1994) 'The Newest Fashion in Fighting Crime is More of the Same', in *Chicago Tribune* (27 January).

Christiansen, K. O. (1973) *Some Consideration on the Possibility of a Rational Criminal Policy* (Copenhagen: UNAFEL Annual Report).

Christie, N. (1981) *The Limits of Pain* (Oslo: Universitetsforlaget).

Christie, N. and Bruun, K. (1985) *Den gode Fiende Narkotikapolitikk i Norden* (Oslo: Universitetsforlaget).

Christie, N. (1987) 'Drugs in Dry Societies', in P. Stageland (ed.), Scandinavian Studies in Criminology, vol. 8, *Drugs and Drug Control* (Oslo: Norwegian University Press).

Christie, N. (1993) *Crime Control as Industry: Towards GULAGS Western Style?* (London: Routledge).

Clark, R. (1970) *Crime in America: Observations of Its Nature, Causes, Prevention and Control* (New York: Simon and Schuster).

Council of Europe (1992) *Prison Information Bulletin June 1992* (Strasbourg: Council of Europe).

Creighton, S. (1994) Opening Statement, *Pelican Bay Prison Express*, vol. 2, no. 3.

Dunbaugh, F. M. (1993) 'Where Should the Movement Move?', in B. D. Maclean (ed.), *We Who Would Take No Prisoners* (Vancover: Collective Press).

Edna McConnel Clark Foundation (1993) *Americans Behind Bars,* a Report of the Edna McConnel Clark Foundation (New York).

Falck, S. and Mathiesen, T. (1981) *Vekter Staten. Om Kontrollpolitkken i det Moderne Samfun* (Oslo: Pax).

Falk, S. (1989) *I Grasonen Rapportt Fra Ila* (Oslo: Pax).

Felson, M. (1994) *Crime and Everyday Life* (Thousand Oaks: Pine Forge Press).

Foucault, M. (1975) *Surveiller et Punir, Naissance de la Prison* (Paris: Editions Gallimond).

Foucault, M. (1977) *Discipline and Punish* (London: Allen Lane).

Frankowski, S. and Wasék, A. (1993) 'Evolution of the Polish Criminal Justice System after World War Two – An Overview', in *European Journal of Crime, Criminal Law and Criminal Justice,* no. 2.

Garland, D. (1990) *Punishment and Modern Society* (Chicago: University of Chicago Press).

Goering, L. (1993) 'Town Calls Prison Its Economic Rescuer', in *Chicago Tribune* (24 October).

Hulsman, L. (1987) *The Participation of the Community in the Prevention of Crime,* International de Criminologia palacio de las Convenciones. Havana, Cuba, 6–10 July (typescript 22 pages).

Human Rights Watch (1988) *Prison Conditions in Poland June 1988* (New York: Human Rights Watch).

Kent, J. (1962) *Elizabeth Fry* (London: B. T. Batsford).

King, R. and Maguire, M. (1994) 'Introduction – Contexts of Imprisonment. An International Perspective', in *British Journal of Criminology,* vol. 34.

Larsson, P. (1991) *Norwegian Penal Policy in the 1980s* (typescript).

Locin, M. and Jouzaitis, C. (1994) 'Our Work Has Just Begun', in *Chicago Tribune* (26 January).

Logan, C. and DiIulio, J. J. (1993) 'Ten Deadly Myths about Crime and Punishment in the United States', in G. F. Cole (ed.), *Criminal Justice: Law and Politics* (Belmont, CA: Wadsworth).

Mathiesen, T. (1990) *Prison on Trial* (London: Sage).

Merton, R. (1968) *Social Theory and Social Structure* (New York: Free Press).

Messner, S. F. and Rosenfeld, R. (1994) *Crime and the American Dream* (Belmont, CA: Wadsworth).

Morris, N. and Hawkins, G. (1970) *The Honest Politician's Guide to Crime Control* (Chicago: University of Chicago Press).

Morris, N. (1974) *The Future of Imprisonment* (Chicago: University of Chicago Press).

Murton, T. (1976) *The Dilemma of Penal Reform* (New York: Holt, Rinehart and Winston).

Newman, O. (1973) *Defensible Space: Crime Prevention Through Environmental Design* (New York: Collier Books).

Pitman, E. R. (1884) *Elizabeth Fry* (London: W. H. Allen).

Platek, M. (1994a) *For Prisoners Rights to Live in Dignity*, a Report on the State of the Prison in the USA, Observatoire International des Prisons (Lyon: Cedex).

Platek, M. (1994b) 'The Great Transition – The Polish Prison System', in *The Keepers Voice* (June).

Platek, M. (1990) 'Prison Subculture in Poland', in *International Journal of the Sociology of Law*, vol. 18.

Platek, M. (1991) 'The Sluzewiec Prison in Warsaw, Poland: A Penal Labour Center or Half-Open Prison', in D. Whitfield (ed.), *The State of the Prison – 200 Years On* (London and New York: Routledge).

Platek, M. (1988) *Underestimated Experiment – The Current State of Penitentiary Practice Towards Women in Poland*, paper presented at the Tenth International Congress in Criminology, Hamburg, 4–9 September.

Porowski, M. (1991) 'Human Rights of Prisoners', in M. Platek, Z. Lasocik and I. Rzeplinska (eds), *Abolitionism in History* (Warsaw: Warsaw University Press).

Reiman, J. H. (1984) *The Rich Get Richer and the Poor Get Prison* (New York: John Wiley and Sons).

Rideau, W. (1994) 'Why Prisons Don't Work', in *Time* (21 March).

Rose, J. (1980) *Elizabeth Fry* (New York: St Martin's Press).

Rothman, D. J. (1994) 'The Crime of Punishment', in the *New York Review of Books* (17 February) vol. XLI, no. 4.

Rothman, D. J. (1971) *The Discovery of the Asylum* (Boston: Little, Brown).

Rusche, G. and Kirchheimer, O. (1969) *Punishment and Social Structure* (New York: Columbia University Press).

Scheerer, S. (1986) 'Towards Abolitionism', in *Contemporary Crisis*, no. 10.

Selke, W. (1993) *Prisons in Crisis* (Bloomington and Indianapolis: Indiana University Press).

Svensson, B. (1979) 'We Can Get By with 3000 Prisoners', in *Sveriges Exportrad Spratjanst*.

Sveri, K. (1975) *Forward in Some Developments in Nordic Criminal Policy and Criminology* (Scandinavian Research Council for Criminology).

Whitney, J. (1937) *Elizabeth Fry: Quaker Heroine* (Boston: Little, Brown).

Zimring, F. E. and Hawkins, G. (1994) 'The Growth of Imprisonment in California', in *British Journal of Criminology*, vol. 34.

4 Penal 'Austerity': The Doctrine of Less Eligibility Reborn?

Richard Sparks[1]

This chapter raises certain arguments and historical analogies which may assist in taking a few preliminary sightings of some distinctive features of the current British penal landscape. I hope to show that some of the present developments, which initially appear rather particular and 'of the moment', interestingly bear comparison with much earlier ideas and events. That comparison may suggest, at least in outline, a way of conceptualizing and responding to the contemporary scene.

I shall begin by sketching some developments in penal policy (and more particularly penal rhetoric) that have occurred during 1993–4, focusing specifically on the claim attributed (via a leaked memorandum) to the British Home Secretary, Michael Howard, that some prison regimes have become insufficiently 'austere', a view which finds ready support in populist media commentary. Secondly, I will suggest that such arguments for more rigorous penal discipline unwittingly but not accidentally reiterate the severe stance that underlay so much of the nineteenth-century penal (and Poor Law) ideology, known as the doctrine of less eligibility. This was, crudely, the view that the level of prison conditions should always compare unfavourably to the material living standards of the labouring poor. Thirdly, I will refer briefly to certain arguments from criminological theory and social histories of crime and punishment which suggest that less eligibility principles are especially characteristic of penal rhetoric during times of economic recession and/or of moments when governments confront crises of popular support and legitimacy. Finally, I will reflect briefly upon how the re-emergence of less eligibility within the penal realm seems likely to impact upon some current debates, especially regarding the privatization of prisons.

THE PENAL CLIMATE IN 1993–4

It can be suggested that 1993 was a year in which the prevailing 'penal climate' in Britain 'cooled' with some suddenness. The year witnessed a general intensification of long-standing fear and censure over lawless youth and their alleged impunity before impotent courts. Newspapers focused with some delighted outrage on instances of undue judicial leniency (especially over rape sentencing), on the frequency of police cautions, on the imputed reluctance of the Crown Prosecution Service to prosecute, and on the alleged inequities of the new (and short-lived) unit fine system. They reported gleefully on the resignations of some magistrates, while social workers were taken repeatedly to task for permissiveness, coddling and extravagance in their treatment of young offenders. Two pieces of major legislation, the Children Act 1989 and the Criminal Justice Act 1991, were called repeatedly into question (at times by members of the Government which enacted them) for their excessive liberality. Key provisions of the latter were repealed by the Criminal Justice Act 1993, effectively destroying whatever coherence its sentencing framework possessed.

Even before the CJA 1993 took effect sentencing and remanding practices (the latter in part stimulated by a rash of 'bail bandit' stories) appeared to undergo a marked reverse. The reductionist agenda of the CJA 1991 which had produced appreciable falls in the prison population during 1991–2 seemed exhausted. The prison population resumed its underlying upward trend at the startling rate of some 500 per month. This largely cancelled any gains created by the government's extensive and expensive prison building programme. During the year as a whole the prison population increased by some 16 per cent (Ashworth, 1993).

All of this rather quashed the mood of (incautious) optimism which had been detectable among Prison Service insiders and liberal pressure groups in the wake of Lord Justice Woolf's (1991) moderately progressive report. It is notable in this context that the first relevant use of the term 'back to basics' known to this author occurred in a lecture given by the then Director General of the Prison Service in 1992 in which he outlined his interpretation of penal progress in light of the opportunities provided by a falling population (Pilling, 1992; Sparks, 1994). Little more than a year later the term assumed rather different penological implications in the regressive moralizing of the 1993 Conservative Party Conference. Any belief that a rough consensus of informed opinion around the reduction of prison numbers and the enhancement of regimes, backed authoritatively by Woolf, would receive continuity of governmental support dissipated abruptly during 1993.

Certain moments stand out in the destruction of that flicker of optimism. In August 1993 a memorandum from Mr Howard's private office was leaked to the press (*Observer*, 22 August) in which the Home Secretary reportedly opined that some prisoners 'enjoy a standard of material comfort which taxpayers find difficult to understand'. In September a destructive riot at Wymott prison in Lancashire received extensive press attention. In contrast to Lord Woolf's attempt to find some intelligibility in prison disturbances the popular press voiced an older and more basic construction of prisons as chaotic cauldrons and of prisoners (see Adams, 1992) as a senseless crowd.

It would be unwise to over-interpret such symptomatic readings taken alone. However, in October, Mr Howard's speech to the annual Conservative Party Conference gave this sensed change in the penal climate an explicit political form. To the rapture of his audience and the joy of the Tory press the Home Secretary unveiled a package of '27 points' to crack down on crime. In addition to his specific amendments to penal policy (the youth training order, six new private prisons, more stringent bail conditions) he announced flatly that 'Prison Works', apparently on a freely interpreted mix of retributive, deterrent and incapacitative grounds. Moreover, he declared, if this should mean that more people go to prison then he 'did not flinch' from that.

It matters little in terms of the political effectivity of this declaration that the sentencing principles espoused by Howard are known by their intellectual proponents to 'stand in open and flagrant contradiction' (Bean, 1981). What matters is that they convey a generic feeling of severity. Mr Howard had articulated a particular kind of rhetorical figure composed principally of the revival of deterrence and a strong implication of rigour. This, it is argued, amounts to the reassertion of the doctrine of less eligibility.

LESS ELIGIBILITY REVISITED

One of the more dispiriting features of the contemporary punitive turn is its apparent ignorance of (or, more accurately, unconcern with) its own historical antecedents. Its populism owes nothing to any developed penological rationale (not even, I will go on to argue, an instrumental control strategy) and everything to an opportunist diagnosis of moral sentiments and popular fears. It is a *discursive* intervention. Its relation to practice, however materially consequential for prisoners, their families and prison staff, is of secondary concern to its author.

Of course, as E. P. Thompson once put it in another context, 'the mind has walked these cliffs before'. The preference for austerity in prison conditions, the elevation of deterrence as a prime aim of punishment, and the association with targeting, discriminating and deserving in welfare provision, are all notions between which a long-standing ideological affinity subsists. This is what the term less eligibility summarizes.

The doctrine of less eligibility received its clearest initial articulation in the late eighteenth century during the period (styled by Foucault as 'the Great Incarceration') when penitentiary imprisonment began to displace more ancient forms of physical punishment, ritual shaming and banishment as a primary penal tactic. The urgent prompting of John Howard and others against the neglect and brutality of the unreformed goals received their sharpest opposition precisely from those who feared that any amelioration in prison conditions would weaken their deterrent effect upon the lower orders. Logically, the more abject the conditions under which the poor survived (or did not) the more extreme the rigours of penal discipline must become.

This is no new discovery of 'revisionist' historiography. In 1939 Hermann Mannheim recorded and anatomized in *The Dilemma of Penal Reform* the hold which less eligibility exerted over all early carceral enterprises. Mannheim explains the inflections which the doctrine underwent. Reactionaries and reformers were divided by their interpretation of it but no one escaped its traces. For the former, whose desire for deterrent control co-existed with a gutsy sense of retributive justice, less eligibility was both practically necessary and morally compelling, since anything else constituted both an invitation and an insult to the honest labourer. For the progressive technocrats of penological engineering such as Jeremy Bentham (for whom considerations of desert were 'nonsense on stilts') the doctrine was moderated into an instrumental requirement of 'non-superiority'.

Such concerns and debates profoundly shaped the forms assumed by early penitentiary regimes. The endlessly careful precautions against comfort and contagion embodied in the silent and separate systems of discipline (Ignatieff, 1978) and the continual debates over the appropriate character of prison labour and diet (Radzinowicz and Hood, 1986) gave the anxiety for less eligibility its material realization. The result was that characteristic ideology of Victorian penality which held that the prison could *perfect* a system of discipline at once unimpeachably humane and unremittingly severe.

These are among the reasons why nineteenth-century penal thought is punctuated by projects for ideal or 'model' systems of imprisonment which are always transfixed between the reforming zeal or philanthropic vocation on the one hand and deterrent criteria on the other. Even transportation (always dogged by allegations of inhuman cruelty) was not immune from allegations of having become self-subvertingly soft when stories of ex-convicts having made good in the new worlds began to filter back to poor relations in the old (Mannheim, 1939; Radzinowicz and Hood, 1986). And the deified icons of Whig interpretations of penal history such as Elizabeth Fry and Mary Carpenter seem never to have disputed that their projects for child saving and the recuperation of fallen women should be consistent with less eligibility principles.

Less eligibility is always sustained by its own sense of justice. Victorian philanthropy was haunted by the knowledge, clearly and repeatedly articulated, of the abject poverty of the mass of the population. Every project of penal improvement was constrained by this knowledge. But such poverty was generally interpreted as a tragic and scarcely alterable fact of nature. Out of a mixture of consideration for the respectable poor and fear of the rough, penal reform could move only within restricted parameters.

The earliest cracks in the dominance of less eligibility, and the counter-assertion of universal criteria in state provision, seem to emerge in the public debate preceding the Royal Commission of 1863.[2] Editorials in *The Quarterly Review* satirize the notion that the rational determination of the prison diet for those in the custody and protection of the state can be pegged to a level believed to exist outside (Radzinowicz and Hood, 1986: 508). But the Royal Commission itself took the standard view, fearing that prisons were 'not sufficiently dreaded'. The meliorist Sir Joshua Jebb died to be replaced by the long ascendancy of the ferocious Sir Edmund du Cane who was absolutely wedded to a principle of uniform deterrence and adamantly resisted any introduction of individuation for prisoners in the guise of rehabilitation (see Garland, 1985, chapter 1).

It is only with the Gladstone Committee of 1895 and the substitution of the rehabilitative 'good and useful life' formula for deterrence as a primary organizing ideology that less eligibility received a serious challenge. The progressivism of early-twentieth-century official penology, registered especially in the institutions of probation and Borstal training, places the doctrine in abeyance as an explicit aim.[3] Among intellectual supporters of rehabilitation, of whom Mannheim is among the most thoroughgoing, less eligibility is identified plainly as an obstacle to be overcome. Mannheim's opposition to less eligibility in *The Dilemma of Penal Reform* is absolute.

Yet Mannheim is only too acutely conscious of the persistence and durability of less eligibility within both lay and jurisprudential penal reasoning. In his view the very contingent and partial status of the victory of rehabilitation during the early and mid-twentieth century penal practice precisely testifies to the doctrine's continued existence as a suppressed but constraining presence. Suffice to say that during periods of penological optimism the dominion of less eligibility is reduced. It is less at home among the development of a universal franchise, welfare entitlement and citizenship than formerly (cf. Jacobs, 1976). Moreover, throughout much of the twentieth century the entrenchment of professional vocationalism (Garland, 1985, 1990) partially insulates penal regimes from the direct impact of less eligibility principles. Thus, even in the wake of the decline of the rehabilitative ideal, the successor languages of 'positive custody' (Home Office, 1979) and 'humane containment' (King and Morgan, 1980) do not betray any marked imprint of less eligibility thinking, even if conservative law-and-order rhetoric, and especially the wilder flights of the *ultras* within Tory ranks (see Pitts, 1989: 41), toy repeatedly with its populist appeal. It is only very recently and for other reasons that less eligibility has resurfaced as an unabashed item of belief and a shaping force in penal politics.

VICTORIAN VALUES AND FREE MARKET EXPERIMENTS

If, as I contend, less eligibility has lately made something of a comeback in the penal politics of Britain and the United States what reasons can be adduced for its re-emergence? In order for less eligibility principles to apply in any strong sense, certain favourable political and ideological conditions appear necessary: first, that the centrality of punishment to social order be strongly asserted, preferably on quasi-classicist deterrent grounds; second, that this demand for order should be linked to a perception that the integrity of the social fabric is threatened by a rising tide of lawlessness; third, that popular *resentment* be invoked against 'soft' or 'cushy' penal measures using a direct comparison with hardships experienced by law abiding citizens; and fourth that there should therefore be significant numbers of the 'truly disadvantaged' (W. J. Wilson, 1987), some of whom are respectable (and hence potentially seen as hard done by in liberal, 'assistantial' penal measures), while others are decidedly unrespectable (and hence eligible principally for deterrent penalties).

Within academic criminology in the recent past this world outlook has been articulated most clearly by James Q. Wilson (1985) when referring to those rationally parasitic criminals whom he terms 'the calculators'. In politics it is a trope deployed with some enthusiasm and success in the crime control rhetoric of the heydays of the Reagan/Bush and Thatcher eras during the early 1980s (Scraton, 1987; Pitts, 1989; Brake and Hale, 1992; Caringella-Macdonald, 1990). It has also recently become central to the articulation of crime policy under the Major administration in Britain too. Why? What are the conditions most propitious for its successful deployment?

There now exists a substantial body of historical evidence and theoretical reflection which supports the view that variations in the level of punishment and in the intensity of punitive rhetoric have at least an elective affinity with recessionary moments in business cycles (fiscal crisis) and/or with critical moments in the popularity and authority of governments (legitimation crises). The scriptural beginning for such concerns is generally taken to be provided by Rusche and Kirchheimer in *Punishment and Social Structure* (1939).[4] The outlines of Rusche and Kirchheimer's argument are well known and need not be rehearsed at length here (for summaries see Cavadino and Dignan, 1992, chapter 3; Garland, 1990, chapters 4 and 5). In essence, Rusche and Kirchheimer argue that both the level and form of punishment are sensitive to variations in labour market conditions. The latter conditions the value assigned to the offender's life and labour power and underlie the various historical mutations in penal strategy. Roughly speaking, the oversupply of labour in late medieval Europe renders life cheap and gives rise to the notorious savagery of physical punishments in this period. By contrast the demand for labour in the early modern 'mercantilist' period increases the value of life and necessitates that the offender be put to use either domestically (in Houses of Correction) or in the service of colonization and conquest (galley slavery, colonization). Later again, the collapse in labour markets during the early industrial revolution swells the ranks of the unemployed rendering prison labour largely redundant. The resulting sense of fiscal stringency and social alarm ('masterless men', machine breaking) gives rise to a deterioration in both Poor Law provision and prison conditions, with prison labour reserved for purely deterrent, unproductive uses (the treadwheel). Thus the first half of the nineteenth century is the high water mark of less eligibility principles (see Ignatieff, 1978, chapter 7).

Rusche and Kirchheimer's thesis has been widely criticized on both empirical and theoretical grounds (Ignatieff, 1983; Garland, 1990; Zimring and Hawkins, 1991), in particular for its alleged assumption of an hydraulic relationship between economic conditions and punishment. Conversely, however, Rusche and Kirchheimer are widely acknowledged, including by their critics, to have extended the possibilities for the social analysis of penality by severing the formerly presumed relationship between crime and punishment and suggesting the punishment may respond to other conditions and pursue other purposes than simply tracking the crime rate. Later commentators have revised and extended the Ruschean thesis to show the historical susceptibility of punishment to a variable range of ideological and political influences (Ignatieff, 1978; Foucault, 1979; Melossi and Pavarini, 1981; Garland, 1985; Box and Hale, 1986; Box, 1987; Hale, 1989; Barlow, et al., 1993). Perhaps most relevantly for the present argument Box (1987: 197) seeks to rescue the contention that political retrenchments during recessionary periods are registered in increasing prison numbers 'from the quicksand of functionalism and conspiracy theory'. For Box the correlation between increasing unemployment and rising prison populations is mediated by the anxieties of policymakers and sentencers acting logically upon their presumption that unemployment increases crime and disorder.

For later revisionists, therefore, it is the discursive politics of punishment and the resulting vocabularies of penal motive that matter most, rather that its instrumental functions for social control. Punishment as a cultural agent and political tactic may perform a number of roles. It affirms boundaries, draws moral distinctions and imposes identities on its subjects. The capacity to punish effectively, appropriately and judiciously in terms of prevailing rules and norms of procedure is a defining element in the legitimacy of states and governments (Melossi, 1993).

It is therefore also necessary to distinguish clearly between, on the one hand, those transformations in the form and function of penal action which occur, as it were, on a long wave of historical development (Foucault's account of the invention of the penitentiary, Garland's analysis of the birth of the welfare sanction) and, on the other, those manoeuvres and shifts of position within its operation which respond to the press of immediate, conjunctural circumstances and contingencies. We may therefore accept a long-standing tendency towards rule-bound, professionally administered, rationalized penal action (which Garland [1990: 4] summarizes as 'penal modernism'), synthesizing a variety of declaratory, supervisory and corrective objectives, without assuming that this wholly displaces prior and more 'basic' discourses and practices. To the extent that the latter, of which less eligibility is an instance, continue to exist, they may also be drawn upon and invoked for tactical advantage (especially in competitive electoral politics) when the need or opportunity is seen to arise. There is every reason to doubt that all the elements that are in play in any given historical moment form a functionally integrated seamless web.

The results are what Mannheim (1940: 41) termed the 'contemporaneity of the non-contemporaneous' – the simultaneous presence of ostensibly incompatible positions and principles. Thus, as Garland notes (1990: 185) the penal realm may look very different from within (to practitioners, administrators and reformers) and from without (to populist politicians, journalists and the public audiences whom they address). The criteria of legitimacy to which each adhere may conflict sharply. The parameters of the cultural politics of punishment are wide, and the scope for political opportunism within them is great.

Both Garland (1985) and Melossi (1985) suggest that during periods of relative affluence and optimism the centrality of punishment to political debate tends to recede (see also Box, 1987). Penality becomes one element among others in a modernizing political settlement. In the case outlined by Garland of the reforming Liberal governments in Britain in the first years of the twentieth century the tenor of the period is set by the extension of the franchise, the institutionalization of labour disputes and the move towards universalism in welfare provision. Penal relations, increasingly depoliticized and professionalized, bear the imprint of that intellectual and political environment. Something similar would hold for the Progressive era in the United States (conventionally 1900–17, see Degler, 1959), or indeed for the Kennedy–Johnson 'Great Society' period of the 1960s. Such moments are not in the main, as Melossi has it, 'a time for punishment'.

However, Melossi argues, during recessionary periods or more particularly during crises of legitimacy and public order (Melossi, 1993: 266), the field of punishment is apt to be reinvested with political contention. At such times, he suggests, a 'chain of punitive discourse' is established which asserts a connection between the restoration of order and the reassertion of penal power (see also Hall et al., 1978). Somewhat similarly, Habermas's (1976) thesis of 'legitimation crisis' proposes that where states are unable to perform the tasks they have set themselves (which in modern welfare states are more demanding and extensive than formerly) then those functions – previously largely consensually defined – become controversial. The state must either divest itself of its obligations or reassert its competence to fulfil them. Where 'the crisis' combines dimensions of both fiscal stringency and public disorder and anxiety, then the articulation between welfare provision and penalty becomes a problem. Arguments arise for the retrenchment of welfare provision. Commentators assert its economically and socially counter-productive effects (Murray, 1984, 1990). Conservative opinion demands the more vigorous imposition of punishment and an end to its confusion with welfarist aims. Hence the suppressed competition between the possible 'worlds of welfare capitalism' (Esping-Anderson, 1988) becomes more open and intense. Expensive, integrationist penal-welfare strategies are less likely to be politically favoured than other kinds of social regulation – on the one hand the 'liberalization' of labour market 'disciplines' (Aglietta, 1987), on the other a more direct appeal to 'the virtues' (see for example Anderson, 1993) in the control of personal conduct.

It is quite well documented that under such conditions the political party or bloc that successfully represents itself as most responsive to public concerns and anxieties about social disorder is electorally advantaged. In the British case the success of the Conservative party since 1979 is generally acknowledged by both sympathizers (Clark, 1990; Anderson, 1993) and critics (Marquand, 1988; Gamble, 1988; Brake and Hale, 1992) to have owed much to such a form of statecraft. At its height Thatcherism folded together concerns with economic efficiency and fiscal prudence with a sense of urgency in the restoration of propriety and public order to immense political effect. On the one hand it offered an appeal to the private virtues of aspiration, property ownership and consumption *enrichissez-vous, mes enfants!*, on the other the remoralization of the public tasks of welfare and punishment. Such a project is inherently both pragmatic and rhetorical. It has in part to do with the restoration of state legitimacy and the provision of stable conditions for accumulation, in part the invocation of the poetry of political ideas – order, authority, national pride. The punitive turn in Anglo-American penality under Reagan and Thatcher organizes respectable fears of dangerous and undeserving others (the Victorian 'residuum' mutated into the contemporary 'underclass').

Of course we need never assume that such strategies achieve their ostensible aims (least of all the reduction of crime) in order to appreciate their cultural and rhetorical power. In fact the empirical failings of neo-conservative crime control strategies are well known (Matthews and Young, 1986; Currie, 1985; Taylor, 1990; Hudson, 1993), but these have rarely been of central importance to their authors. Rather, the exploitation of ever more well-founded fear may be deployed to buttress the intensification of precisely those same techniques. To the extent that the state grounds its claim to legitimacy in the maintenance of order it must at least symbolically communicate its order-making prowess (Mathiesen's 'action function' of punishment [1990: 138]). In all these respects the politics of punishment necessarily exceed considerations of instrumental social control.

One weakness, therefore, of those commentators who have most closely followed and revised Rusche and Kirchheimer (Box, 1987; Hale, 1989) is their overwhelming preoccupation with punishment *numbers*. The easiest and apparently most conclusive way of demonstrating the turn back towards punishment lies in showing quantitative increases in the allocation of penalties, and especially of prison sentences. Of course this is an important matter and the evidence is indeed startling, especially with respect to the United States where the 'mega-shift' in the prison population since 1980 makes it hard to calibrate on the same scale as those of other advanced societies (Mathiesen, 1990; Christie, 1993; Caringella-Macdonald, 1990). What is frequently forgotten here (though *not* by Rusche and Kirchheimer themselves) is the independent significance of *qualitative* changes in penal style or method, in the conditions under which punishment is undergone, and in vocabularies of motive.[5] But, for Rusche and Kirchheimer it is not just quanta of punishments that matter. Rather, it is less eligibility itself that provides 'the leitmotiv of all prison administration down to the present time' (1939: 94).[6]

Why then should less eligibility – after a quite extended period of comparative abeyance – have recurred with some vigour recently? The reasons, I suggest, are not so very difficult to discern. Much social analysis of the 1980s in Britain (Walker, 1990; Gamble, 1988) and the United States (for example, Currie, 1990) suggests an increasing polarization of shares of national wealth. Such a 'strategy of inequality' is justified by its true believers on the grounds that trickle down effect of affluence for the more successful in Sir Keith Joseph's expression 'lifts all the boats'. Relative inequalities are unimportant by comparison with the optimization of economic performance for the national economy as a whole. Such a view demands the attribution of virtue to the economically successful and insists that any disincentive to free enterprise (redistributive taxation, over-generous transfer payments) is economically irrational. Just as entrepreneurs must be incentivized by the freeing of the market forces, so much concern focuses on the alleged disincentives to the poorest against participation in the labour market presented by the consoling but ultimately disabling embrace of welfare (Murray, 1985; Dennis and Erdos, 1992; Anderson, 1993).

For purists the 'negative freedoms' (Berlin, 1984) of classical liberalism are to be preferred to the positive ambitions of social democracy. The latter inevitably entail an unwelcome and perhaps disastrous over-extension of state action into the private sphere, sapping initiative and personal responsibility. The state should in principle confine itself to the minimally necessary tasks of macro-economic management and the maintenance of law and order. The most appropriate model of social organization is in essence of that social contract theory, in which there may be a sovereign power and an 'invisible hand' but certainly no such thing as 'society'. Individuals are radically accountable for their own character and conduct and must be encouraged to make the best of the benefits and burdens which the moral luck of their market situation affords them. There is thus a necessary symmetry between rewards and deterrents.

One penological sidelight on this world outlook is ingeniously provided by Wilkins (1984) and Pease (1990) in the form of a 'tolerance of inequality' thesis. For Wilkins and Pease punishment and reward in free market societies can be thought of most simply as the two ends of a single polarity. Those western societies with the widest ranges of income distribution (the USA, Great Britain) tend also to have the widest spread of penal values. That is, the concept of proportionate punishments is translated on to a more 'stretched out' tariff of penalties than in other comparable societies. It tends to follow that prison populations will be larger in part because a higher proportion of very long sentences will be imposed than in, say, Scandinavia or Japan where income distributions and penal ranges are both more compressed. Where does this argument lead? The greater the tolerance of inequality of outcomes the more censoriously a society regards its deviants? The more rigorously it polarizes punishment and reward the more centrally it relies upon a system of incentives and deterrents as the calculable levers towards desired conduct? If so, the rational economic man of classical theory naturally takes as his criminological counterparts either the successful free rider (Wilson's 'calculators', Clarke's 'reasoning criminal') or the unsuccessful outsider (the Victorian pauper or ruffian; the contemporary New Age traveller, the 'social junk' of the urban underclass).

Pease freely acknowledges that his schema is not much more than a thought experiment, a statistical *jeu d'esprit*, albeit a provocative one. What it particularly lacks is any developed awareness of its own potential links to an actual world of structure and contingency, discourse and action. That connection seems to me to run somewhat as follows. On the level of theoretical principle, the economic strategy of inequality speaks a language of reward and penalty based on its assumption of hedonic rationality. Its vocabulary of motives emphasizes a connection between deserving and rewarding whose mirror image lies in a structure of justly deserved penalties. But rewards and sanctions are also instruments. Whenever such a society senses a special difficulty in ensuring desired (or at least compliant) behaviour, or experiences a heightened sense of threat, the discourse of justice is liable to be supplemented or indeed supplanted by that of deterrence. At such moments the special mixture of censure and coercion implied by the notion of less eligibility again offers itself as a favoured option.

This seems to me to describe just the sort of shift of rhetorical gear which has occurred in British penal politics in recent years. There was a period in the later 1980s when law and order issues were much less central to political campaigning than they had been in the early heyday of radical Thatcherism (indeed they were largely absent from the foreground of the 1987 General Election). Penal policymaking, while still marked by the liberal individualism of the times took a rather more studied and less ideologically charged form. The principal result was the 1991 Criminal Justice Act with its formalist 'just deserts' framework. 'Law and Order', however has now returned to the political agenda with something of a vengeance. It has done so, moreover, in consequence of a specific conjunction of political circumstances. A successor government presides over an extended and painful recession and stubbornly high unemployment. It stands accused by the ideological ultras within its own ranks (some of whose paternally challenged members are within the Cabinet, indeed the Home Office itself). The government experiences low opinion poll ratings. The governing party is sharply divided on some key issues, especially European policy, in ways which directly bear on its claim to defend the integrity of that key rhetorical entity of Thatcherism, the nation.

Moreover, it is forced to adopt tactics of economic management – first high interest rates, latterly tax increases – which consciously target both private consumption and public expenditure. This tends to induce a sense of relative deprivation (especially compared with the Lawson 'boom' years). This is not just for low income groups. It also squeezes those whose membership of the middle class (especially defined by home ownership) is insecure – people on occupational pensions, the self-employed, older white collar workers who lose their jobs, and so on. And the rage for public spending cuts affects controversial areas – not just welfare provision but, unthinkably to Mrs Thatcher, the police. Key thresholds in social stratification – benefit entitlements, access to housing, access to employment – become politically controversial. They are scarce resources.

The language of discussion that surrounds them comes more and more to include considerations of targeting, discriminating and deserving. It is not simply that any programme of fiscal austerity has implications for the prisons as it does for other public services. Nor is it just that they stand to become overloaded. It is also the case that when governments call upon the general public to accept certain burdens 'in the national interest', they will tend to speak a language of moral injunction which bears down with increasing sharpness on the undeserving and non-contributing, and which underscores more sharply than before the boundary between those who are 'in good standing' and those who are not. A society in such a condition is apt to identify its excluded minorities rather more in terms of their capacity to create trouble than in terms of their needs.

It would appear then that there are moments when a politician's or a party's seizure of a moment of opportunity for self-promotion and the surrounding logic of the situation coincide. The apparent failure of the governing party to deliver on its long-standing undertaking of enhanced community safety and public order itself becomes part of the moment of opportunity, provided that the diagnosis of such failures can be re-interpreted as lying elsewhere – in undue leniency, undiscriminating generosity, middle-class permissiveness. It becomes in itself a reason for reassertion of robustness and hence part of the strategy for coping with a legitimacy deficit. Thus John Major's assertion that we should 'condemn a little more, understand a little less' suppresses and denies what in fact we know of the recent past (the record prison numbers, the drastic public order legislation, the whole uncomprehending and condemnatory dis-course of Thatcherism) and insists instead that the remoralization of penalty starts *here*.

CONCLUSION: LESS ELIGIBILITY, PENAL VALUES AND PRIVATIZATION

It is now, as it has always been, the case that the weight of penal discipline falls disproportionately on the poorest (Hudson, 1993). Recalling the historical tenacity of the discourse of less eligibility reminds us that it is *designed* to do so.

Garland (1985) suggests that the general direction of the twentieth century penal-welfare strategies has been away from less eligibility as a dominant principle and towards reconciling penal action with techniques of inclusion. However 'disciplinary' and invasive the normalizing tech-niques of the welfare sanction, they were also about the connecting and assimilating properties of social control. Even imprisonment, the most segregative and still stigmatizing penalty, came to be seen in terms of a specific deprivation (of time at liberty) rather than in terms of the deliber-ate imposition of other hardships; and at least some of its institutions (for example the Borstal) claimed strongly to incorporate a remedial and rehabilitative element, however distantly removed this ideology may have been from practice and real outcomes.

My guess is that the vocational attachments of most penal professionals (whether in the prisons or the 'community') remain to that earlier model of penal action rather than to the present renaissance of a harder edged view. Hanging on to their well-thumbed copies of Lord Woolf's (1991) report and their mission statements, working diligently on their model regimes, prison governors and officers want in the main to be left out of the new vogue for more frequent and more austere punishments. They want to run decent, hygienic, uncrowded, unsmelly prisons. Their professional pride is invested in pre-release schemes, bail information units, visitors' centres, alcohol and drug groups, edible food, suicide prevention initiatives and other signs of penological decency. If they hope that the new renaissance of less eligibility rhetoric will pass them by they may well turn out to be lucky. For its opportunism is palpable. Moreover, it is a language that goes over the heads of those professionals and their practices and speaks directly to 'sound popular feeling' via the medium of the popular press. Maybe then the 'discourse' really is just 'talk'. It does not actually have to be delivered.

Moreover, the vicissitudes of the English prison problem have already had some ironic effects. The nadir of April 1990 and the Strangeways siege generated the somewhat progressive moment of Woolf. Meanwhile, if the politicians give grounds for thinking that they have quit any form of consensus for penal improvement other alliances emerge. Already one can begin to detect a new friendliness between the prison governors, the respectable pressure groups and perhaps the Prison Officers Association (POA) not easily imaginable a few years ago. Those who know better are shrewdly aware that the fragile legitimacy of the prison system, and its avoidance of riot and scandal, depend on defending the gains, not great but real, of the last few years. Taken together these groups form a bloc that even the most studiously reactionary Home Secretary cannot altogether ignore.

But there are also new ingredients in the stew of penal politics. The first is that overcrowding is back, and in no small way. In that respect conditions are again turning in an adverse direction, whatever the best efforts of governors and staff might be. Second, there is privatization. Its position is rendered enormously more complicated by the current harder rhetorical turn. Privatization was mooted and conceived during the eras of just deserts and humane containment. Private imprisonment is thought of by governments principally as a means to certain ends, namely the flexible and cost-effective provision of additional space in which humanely to contain. Private sector agents are not called upon to *want* to punish more people, still less to punish them more. Rather, it is simply that the market only comes into being when governments determine that more prison places should be provided (Sparks, 1994; Shichor, 1993; Lilly and Knepper, 1992a, 1992b).

In the main politicians (Clarke, 1992) and intellectual advocates of privatization (Logan, 1990) argue in conventional terms, but presumably in good faith, that market disciplines and new thinking will produce better and more humane penal environments. However, what has not been thought about in this debate (and certainly not anticipated by the private players) is what happens if better and more humane penal environments are no longer what are desired. The attraction of the privatization case depends on a distinction between the allocation of punishment by the state and the delivery of penal services by its delegated agents. Private sector operators disclaim any interest in making the conditions of imprisonment punitive in themselves (rather than reverse). Many private prison personnel are disillusioned liberals, frustrated at conditions prevailing in the public sector. They posit a close connection between their intervention and penal reform or amelioration. If private sector prisons have preferred penal rationales they lie in the region of neoclassical 'just deserts' thinking and/or selective incapacitation. In either case they are about normalized containment.

But what happens to this argument when the assumed consensus (that prison conditions should be made progressively more tolerable) dissipates? That is, if deterrence is reinstated and less eligibility comes back into the penal equation? For present purposes what is most clearly apparent from these developments is that the more implicit progressivist teleology of Kenneth Clarke's earlier statements during his tenure as Home Secretary (flatly equating privatization with penal improvement) can hardly survive such a deterioration in the surrounding political environment. The idea that the terms on which contracts are offered must inevitably make private prisons preferable from the prisoner's point of view seems more and more open to reasonable doubt. Rather the vaunted responsiveness of the private sector signifies if anything the reverse, namely that prison regimes can be made to react barometrically to the external penal climate (in part by virtue of not being mitigated by the vocational culture – the 'restrictive practices' – of a cadre of administrators and staff steeped in a meliorist public service ethic). The prospect that penal services might be provided by a private sector not 'incentivized' towards relentless improvement but instead constrained by a rhetoric of austerity exposes a range of impending troubles for the legitimacy of the private corrections industry which have until now been largely suppressed. In short, market conditions will have changed because those conditions only exist by grace and favour of the prevailing penal ideology. Either private sector contributors must throw their weight decisively against the deterrence/less eligibility dyad or they must accept the full implications of free market premises, namely that if austerity is what the customer wants, austerity is what they will have.

Notes

1. I am most grateful to Pat Carlen, Chris Hale, Nicola Lacey and Joe Sim for their thoughtful comments on an earlier draft of this paper.
2. The Royal Commission itself and the *Penal Servitude Act 1864* which followed were harshly dominated by less eligibility thinking. This was even more clearly true of Lord Carnarvon's 1863 House of Lords Select Committee into prison discipline which called for more uniformity and deterrent discipline in prisons and for intensified dietary restrictions. This is well summarized by Sim (1990: 33–5).
3. This does not mean of course that prison conditions uniformly improved or, as Sim (1990) makes clear, that the provision of medical and other facilities to prisoners ceased to be subject to special restrictions. Sim also reminds me (pers. comm.) that in all manner of routine and unacknowledged ways (food, underwear changes, bathing and toilet facilities) prisons remain marked by less eligible features well into the present century.
4. It is less often remembered (curiously, since Mannheim is generally assigned the role of 'mainstream' commentator to Rusche and Kirchheimer's Marxist outsiders) that the same year also saw the publication of *The Dilemma of Penal Reform*, similarly preoccupied with less eligibility. For all their differences, and Mannheim's sharp criticisms of Rusche and Kirchheimer's economism, both books (but Mannheim's more explicitly) are haunted by the implications of Nazism for the politics of punishment.
5. In fairness to Box and Hale, of course, one could reasonably argue that under the conditions prevailing in the English prisons during the 1970s and 1980s the problem of less eligibility took care of itself. One did not have to *will* or intend that conditions should become increasingly less eligible; problems of overcrowding and shortage simply made it so willy-nilly (see also McDermott and King, 1989). Moreover, it may well be that, with the notable exception of the 'short, sharp, shock' experiments, that demands of Thatcherite 'law and order' concerns were satisfied by the assurance that more people were in prison, parole conditions made tighter and so on.
6. This, they go on to say, is the 'inner contradiction' that underlies every reform programme. In this respect they are of course in entire agreement with their contemporary Mannheim. Rusche and Kirchheimer's concern is that each gain in humanitarian reform may be 'surrendered ... to the mercy of every crisis in the market'. Conversely, their hope that the spread of affluence may contribute towards a 'more rational and more humane praxis' again suggests more commonality between the 'marxist' and the 'mainstream' commentators than is generally admitted.

References

Adams, R. (1992) *Prison Riots in Britain and the USA* (London: Macmillan).
Aglietta, M. (1987) *A Theory of Capitalist Regulation* (London: Verso).
Anderson, D. (ed.) (1993) *The Loss of Virtue* (London: Social Affairs Unit).

Ashworth, A. (1993) 'Sentencing by Numbers', *Criminal Justice Matters* (Winter 1993–4).

Barlow, D.; Hickman Barlow, M.; and Chiricos, T. (1993) 'Long Economic Cycles and the Criminal Justice System in the U.S.', *Crime, Law and Social Change*, 19: 143–69.

Bean, P. (1981) *Punishment* (Oxford: Martin Robertson).

Berlin, I. (1984) 'Two Concepts of Liberty', in M. Sandel (ed.), *Liberalism and its Critics* (Oxford: Blackwell).

Box, S. (1987) *Recession, Crime and Punishment,* London: Macmillan.

Box, S. and Hale, C. (1986) 'Unemployment, Crime and Imprisonment and the Enduring Problem of Prison Overcrowding', in R. Matthews and J. Young (eds), *Confronting Crime* (London: Sage).

Brake, M. and Hale, C. (1992) *Public Order and Private Lives* (London: Routledge).

Caringella-Macdonald, S. (1990) 'State Crises and the Crackdown on Crime Under Reagan', *Contemporary Crises*, 14: 91–118.

Cavadino, M. and Dignan, J. (1992) *The Penal System: an Introduction* (London: Sage).

Christie, N. (1993) *Crime Control as Industry* (London: Routledge).

Clark, J. C. D. (ed.) (1990) *Ideas and Politics in Modern Britain* (London: Macmillan).

Clarke, K. (1992) 'Prisoners with Private Means', *The Independent* (22 December): 17.

Currie, E. (1985) *Confronting Crime* (New York: Pantheon).

Currie, E. (1990) 'Heavy with Human Tears', in I. Taylor (ed.), *The Social Effects of Free Market Policies* (Hemel Hempstead: Harvester Wheatsheaf).

Dennis, N. and Erdos, G. (1992) *Families Without Fatherhood* (London: Institute for Economic Affairs).

Degler, C. (1959) *Out of Our Past* (New York: Harper & Row).

Esping-Anderson, G. (1988) *Three Worlds of Welfare Capitalism* (Cambridge: Polity).

Foucault, M. (1979) *Discipline and Punish* (London: Paladin).

Gamble, A. (1988) *The Free Economy and the Strong State* (London: Macmillan).

Garland, D. (1985) *Punishment and Welfare* (Aldershot: Gower).

Garland, D. (1990) *Punishment and Modern Society* (Oxford University Press).

Habermas, J. (1976) *Legitimation Crisis* (London: Heinemann).

Hale, C. (1989) 'Economy, Punishment and Imprisonment', *Contemporary Crises*, 13, 4: 327–49

Hall, S.; Critcher, C.; Jefferson, T.; Clarke, J.; and Roberts, B. (1978) *Policing the Crisis* (London: Macmillan).

Home Office (1979) *Committee of Inquiry into the United Kingdom Prison Services* (May Committee) (London: HMSO).

Hudson, B. (1993) *Penal Policy and Social Justice* (London: Macmillan).

Ignatieff, M. (1978) *A Just Measure of Pain* (Harmondsworth: Penguin).

Ignatieff, M. (1983) 'State, Civil Society and Total Institutions: A Critique of Recent Social Histories of Punishment' in E. Cohen and A. Scill (eds), *Social Control and the State* (Oxford: Blackwell).

Jacobs, J. (1976) *Stateville: the Penitentiary in Mass Society* (Chicago University Press).

King R. and Morgan, R. (1980) *The Future of the Prison System* (Farnborough: Gower).

Lilly J. R. and Knepper, P. (1992a) 'The Corrections-Commercial Complex', *Prison Service Journal*, no. 87.

Lilly, J. R. and Knepper, P. (1992b) 'An International Perspective on the Privatization of Corrrections', *Howard Journal of Criminal Justice*, 31, 3: 174–91.

Logan, C. (1990) *Private Prisons: Cons and Pros* (Oxford University Press).

McDermott, K. and King, R. (1989) 'A Fresh Start: The Enhancement Of Prison Regimes', *Howard Journal of Criminal Justice*, 28: 161–76.

Mannheim, H. (1939) *The Dilemma of Penal Reform* (London: George Allen and Unwin).

Mannheim K. (1940) *Man and Society in the Age of Reconstruction* (London: Routledge and Kegan Paul).

Marquand, D. (1988) *The Unprincipled Society* (London: Fontana).

Mathiesen, T. (1990) *Prison on Trial* (London: Sage).

Matthews, R. and Young, J. (eds) (1986) *Confronting Crime* (London: Sage).

Melossi, D. (1985) 'Punishment and Social Action: Changing Vocabularies of Motive within a Political Business Cycle', *Current Perspectives in Social Theory*, 6: 169–97.

Melossi, D. (1993) 'Gazette of Morality and Social Whip: Punishment, Hegemony and the Case of the USA, 1970–92', *Social and Legal Studies*, 2: 259–79.

Melossi, D. and Pavarini, M. (1981) *The Prison and the Factory* (London: Macmillan).

Murray, C. (1984) *Losing Ground* (New York: Basic Books).

Murray, C., (1990) *The Emerging British Underclass* (with responses by Frank Field, Joan C. Brown, Nicholas Deakin and Alan Walker) (London: Institute for Economic Affairs).

Pease, K. (1990) 'Punishment Demand and Punishment Numbers', in R. V. Clarke and D. M. Gottfredson (eds) *Policy and Theory in Criminal Justice* (Aldershot: Avebury).

Pilling, J. (1992) 'Back to Basics – Relationships in the Prison Service', The Eve Saville Memorial Lecture, Institute for the Study and Treatment of Delinquency. (London: ISTD).

Pitts, J. (1989) *The Politics of Juvenile Crime* (London: Sage).

Radzinowicz, L. and Hood, R. (1986) *The Emergence of Penal Policy* (Oxford University Press).

Rusche, G. and Kirchheimer, O. (1939) *Punishment and Social Structure* (London: George Allen and Unwin).

Scraton, P. (1987) *Law, Order and the Authoritarian State* (Milton Keynes: Open University Press).

Shichor, D. (1993) 'The Corporate Context of Private Prisons', *Crime, Law and Social Change*, 20: 113–38.

Sim, J. (1990) *Medical Power in Prisons* (Milton Keynes: Open University Press).

Sparks, R. (1994) 'Can Prisons Be Legitimate?', *British Journal of Criminology*, 34, 1: 14–28.

Taylor, I. (ed.) (1990) *The Social Effects of Free Market Policies* (Hemel Hempstead: Harvester Wheatsheaf).

Walker, A. (1990) 'The strategy of inequality', in I. Taylor (ed.), *The Social Effects of Free Market Policies* (Hemel Hempstead: Harvester Wheatsheaf).
Wilkins, L. (1984) *Consumerist Criminology* (London: Heinemann).
Wilson, J. Q. (1985) *Thinking About Crime* (New York: Basic Books).
Wilson, W. J. (1987) *The Truly Disadvantaged* (Chicago University Press).

5 Modernity, Imprisonment, and Social Solidarity

Wayne Morrison

We may define modernity as the time – dating from an historical period in the late seventeenth and eighteenth centuries we call the enlightenment – when a rather peculiar image of the relationship of mankind and the world became possible. First, confined to a small group of intellectuals, then gradually spreading to larger groups of people, modernity is based on the belief that social order is a human creation. Society is a human artifact. Fitting with this belief was another – that with the possession of secure knowledge concerning the basic entities of nature and the laws by which nature operated, we could develop social order in such a way that, gradually but progressively, individuals and societies could become happy, could become stable, could become free, could enjoy a range of social goods, could become *just*. There was a vision of a future age of peace and prosperity, of freedom and justice. This would be our destiny, if only we did not lose our confidence. But as we enter late modernity those aspirations do not appear to have been fully realized. Instead we are confronted daily with multiple injustices, inequalities, segregation and significantly, the increased use of incarceration.

In both the United States and England and Wales over half the con-victed inmates in each country has a record of adult custody before their current confinement. In the adult prisons in each of these countries only about a third of inmates are imprisoned for violent offences – murder, rape, robbery, or assault. The adult prison population in the United States is 1.2 million (including both State and Federal prisons), while the number in England and Wales in 1994 was approximately 50 000. This involves an incarceration rate of 640 per 100 000 in the United States and 119 per 100 000 in England and Wales. Moreover the prison population of each country appears likely to rise sharply throughout the 1990s. The increase in use of imprisonment in the United States is startling, rising from 230 per 100 000 in 1979 to 640 per 100 000 in 1991. But even more shock-ing is the ethnic imbalance. As apartheid ended in South Africa, the figures for imprisonment revealed that black males in the United States were subjected to a greater level of penal constraint than in South Africa. In 1989 there were 14 625 000 black males in the United States and

15 050 642 in South Africa, but in 1990 the United States incarcerated 499 871 while South Africa held 107 202. This gave a incarceration rate of 3370 per 100 000 black males in the US and 681 for South Africa. This meant that 4 per cent of black males were in prison in the United States (Christie, 1993). Elsewhere in the western world the use of imprisonment has also experienced an upward trend. Only imprisonment levels in the former communist countries – which appeared to be declining from the high uses of the 1950s and 60s – bucked the trend, but even in these countries increases have been predicted as the dislocation effects of free market policies have become more severe (see Mikhlin and King in this volume).

In Britain, under variations of the same political party in government (the Conservatives), penal policy has gone through several U turns. The 1979 election campaign politicized the issue of law and order, with the Conservative platform including a tough deterrent strategy of strengthening the police, increasing sentence lengths and building more prisons. In the later part of the 1980s, the evident failure of this policy to dent the rise in crime, led to Home Secretaries adopting a more pragmatic approach with increased emphasis on crime prevention, the development of a broader service based and problem-focused style of policing, and to a conception of the prison as part of the problem rather than the solution. The 1990 White Paper *Crime, Justice and Protecting the Public*, which led to the 1991 Criminal Justice Act, declared imprisonment was 'an expensive way of making bad people worse'. Imprisonment rates declined sharply immediately the Act came into force, but shortly afterwards a new Home Secretary made a dramatic change back to the harsh rhetoric of the early 1980s. This culminated in Michael Howard's 'Prison works' speech to the 1993 Conservative Party Conference. Prison worked, Howard claimed, in that it kept known offenders out of circulation, while hard work and discipline would put fear in the minds of potential offenders. Overriding his advisers, Howard engineered a spectacular U turn in prison policy, dropping schemes to reduce the numbers sent to prison, with the consequence that between January 1993 and September 1994 – a period of 21 months – the prison population for England and Wales grew by 25 per cent from 40 000 to 50 000.

What are we to make of this? Certainly the reliance upon imprisonment can not simply be explained by the increase in crime rates, since countries vary greatly in their use of imprisonment (Christie: 1993). Moreover why did the increase in imprisonment take place at a time when criminology claimed not to support it? Criminology appears to be of increasingly little relevance. Certainly, contemporary criminology faces several problems. These include:

1. A dramatic increase in crimes rates throughout the western world since the 1950s which, along with an increase in fear of crime, has created an image of a breakdown of internal social order.
2. An aetiological crisis arising from the difficulty of developing coherent and general explanations of crime and criminality.
3. A scepticism towards the theorization of crime, and towards integrating the various information bytes that research has thrown up.
4. A more modest assessment of the effectiveness of the criminal justice system particularly in relation to imprisonment which increasingly appears stripped of legitimacy.
5. An apparent relentless increase in punishment and a dramatic take off in the use of imprisonment which is most apparent in the United States but also evident in several other countries.

Thus there appears to be a disjuncture between the claims of criminology, or the scientific knowledge concerning crime, and the operation of punishment and the practical reality of criminal justice. A major question arises: Why is it that imprisonment currently appears stripped of legitimacy but increases in usage? Part of the answer may lie in the political uses the rhetoric of law and order has been put, particularly by the conservative right, but a deeper set of issues concern the underlying nature of contemporary social order. Put simply, we can no longer hold to our certainties concerning the nature of our societies and our social ordering. We tend to think of modern society as producing vast amounts of information and of modernity as subjecting all subject to critical analysis – that modernity strips the world of its mystery in pursuit of rationality – but the truth appears to be that as the amount of knowledge we produce increases, the more complicated and ultimately mysterious the overall picture gets.

Surrounded by the sea of diverse knowledge(s), or information bytes, wisdom becomes more difficult to achieve and simplistic messages gain in appeal. Thus it is possible for politicians, such as Michael Howard to ignore criminological 'wisdom' concerning the weakness of using the formal systems of social control to tackle crime, in favour of short-term improvements to the system so as to make it easier for the police to catch criminals and for the courts to convict the guilty.

Imprisonment is currently a system in expansion. The Norwegian Nils Christie (1993) is not alone in seeing contemporary *Crime Control as a form of Industry*, and wondering if we are witnessing a movement towards western style Gulags. Specific problem groups – for example, drug users or the unemployed – become loosely grouped into a category reminiscent of the dangerous classes of the nineteenth century and for which only the loose label 'underclass' appears applicable (Morrison, 1995). It appears that little has changed from the reality of the Victorian penal policy which Garland (1985) had seen as focused upon the lowest sections of the working classes. Imprisonment is concentrated in its effects on certain, albeit reasonably large, sections of the population. This raises for some criminologists at least, the difficult question of why the populations with the least stake in society and with the least social and economic resources, should also be the sections most subjected to intensive policing and the recipients of harsh penalties. For critical scholars of the criminal law, which stresses an image of a legal subject which is not only a rationally calculating individual but one who acts as a reasonable man, can claim universality when the real people who come before it overwhelmingly are located at the 'bottom end' of the social structure, with the least to gain from 'playing the game' (Norrie, 1993: 202).

Outside the radical criminology and critical legal studies these questions remain largely ignored. Moreover, we remain, as a society, unsure of how exactly to view imprisonment. At times it is difficult to break with the notion that it is natural and therefore necessary for social order. Thus while the director of NACRO may describe British prisons as *Bricks of Shame*, and 'an affront to civilized society' (Stern, 1989), for a long time imprisonment was held out as a rational advance upon pre-modern modes of punishment and as an expression of humanitarian values, reflecting our commitment to calm, rational calculation.

Western societies have a phrase which lawyers, and occasionally politicians, are very fond of. It defines modern western societies as *Rule of Law States*. Everyone is presumed to be subjected to the law and none, including the government, is above it. The law decrees that although the institutions of government and state are staffed by individuals, they act in their legally defined capacity and it is the law which indicates the various outcomes. In this image the prison is an institution which belongs to the sphere of legality. It is a logical and necessary counter-point to criminal law, and both the decision to imprison and the amount of imprisonment should be determined by the level and seriousness of the crime. The operation of the judicial decision does not require a conception of social justice. Social knowledge concerning the background and circumstances of the offender is not required for the operation of the judicial apparatus. The opposite is more the case; the operation of the liberal criminal justice system institutionalizes a purified notion of individual selfhood – a pure judicial subject. The effect of this is to operate upon a distanced self – but this means that the operation of criminal justice depends on a structure of rationality and principles at odds with the empirical forms which constitute its reality.

Of course this has been known for sometime. Writers sharing the perspectives we know as positivist criminology have criticized the structure of liberal criminal justice for being based on a philosophical metaphysics, at odds with what they perceived as proper science. Their criticisms led to a new rationality for imprisonment involving forms of treatment and rehabilitation. The positivist theories of rehabilitation and individual reform, which sought – albeit under a 'correctional' gaze – to gain knowledge of the person, were, however, largely undermined by the rhetoric of 'just deserts' which accompanied the increasing use of imprisonment in the 1970s and 1980s. This return to a strict equivalence of crime to punishment (most openly expressed in the concept of sentencing tables) centered around the deterrent potential of punishment.

For writers, such as James Q. Wilson, who was in the mid-1970s an early exponent of the return to justice/punishment, the function of the penal system was 'to isolate and to punish'. While appearing to be an admission of a return to the 'cruel, even barbaric' sentiments of yesteryear, it was 'a frank admission that society really does not know how to do much else' (Wilson, 1975). Wilson was soon joined by a flood of fellow thinkers. For others, this shift in direction and emphasis amounted to a declaration of defeat, indicating the dreams of a progression and humanitarian modernity were over. Not only was it now politically correct in America to watch executions, to announce them on the radio and seek to make the prize in local radio contests a seat in the execution chamber, but this embrace of imprisonment appeared to go against one of the fundamental items which made us modern – namely that every institution and practice had to pass the test of effectiveness and rationality. By most accounts imprisonment simply did not work. There is a long line of studies which specify that imprisonment is a failure, illegitimate, and that whatever ideological forces support it, imprisonment does not achieve those purposeful activities which penal reason specifies. In a critical overview of imprisonment, Thomas Mathiesen (1990) concludes that 'the prison does not have a defence, the prison is a fiasco in terms of its own purposes'.

How may we conceptualize the paradox that the use of imprisonment is increasing while at the same time losing its legitimacy? A body of social theory has developed which directly and indirectly allows us to engage with this question. While we are conscious of the narratives – such as those of political economy of Rusche and Kirchheimer (1968), the mistaken consequences of reform (clearly influenced by humanitarian and religious sentiments), or the liberalism of good intentions with unanticipated effects (Ignatieff, 1978, 1983), our own narrative in this chapter will outline a perspective based on the constitutive role of knowledge in constructing modern society. As David Garland (1990) has pointed out, punishment is an institution with a variety of determinations and functions. There is no one master perspective which tells us the final answer to why punishment occurs or explains the forms in which it does. The prison is a surface reflection of underlying forces and structures which constitute modernity; there are a variety of forms and structures, and the prison is implicated in the dialectic of modernity of freedom and repression of liberty and discipline. In short this chapter contends that modernity has been constructed around an ideal type of a self-regarding, self-controlling, self-esteeming, rational individual and that social development should provide a rational terrain for this type of individual to function, while disciplining those who fail to achieve these objectives. This is a story of progress and reflexivity, of confidence and ambivalence which I can only sketch here. I shall start with a brief look at one of the founding fathers of modern sociology, Emile Durkheim, who gave an essentially optimistic narrative of the development of individualism, the prison and social solidarity.

DURKHEIM'S MISTAKEN PREDICTIONS FOR PUNISHMENT AND SOCIAL SOLIDARITY IN MODERN SOCIETY

It is widely accepted that Emile Durkheim, the first University Professor of Sociology in the world, was sadly mistaken with his empirical predictions on the severity of punishment in modern society. Writing in the late nineteenth century, Durkheim saw the driving force behind the changing social structure of modern western societies as an increasing division of labour. He created two ideal types of social solidarity and argued that the increasing differentiation and complexity of social structure changed the form of social solidarity from a rather simplistic mechanical solidarity, based on a limited store of social knowledge with a religious core which was strongly defended by repressive sanctions, to organic solidarity, a more flexible and pluralist social order based on the sanctity of the individual. Specific forms and types of punishment characterized each of these stages and it was possible to discern two laws of change.

The variations through which punishment has passed in the course of history are of two sorts, quantitative and qualitative. The laws governing each of these are, of course, different. The law of quantitative change posits that the intensity of punishment is the greater the more closely societies approximate to a less developed type and the more the central power assumes an absolute character. The law of qualitative change suggests that deprivations in liberty, and of liberty alone, varying in time according to the seriousness of the crime, tend to become more and more the normal means of social control (Lukes and Scull, 1983). The changing forms of punishment were an index of the invisible moral phenomena of social solidarity. Durkheim believed that modern society was replacing the harsh punishments of public executions and exile with less repressive punishments, specifically imprisonment. The infliction of punishment was becoming both more reflective and more rational. While the central feature of punishment was emotive, the strong emotionality of punishment in pre-modern times would give way to a calmer and more reflective emotion provoked by offences which take place between equals. Blame is no longer the same and does not exclude pity. By itself it calls for moderation.

Punishment according to Durkheim would lesson in intensity as moral individualism became the organizing philosophy of criminal justice. As the religious underpinnings of the collective conscience of pre-modern society declined, a more humanist understanding of social interaction and interdependency ensured that crime would be seen as an action between individuals. Earlier societies were focused around certain fundamental beliefs as to the 'truths' of the human condition, by contrast they had down-played individuality. Modern society was increasingly structured around the idea of the autonomy of the individual. Durkheim believed that individuality was a condition only created by a specific set of social forms, specifically the normative drive of modern society was towards moral individualism. Moral individualism denoted a social and cultural structure which stressed the dignity and worth of the human individual. Individuals come to apply this feeling to themselves and to their relations with fellow citizens. As the social structure progresses, individuals become more sensitive to their feelings and to their fellows. In this social milieu we would come to appreciate and value the 'other', even as we understood his or her difference.

The repressive moral authority of traditional society, which did not know of a free and autonomous individuality, required a similarity of thought and limited variation in behaviour. By contrast the increasing division of labour of industrial society was ushering in a highly differentiated society with a plurality of values and lifestyles characterizing a growth of civilization. Punishment levels became less repressive and addressed the situation of the individual. Moreover, traditional forms of punishment would often be replaced by measures designed to facilitate social ties and social bonds. Above all, the social bond of modern society was to be a psychological understanding. Moral individualism was the acceptance of the inescapable sociality of individuality. The individual was a modern creation and we could not conceive of individuality outside specific social conditions. Durkheim asked how could moral individualism be achieved and strengthened in modernity. While Max Weber pessimistically foresaw the necessity for bureaucratic modernity, Durkheim argued that durable social order came about in a more spontaneous or organic fashion. Society was ultimately a moral phenomenon, and the strength and flexibility of this new social bond came from an understanding of interdependency and the respect we had of our very individuality – our very modernness – a respect we gave to our fellow moderns.

Durkheim stresses that punishment is a moral phenomenon closely linked to shared social understandings and emotions. Thus, we might ask what are the understandings and emotions which surround the contemporary turn to imprisonment and what are the emotional states which surround it. Instead of Durkheim's belief that punishment was at core an expressive activity communicating moral condemnation, contemporary punishment systems can also be seen as a managerial or rationalized process (Garland, 1990). Moreover modern society has witnessed a social distancing of punishment and a decline in the spectacle of penal suffering. This is a feature which various writers have commented upon. Most famously, it provides the dramatic beginning to Foucault's *Discipline and Punish* (1977) where the public punishment of Damiens, who made an unsuccessful assassination attempt against King Louis XV, is contrasted with the meticulous timetable of a juvenile reformatory.

Under the *ancien régime* punishment was a factor of status and organized around the poles of display and humiliation. Punishment was mostly conducted in public (this was not peculiar to punishment since there was little conception of privacy as we know it today in most activities) and the principal kinds of death penalties in France were quartering, the wheel and the gallows. An execution was usually a great festival. Many of the French executions took place on the Place de Grève in Paris. Several became enshrined in folk memory, similar to our great sporting contests.

Montesquieu in his *Spirit of the Laws* as well as Voltaire and many others, declared that the spectacle made the people more cruel in spirit. Others were more favourable in their regard for the executions as pleasurable spectacles. Not only was humiliation at stake, but power was ritualized and openly displayed. The details of Damiens' slow and horrific death stood out. We may note, however, the sense of occasion. The execution of Damiens had packed Paris: citizens from near and far provinces, even foreigners, came for this festival. The windows, roofs, streets were packed head on head. And while pickpockets were a nuisance, a good sum was to be made wagering on the length of time it would take for Damiens to die. In the event it took nearly four hours.

To those enlightenment philosophers who believed in the power of reason to advance human affairs, the public executions came to stand for a mass of ills, from irrationality to stirring the rabble of excesses. No wonder that imprisonment appeared progressive to intellectuals such as Durkheim. It not only took away the public spectacle and its connection with mass or popular culture, but appeared humanitarian and part of the growing institutionalization which seemed to offer frameworks capable of rendering modern life predictable and stable.

Thus, to say that Durkheim was optimistic is to make an understatement. At a time where the knowledges of anthropology have destroyed simplistic theories of eurocentric domination, where we enjoy mixing and matching entries of ethnic identification in creating the 'international' style of the late-modern urban professional, at a time where we witness the globalization of the world economy, it seems more realistic to claim we live in (non)-communities whose social bond comes from objects and technologies, many of which originated in experiments conducted in laboratories (and later gave rise to television, video, computer networks, etc.). While tolerance and openness are essential, practices and networks are more important than universally shared understandings. Instead of some community, or some integrative collective conscience (which Durkheim certainly thought was becoming more difficult under the conditions of modern society), the social is increasingly a multiplication of private spaces, connected randomly by various strategies of transcendence. The apex of punishment is a case in point.

While we may wish to consider ourselves as subjects of a 'Law's Empire' wherein the legal structure embodies our communities moral principles – to use Ronald Dworkin's (1986) description of modern western states – other commentators, such as MacIntyre (1985) deny that a coherent moral structure is possible in the conditions of liberal modernity. For Christie (1981, 1993), not only has our penal system become divorced from any necessity to reflect a moral community, he also asks how many of us (apart from 'we' professional criminologists) have actually witnessed the infliction of the pain of penality? Aside from the technologies of representation, and the fabrication of penality in film and television programmes, how public is penal pain? The advanced division of labour means that decisions made about the offenders are made by professionals (lawyers, judges, probation officers, doctors, psychiatrists, prison governors, parole boards) using specialized techniques. The behaviour of the person becomes institutionally criminalized or pathologized (medicalized).

The criminal becomes the subject of general knowledge and rules rather than vocal knowledge about his or her particular environment and conditions. This process has intensified in recent years with the introduction of sentencing guidelines and tables which indicate the disposition that particular crimes should receive. As Christie has argued:

> A political decision to eliminate concern for the social background of the defendant involves much more than making these characteristics inappropriate for decision on pain. By the same token, the offender is to a large extent excluded as a person. There is no point in exposing a social background, childhood dreams, defeats – perhaps mixed with some glimmer from happy days – social life, all those small things which are essential to a perception of the other as a full human being. With the Sentencing Manual and its prime outcome, the Sentencing Table, crime is standardized as Offence Levels, a person's life as Criminal History Points, and decisions on the delivery of pain are reduced to finding the points where two lines merge.   (Christie, 1993: 138)

The social distancing and demarcation continues in the prison – out of sight, out of mind. Cruelties occur which no philosophy of punishment appears to include. The conditions of life in crowded facilities only too often means subjection to indignities, the possibility of severe injury or loss of life, or rape, with the result of deep bitterness and increased motivation toward criminal behaviour.

Should we be surprised at this systematizing and distancing of penality? Should we feel surprised at the ease with which the underclass become the fodder for this ritual? The answer suggested in this chapter is no. Such distancing, abstraction and rationalization – this ritual of segregation and exclusion – has been a fundamental part of the modern project. But how do we manage to hide its normative nature? How do we manage to escape feeling implicated in its processes? How do we keep our appearance of innocence and belief that imprisonment is rational and effective in the face of the criminological discourse which declares it isn't?

MODERNITY AND LEGITIMACY

The ingenuity of liberal-democratic modernity is that the processes of administration and decision-making, designed perhaps to achieve substantive ends, become their own justification. Once in place we tend to think of a practice in terms of its own justifications, its own rhetorical devices, which serve to make it natural and acceptable. But does this constitute a form of legitimation? Or do we witness a de-legitimation of legitimacy? Perhaps Max Weber gave the answer in his typologies of legitimation, specifically the argument that modernity developed a form of legal-rational legitimation linking the search for reason and legality with bureaucratic administration; whatever is done according to the correct procedure is legitimate. Legal-rational domination makes legitimation largely redundant. As long as the procedure obeys certain methodological percepts, it does not have to be substantively rational. In other words, the legitimacy of the authority of the modern state can be procedural rather than substantive. Technique can become the major characteristic of the operation of the modern state.

There are various forms of techniques. Techniques can exist without a normative conception of the overall context in which they are used. Many commentators visualize late-modern life as a series of social games. From Wittgenstein to H. L. A. Hart to Jean-François Lyotard, the notion of late-modern life as language games, or an analogy with games, or actually, 'just gaming' dominates. Instead of the synthesis which a full system of legitimation would require (that is one which tied together formality and substance, which concerned substantive rationality) late-modernity has an interacting structure of forms and processes which constantly need to be negotiated and played with. Late-modernity has two complimentary techniques of social control – one for those players with good social skills and a range of capital, another for those who have few skills and little capital. Bauman (1988) terms these seduction and repression. In short we as members of the superclass are the subjects of a different form of social bonding and control than the others. The thought processes which we can consider as universal – the rationality of the calculating individual – may apply to us. But the social world of the underclass – a world of deprivation, powerless in the face of bureaucracy – makes our terms of rational calculation largely redundant.

Seduction is the paramount tool of integration in a consumer society. Once the market succeeds in making consumerism dependent upon itself, a process of desire, attempted satisfaction through consumption, dissatisfaction, satisfaction through more work and consumption is set up. The worth of the individual increasingly becomes a question of relating to the market and market dependency is deepened by the destruction of such skills (social, technical, psychological, existential) which do not entail the use of marketable commodities. The more complete the destruction of these non-market skills, the more necessary it becomes to acquire skills which relate to the market. Once men and women cannot proceed with the business of life without tuning themselves to the logic of the market, dependency is dominant and self-perpetuating. Life becomes a circle of desire, the purchase of commodities, temporal enjoyment, dissatisfaction, desire and yet more commodities.

Repression is the other side of domination consisting of a mixture of enforced disciplines with the traditional juridical regimes of deterrence punishments under the authority of law. Its most obvious forms consist of military-style policing, wars on drugs and imprisonment. It also involves newly developing techniques of surveillance aimed at the regimentation of the body. For Bauman:

> Repression as a tool of domination-reproduction has not been abandoned with the advent of seduction. Its time is not over and the end of its usefulness is not in sight, however overpowering and effective seduction may become. It is the continuous, tangible presence as a visible alternative which makes seduction unchallengeable. In addition, repression is indispensable to teach the areas seduction cannot, and is not meant to, reach: it remains the paramount tool of subordination of the considerable margin of society which cannot be absorbed by market dependency, and hence, in market terms, consists of 'non-consumers'. Such 'non-consumers' are people reduced to the satisfaction of their elementary needs; people whose business of life does not transcend the horizon of survival. Goods serving the latter purpose are not, as a rule, attractive as potential merchandise; they serve the needs over which the market has no control and thus undermine, rather than boost, market dependency. Repression reforges the market unattractiveness of non-consumer existence into the unattractiveness of alternatives to market dependency. (Bauman, 1988: 222)

How did we get here? What happened to the regulative idea of the universal rational society? To what extent is the search for knowledge implicated in this segregation?

MODERNITY, CONTROL AND KNOWLEDGE

Central to modernity is an emphasis upon control and the reduction of the world to sets of phenomena to be analyzed and mastered. Questions of knowledge – questions of epistemology – are also questions of social order. We choose a style of knowing, and a style of living, interdependently. Our style of knowing – our epistemology – is a crucial supporting basis for social order. The way we seek knowledge and convey its entities both reflects, and impacts upon, society. If modernity was to be rational, then the power of law in the form of legislation and decision-making 'ought' to reflect knowledge. In the eighteenth century Goodwin declared that conflict in modernity could be resolved by agreeing to follow the results of the pursuit of knowledge. The role of law was to reflect our knowledge of basic natural and social laws.

The central instrument of modern formal control, the prison, has both reflected a form of knowing, and helped continue specific knowledge(s). Its roles have reflected dominant styles of living. While no one framework need give answers, one popular theory linking developing forms of knowledge and the prison has been put forward by David Garland (1985). Garland argues that in the late nineteenth century a specific relationship, involving new forms of criminological knowledge and the institutions of punishment, developed with particular relevance to the prison. The emergence of an individualistically oriented positivist criminology was closely linked to the institution of the prison. Hence there became a specific connection between the analysis of the prison and knowledge(s) which sought to answer the question of what the offender was. The development of a specific body of knowledge on the institution of punishment was, thereby, compromised. As Ruggles-Brise (1925) put it: '*la science penitentiary* develops gradually into the science of the discovery of the causes of crime – the science of criminology' (quoted in Garland, 1985: 82).

The developing penology was limited in the questions and theoretical frameworks it could pose for the institutions of punishment. It simply could not pose the issue of criminalization (as Durkheim had hinted) in terms of culturally specific patterns of labelling. Instead of seeing the processed offender (the person in prison) as the end result of an interactive process wherein the institutional arrangements were partly responsible for the end product, the offender was treated as if his or her own constitution (or the constitution of his immediate environment) was deviant. For Garland, the study of the institutions was constrained by the two concepts of criminology, those of individualism and differentiation. Penology's understanding of penal institutions became how best to put these concepts into institutional reality. Positivist criminology thus produced knowledges which legitimated the prison, and fed-back 'knowledges' which legitimated social demarcations while philosophical modernity declared participation was open to all, the knowledges of pathology offered forms of differentiation by which the 'other' was kept at bay. For Garland these knowledges obscured the class antagonisms beneath the universal pretensions of the rule of law.

We still live with these obscurities and antagonisms, but they do not originate solely with the advent of positive criminology. Rather they are fundamental to the linkage of knowledge and the construction of modernity. Sociological and philosophical theorizing has served as an adjunct to the (re)-constructive processes of modernity. Its intentions for the prison have served on its own terms as a support for the constitution of the modern. In order to explore these tensions we need to examine the work of Beccaria, Bentham and Mill.

BECCARIA TO MILL: FROM SOVEREIGNTY TO LEGITIMACY

The movement from sovereignty to legitimacy occurs when the discussion moves from ascertaining who is the rightful ruler(s) and what makes him or her or them rightful, to the issues of what the ruler(s) ought to do and what are the tasks of good government. It is only really possible to talk of legitimacy (that is to become reflexive), when we can scrutinize various forms of social and political life. The discourse of Beccaria (1764) was soothing. Beccaria is not concerned to establish sovereignty – that had already been achieved by Hobbes and others – instead it is legitimacy, or the rational performance or power, that is at stake. The language is calm and infused with the motifs of progress, truth, reason and equivalence.

Throughout *On Crimes and Punishments* (1764) is the belief that law must reflect the rationality of existence; we are looking for the truth of the secular human condition. For example, the first step Beccaria takes is the critique of religion as the legitimation of law. For Beccaria the problem with God is that he knew too much. No human judge could make the sort of absolute decision that God could. The human judge cannot judge the weight of evil or sin. Rather the human judge must be bound by the law. The source of judgements for punishments carried out under the criminal law must be the law itself and this law is to be created, or posited, by humans in political society acting in accordance with their human sciences, offering 'truths' of the human condition.

The authors of *The New Criminology* (1973) point out the contradictory tensions within Beccaria's work in both proposing the notion of equality and also defending the possession of property. Taylor, Walton and Young saw the democratic stress of early philosophical utilitarianism as nothing more than the ideology of the rising bourgeoisie, and social contract theory as ideologically part of their protection against feudal interference. A system of classical justice of this order could only operate in a society where property was distributed equally but such distribution was never contemplated. The authors imply that the contradiction would be too great to be sustained. Classicism, however, has not only survived, it has strengthened in recent years and currently reinforces the increased use in imprisonment. Its great achievement was to create a methodology, a technique which can fit over the secular mystery of the human condition; a technique which fits two vital elements of liberalism – those of self-interest and utility. Liberalism can assert that individuality and possessive individualism are the guiding forms of the legal structure, since they seem to reflect human nature. Social justice can be determined by utility.

The paradox of crime was that it was both rational and irrational. It was rational for an individual to choose to commit a crime – he may well have his reasons which Beccaria acknowledged were possibly political – and yet crime was a social irrationality. The irrationality of crime stems from its contravening the progressive rationality of the social contract. Man's selfish rationality has identified subjection to the power which the social contract grants as the most beneficial mode of social existence. It is this subjection that creates the social space for exchange and accumulation of social goods via trade and investment, while the rational choice of an individual to choose criminal behaviour is to choose the irrationality of behaviour beyond the social contract. It is an irrationality to be constrained by a fully rational crime control mechanism.

This mechanism is based on the central site of social development. It must defend power from scepticism and disruption. The criminal justice system would pacify the arbitrary and disruptive influences of social life, and give the social engineering required for progress through the systematization of penology rather than some simple humanization. We can see this in the particularity of Beccaria's replacement of capital punishment with penal servitude. Thorsten Sellin (1977) labels it a punishment worse than death, a living death. Penal servitude, and the associated repeated public sighting of the prisoner, is a rational advance since Beccaria argued that it is not the intensity of punishment that has the greatest effect on the human spirit, but its duration. Our sensibility is more easily, and more permanently, affected by slight but repeated impressions than by a powerful, but momentary, action. The death penalty can only create an impression which, for all its immediate force, men soon forget, but:

> In a free and peaceful government the impressions should be frequent rather than strong ... The death penalty becomes for the majority a spectacle and for others an object of compassion mixed with disdain: these two sentiments rather than the salutary fear which the laws pretend to inspire occupy the spirits of the spectators. (Beccaria, 1764)

This version of the penal spectacle will be able to deter any potential justifications that the aggrieved sections of the populace may have in breaking a law which they consider creates or reinforces an unjustified situation. The penal equation reinforces the radically unequal economic and social structure which an offender may view as 'fatal to the majority'. Beccaria uses a materialist science of human nature in discussing the idea of 'motive' and thereby considers the rationality of thieves or assassins as calculable: the offender(s) are those individuals who find no motive weighty enough to keep them from violating the laws, except the gallows or the wheel. Although they cannot give a clear account of their motives this does not make them any the less operative. It is not that Beccaria refuses to understand the predicament of the offender, but the social discourse of politics and desire (even for social justice) are not legally recognized items of communication. Beccaria recognizes that the offender may have an understandable set of motives for his crime, but this is of no legal consequence. We could offer a social explanation for the crime committed. We could locate it within a set of social processes, but that is of no matter. The crucial issue is the exercise of power according to the core rationality and the set of knowledges which serve to guarantee social progress. Criminal justice must defend not only the structure of societal power, but also protect the epistemological framework from disruption.

Bentham, too, was confident of the ability of the system to ensure social progress. But his dislike of irrational and barbaric criminal punishment becomes transformed into tyranny when one analyzes the grandest reform proposal of all: his Panopticon or Inspection House. This life-long project protected his jurisprudence, integrating it with utilitarianism in an attempt to make it a practical possibility. This item of work, which Foucault (1977) picks up as the ideal mode of disciplinary technology, is based on the idea of the panoptic gaze and of continuous and concealed surveillance. Bentham believed he had found the 'Columbus Egg' of politics and argued it provided a technique with a multitude of purposes:

Morals reformed, health preserved, industry invigorated, instruction diffused, public burdens lightened, economy seated as it were upon a rock, the guardian rock of the poor-laws not cut but united – all by a simple idea in architecture....

No matter how different, or even opposite the purpose; whether it be that of punishing the incorrigible, guarding the insane, reforming the vicious, confining the suspected, employing the idle, maintaining the helpless, curing the sick, instructing the willing in any branch of industry, or training the rising race in the path of education; in a word, whether it be applied to the purposes of perpetual prisons in the room of death, or prisons for confinement before trial, or penitentiary-houses, or houses of corrections, or work-houses, or manufactories, or mad-houses, or hospitals, or schools.   (Bentham, 1791: 39–40)

All these disciplinary institutions would share the regulated coding of human conduct in a restricted space, continuously controlled by officials; a technology of division of space into separated parts, partition of time into a routine, the detailed coding of human action of the inmates, and the use of the panoptic gaze. The idea reflects the epistemological basis of the growing scientific approach; that of control through transparency or 'seeing without being seen' (1791: 44). The panopticon provides a technology to reinforce the conscious intentions of power. Circular in shape, the cells are located on the outer frame with the inspector's lodge at the very centre of the circle, while the area in between is left open and all the inmates' cells face the inspector's lodge. The cell walls facing the inspector's lodge and the ones on the opposite side are made of glass, so that a guard situated in the central lodge can easily control each and every one of the inmates, and by turning around can capture all in his gaze. The inmates cannot see their overseer, since the walls of the inspector's lodge are darkened with blinds and screens. As well as the cells, the Panopticon accommodates a chapel and a separate hospital department.

The panoptic gaze is ever present, penetrating every part of the cells and corridors of the building. It follows the smallest movements of the inmate, who is always within the gaze and understands this. Even if the inspector's lodge were left empty for some time, the inmate would never be able to tell. The guards, additionally, needed to be constantly watched; the inspector's lodge also monitored the activities of all the staff. Hence we have a hierarchy of continuous surveillance; the institution itself is open to the general public and the inspection of a judge or governor. The panopticon was to have no closed areas, no secrets; it was to be open to the inspection of the world and, thereby, abuse of power was impossible. Is this the model of hell, or of a perfect organization? And what of the effects upon the inmate? Bentham himself pre-empted the critical question:

Whether the liberal spirt and energy of a free citizen would not be exchanged for the mechanical discipline of a soldier, or the austerity of a monk? – and whether the result of this high-wrought contrivance might not be constructing a set of machines under the similitude of men? ... Call them soldiers, call them monks, call them machines: so that they be happy ones, I should not care.   (Bentham, 1791: 64)

Foucault points out that the era of the Enlightenment both discovered the political rights of the citizens and invented the disciplinary techniques for the deprivation of the newborn liberties. The roots of the modern prison were founded in the great incarceration which swept over Europe in the seventeenth century: Bridewell in London (from 1557); the *Tuchthuis* for men (1596) and *Spinnhuis* for women (1597) in Amsterdam; the *Zuchthausern* in Germany (Bremen, 1613; Hamburg, 1622); the *hôpitaux généraux* in France (Paris 1656); and the houses of correction, and work-houses in England. Foucault locates the history of the prison within a history of bodies, of the political investment in the body, part of a closer penal mapping of the social body providing:

A whole technique of human dressage by location, confinement, surveillance, the perpetual supervision of behaviour and tasks, in short, a whole technique of 'management' of which the prison was merely one manifestation. (Foucault, 1988: 105)

So while Hobbes' *Leviathan* came to symbolize the contractual model of society, Bentham's *Panopticon* was seized upon as the ideal model of routinized discipline and habituation. For Foucault, the Enlightenment gave us a new capacity, a new power for life, but the consequence was that we became the subjects of a dual constitution: law and positive knowledge. And while we could see the tyranny and openness of the coercion behind the law, we failed to see the tyranny underneath the power to discipline. We thought it was normal.

Bentham's plans for the Panopticon was only the extreme of the connection between the developing sciences of man, as expressed in utilitarianism, and the prison. Bentham's close friend, James Mill, used more usual terms in his essay on *Prisons and Prison Reform*. James Mill argued that prisons served three purposes: First the provision of safe custody for those who are to stand trial; secondly the punishment of convicted criminals; and finally the reformation of criminals. There are three types of individuals in prisons: those who are to stand trial; persons already convicted who are awaiting the punishment stipulated by the court; and debtors. Speedy trails would rid prisons of the first group and rational debtor legislation would rid them of the last. Since all three classes of men are in prison, however, debtors and those detained before trial should not be 'punished' while in prison. Neither are they there for 'reformation'. For these men, the prison should provide a subsistence level sufficient to prevent impairment of health. They should be permitted through voluntary paid labour or by use of savings to purchase 'unexceptional indulgences' to supplant the subsistence standard. These men should be treated with 'benevolence consistent with economy'.

Mill did not accept that prisons are an effective instrument of punishment. He dismissed the argument that confinement as such might be thought of as punishment; criminal punishment is involuntary physical pain or bodily harm. Prisons can be used to confine and perhaps reform men but not to punish them. The practice of forced labour is an example. Accepting that most of the persons who come to prisons as criminals, are bad, because they have hated labour, and men seldom become in love with their punishments, compulsory labour as a punishment would make reformation impossible. Mill asked what sort of lesson do you teach those outside whose lot is hard labour, harder than any which is in your power to impose. Instead a simple form of learning, or conditioning psychology, is to be utilized. The prison should provide a basic subsistence economy. Work is to be provided at a set wage. The earnings can be used to purchase additional items. The jailer receives funds to pay for wages and subsistence expenses from the sale of the products of convict labour to the world at large. Reformation seeks one outcome, namely:

> what are the best means of producing the performance of those acts, the habit of performing which we desire to render so perfect, that it may be relied upon for effect, even in a state of freedom? (*Encyclopaedia Britannica*, 7th edn: 575–8)

His answer is lawful labour for reward. The only way that labour can be a means of reformation is that it be a source of pleasure, not pain. The way in which labour becomes agreeable to men out of a prison, is the way in which it can be made agreeable to them in prison, and there is no other. The jailer re-enacts the system of political economy outside the walls, but artificial means must be created to prevent their monopoly position as buyer of labour and seller of commodities from being misused. If the jailer maintains the subsistence floor, the profit will come only if he or she can motivate prisoners to labour. James Mill would establish additional checks. The jailer gets his position by competitive bid; he is fined if the death rate within a prison population is greater than actuarial equivalents in the world outside; if convicts commit crimes when released, he is fined proportionate to the amount of time these convicts were under his care; he must publish audited accounts of his enterprise and, without legal immunities, answer to inspecting magistrates. The prison so reflects and emphasizes the economic and motivational mechanism of civil society that Mill closes his essay by answering charges of unfair competition with the larger economy.

The purity and straight lines of the knowledges and calculations under-lying utilitarianism mirrors the outlines of prison walls. John Austin – the first professor of Jurisprudence at the University of London lecturing in the late 1820s – was specific: the structures of political power and prison walls are both general contexts of suffering within which we involuntarily find ourselves. We do not will or desire to be born in a particular political society any more than we would voluntarily walk through the gate of a prison. Both contexts, however, shape our character: 'Change in the mind may be wrought or prevented, whether we desire the change or whether we do not desire it' (Austin, 1873: 467–72). Our way of life is bound by the strictest servitude, necessity itself; our unending desires cannot be granted the widest liberty. Prisons and governments surround and protect a realm of civil law and – if rightly ordered – vouchsafe the liberty which civil law sustains.

For Austin the plight of those who end up in prison, the poor and wretched, could be prevented if only they would come to understand and use the truths of political economy. Those who do not understand the necessity for the institutions of property and unequal distribution of resources are capable of crimes which destabilize governments. Thus they must be contained. Their fault lies in their failure to understand the demands of societal rationality.

In this managerial society the insiders are the possessors of knowledge; the outsiders are those who will not operate in a rational fashion. But who are the criminals? The criminals are those defined as such by those who have the power to define the basic knowledge that the society will operate upon. We have the ultimate connection: power gives knowledge, power determines crime, power determines rationality.

As is well known, James Mill's son, John Stuart Mill, having been raised by his father and Bentham to be the utilitarian par excellence, suddenly called an end to the totalizing aspirations of the utilitarian party. Mill's rejection of the generalisability of utilitarianism was not so much that it needed prisons to discipline those who did not understand the truths of political economy, but that it became difficult to work out where the walls of the prison were located. In other words the doctrine so determined the calculations of its believers that it was self-enslaving. How could one measure happiness? All we could measure in a reductionist language of physics or mathematics was pleasure. Happiness involved debates over the quality of activities, over the meaning of human existence. But this brought back into general calculation the mystery underlying the human condition that Hobbes had defined as the secret of the intellectual not to be shared with the masses least social chaos result. How then could we be sure that our society was socially progressive? In one powerful image our confidence lies in the fact of underlying laws of social development and functional structure, which we need to find and construct social relations upon. We can call this the dream of positivism. While society is an artifact mankind must build according to the dictates of scientific (positive) knowledge.

POSITIVISM

We have already noted Garland's (1985) reading of the link between positive knowledge and the prison. Criminological positivism was premised on the idea of a natural differentiation of the deviant from the normal. The writings of early criminological positivism are too large to survey here (see Morrison, 1995), but the assumption of a pathology or a condition, which could create 'criminality' leads to the logic of an institutional or a segregational remedy. Extermination, sterilization, incarceration – ultimately the Holocaust – were versions of what Bauman (1989, 1991) has termed the 'gardening ambitions' of (organized) modernity.

There was, however, a tension in the correctional orientation of positivism. For while classical criminology was content to accept a continual demarcation between the insiders and the outsiders, positivism, ideally, believed in a solution to the crime problem. Either the pathology of the individual could be corrected, or the pathology of the social conditions could be remedied. The French social theorist of the early nineteenth century Auguste Comte distinguished between progress in human nature and progress in the external conditions of life. As the conditions of man's existence improved, a slow and gradual improvement in individual man's facilities resulted:

> The lower instincts continue to manifest themselves in modified action, but their less sustained and more repressed exercise must tend to debilitate them by degrees; and their increasing regulation certainly brings them into involuntary concurrence in the maintenance of a good social economy. (Comte, 1855: 468)

The advance of knowledge assures us of the inevitable progress in the conditions of life, moral and organic improvement of the human species will follow. As the basic conditions of life improve for all, the causes of social despair disappear. Ultimately positivism led to Durkheim. Society is a moral phenomenon which has an underlying set of natural laws we need to uncover and develop. Only this writing turned out to be prescriptive, rather than describing a template which guarantees a normatively committed social order. With time, confidence in utilitarianism had faded – while the search for a secure theory of social justice has thrown up competing candidates – increases in social goods has not lessened crime but increased it. But this does not mean that criminology has no explanations for crime. On the contrary, within the writing on relative deprivation, culture, desire and social structure there are a host of theories and insights. What becomes more difficult is to believe in any positivist utopia. Instead of history being over, we may be doomed to its perpetual reoccurrence.

THE PRISON AND THE POST-POSITIVIST KNOWLEDGES OF THE SOCIAL

We no longer believe in utopia. There is no grand society of equality, harmony and justice awaiting our discovery. The dream is over. We are told, therefore, that we cannot construct general theories. For Lyotard (1984) that would be to engage in constructing grand narratives and 'we have had enough of the claims of totality'. The pragmatic pursuit of short term research contracts, situational crime prevention, decontextualized rational choice theory – all deny the need (if not denying the ability) to construct large-scale pictures of our societies. Criminologists of the right, while they assert that a social theory of crime must involve a general social theory do not feel the need to construct one (Wilson and Herrnstein, 1985; Gottfredson and Hirschi, 1990; Morrison, 1995).

Instead of images of society which allow us to perceive it in normative terms, we are told that it is more realistic to offer narratives of system functioning. Perhaps the implicit message of such systems narratives is that society works for those who key themselves into the system, accepting the rules of the social game and sharing in the benefits. Sometimes this is acknowledged without any sense of irony or contingency. This was nowhere more evident than in the modern positivist jurisprudence of H. L. A. Hart in his classic book *The Concept of Law* (1961), where he divided modern citizens into insiders who understand the normative bind of the social rules, and outsiders who adopted an external attitude.

The cultural revolution of the 1970s and 1980s, the globalization of the world economy and the rise in economic strength of Asia, accompanied by a growing division between rich and poor in the West, may have turned the insiders to those who gain social goods from the system, and thus have a stake in playing by the rules (the seduced), and those who both in relative and real terms are losing out and who have no normative reason to abide by the rules of a social order which does not respect them or offer a viable path to achievement and self-esteem (the repressed).

Perhaps we have few options; as the underlying dream of the construction of a just society has disappeared so too has a normative commitment to the good society. This has been replaced by privatization, including the 'privatization of public space'. Globalization, equality of employment opportunity, the free-market, the decline of public services, the arrival of post-modernism and its revolution in industrial structuring has resulted in the decreasing demand for the services of the unskilled working-class male. Thus, while for Bentham imprisonment could offer labour and carry out tasks which were earlier performed by slaves or indentured labour, this notion became redundant when even the modern factory came to require greater levels of skill and flexibility than imprisoned labour could offer. The contemporary western prison, existing in a (post-modernist) social order which does not require a high level of manual labour can now cycle and recycle the unwanted (non-)labour of a post-fordist economic structure into a place of mere containment. It was no coincidence that a fashionable slogan of the return to justice ideology of the late 1970s was of 'humane confinement'. There was nothing else to ask for. The simple fact is that those who are currently sent to prison are largely unwanted outside the prison walls and have no skills which are in demand.

It is undeniable that those who are sent to prison have committed offences. They have lost in playing the games of everyday life and the game of criminal justice – their crimes are mostly those which are easily apprehended while their personal characteristics reflect a lack of social and personal resources. Successful late modern life, or post-modern 'seduction', is not a passive state. On the contrary it requires a finely tuned set of social skills as well as social, human and economic capital.

> The individual is forced permanently to choose, to take initiative, to inform himself, to test himself, to stay young, to deliberate over the simplest acts: what car to buy, what film to see, what book to read, what therapy to follow. Consumption compels the individual to take charge of himself, it makes him responsible, it is a system of ineluctable participation, contrary to vituperations against the society of the spectacle and of passivity.   (Lipovetsky, quoted in Callinicos, 1989: 153)

The late-modern self is the result of an historical process of individuation and privatization. Our contemporary economic privatization policies may only be one oscillation in the historical movement of modernity of 'personalization' which, contrary to Durkheim's wish for a moral individualism, currently involves an intense investment in our private lives and the reduction of the public sphere to the status of the context of our activity. But we are not some set of abstract, formal selves. Rather we are real people. We are the products of the projects of constituting individualism of modernity; both the individuals with the capital to play the games of seduction, and the individuals with weak capital who form the grist for the repression mill. We are all the creations of social processes.

There is a subtle dialectics in play. Participation in the differentiated roles opening up with modernity results in experiences and forms of self-scrutiny which create the fully modern person. But only the fully modern person is deemed fit to participate in these roles. The non-modern, by contrast, finds his or her natural home in the prison; in passivity. Late-modernity may produce a new alignment of Hobbes' three groups: first the intellectuals who despair at the superficiality of the images of (non-) reality; mystery has become hyper-reality; second those who play the game of social life – who obey out of their socialized civilized self-control, and thirdly those who have no stake in obeying the rules of the game. To the first two groups flow the rewards of modernity. The third receives imprisonment. Under this narrative to engage in crime is a personal calculation. It is a question of balancing opportunity, risk, profit and the possibility of loss. Crime and normalcy are the products of desire.

Modern conservative criminology tries desperately hard to indicate that some means of demarcation exists in nature. For Gottfredson and Hirschi (1990) the underlying propensity to commit crime is tempered by the degree of self-control. Those who commit crime, who cause accidents, who use drugs, have less self-control than the others. The others have a personal ability to play the market better. As with other commentators such as Murray (1984, 1990; and with Herrnstein, 1994), we need to recognize the failure of social policies which were designed to encourage social integration. We are told that policies of equal opportunity cannot overcome differences in group and personal differentiation in characteristics such as IQ or self-control. Consequently they argue for a reduction in the role of the state, the encouragement of personal responsibility and the punishment of those who breach the rules.

This surrender to the market and to the image of the self-regulating system, amounts to renouncing any of the universalistic pretension of the Enlightenment project. It amounts to a resistance to allowing the 'others' to becoming truly modern. But we should not be surprised. While the philosophy and the rhetoric of modernity declared it was open to all, the underlying reality was different. The freedom of the modern was always at the expense of the subjugation and obedience of the 'other'. Modernity was, after all, founded on slavery, the exploitation of nature and the non-European worlds. It replaced slavery by the Holocaust, and ignorance by 'truth'. But power has always the modality.

What can we do? Some voices ask us to encourage the empowerment of knowledge. Reduce the power of the centre of knowledge, and increase the knowledge of interdependence. From Foucault to post-modernist deconstruction, the demand is to allow knowledge(s) and people(s) to participate. What have we to lose?, these voices ask. Only domination, they suggest. But domination is not so easily overcome. All life involves ranking, classifying, demanding, denying, urging, punishing and knowing. Paradoxically, the time when we appear to have lost our confidence, is also the time of our greatest knowledge. We are surrounded by information, but with so much information it is difficult to gain wisdom. But the pursuit of knowledge was also the search for some position by which to escape the trap of locality, to attain a vantage point by which to know more than that which was otherwise provided for us. Knowledge was the power to become modern. The search for a normatively acceptable modernity cannot be achieved without acknowledgement of the real identity and locality of the offender, not of the reality of the things done in the name of reason. The aspiration to be modern is too important to be surrendered to the totalitarianism of only partial realities and partial truths. The tension between the surface and the underlying forms may never be overcome, but acknowledgement of that tension is an indispensable part of the truth of modernity – a precondition of true social solidarity.

Both we, the successful individuals and the 'winners' of modernity, as well as the inmates – those who have been labelled as suffering from 'criminality' – are equally the products of large-scale social processes. These need to be understood and examined for tactics and resources to combat forms, structures and trends we cannot normatively accept. Only our contemporary knowledge projects – projects which deny the possibility of true 'general theory' – prevent this process from disturbing our normative expectations of social order. In giving up any solace of underlying truths of nature that will guarantee our society, we ought not to condemn ourselves to merely playing the system, but acknowledge that it is ours absolutely. And thus still ours to (re)construct. If only we want to.

References

Austin, J. (1873) *Lectures on Jurisprudence or the Philosophy of Positive Law*, 4th edn, R. Campbell (ed.) (London: John Murray).

Bauman, Z. (1987) *Legislators and Interpreters* (Cambridge: Polity Press).

Bauman, Z. (1988), 'Is There a Postmodern Sociology?', in *Theory, Culture and Society: Special Issue on Postmodernism*, vol. 5 (June).

Bauman, Z. (1989) *Modernity and the Holocaust* (Cambridge: Polity Press).

Bauman, Z. (1991) *Modernity and Ambivalence* (Cambridge: Polity Press).

Beccaria, C. (1764; 1986) *On Crimes and Punishments*, trans. D. Young (Indianapolis: Hackett).

Bentham, J. A. (1791) *Comment on the Commentaries and A Fragment on Government*, J. H. Burns and H. L. A. Hart (eds) (London: University of London, Althone Press).

Bentham, J. A. (1838–43) 'Panopticon, or the Inspection House'; 'Panopticon, Postcript', Parts I–II; 'Panopticon vs New South Wales' in *Bentham's Collected Works,* Bowring edn, Edinburgh, vol IV.

Callinicos, A. (1989) *Against Postmodernism: A Marxist Critique* (London: Polity Press).

Christie, N. (1981) *Limits to Pain* (Oxford: Martin Robertson).

Christie, N. (1993) *Crime Control as Industry: Towards GULAGS, Western Style?* (London: Routledge).

Comte, A. (1885) *The Positive Philosophy of Auguste Comte*, trans. H. Marineau (New York: Calvin Blanchard).

Connor, S. (1989) *Postmodernist Culture: An Introduction to Theories of the Contemporary* (Oxford: Basil Blackwell).

Dworkin. R. (1986) *Laws Empire* (London: Fontana)

Foucault, M. (1977) *Discipline and Punish: The Birth of the Prison*, (Harmondsworth: Penguin).

Garland, D. (1985) *Punishment and Welfare* (Aldershot: Gower).

Garland, D. (1990) *Punishment and Modern Society* (Oxford: Clarendon Press).

Gottfredson, M. and Hirschi, T. (1990) *A General Theory of Crime*, Stanford, CA: Stanford University Press.

Hart, H. L. A. (1961) *The Concept of Law* (Oxford: Clarendon Press).

Hernstein, R. J. and Murray, C. (1994) *The Bell Curve: Intelligence and Class Structure in American Life* (New York: Free Press)

Hobbes, T. (1950) *Leviathan* (London/New York: Everyman's Library).

Hobbes, T. (1949) *The Citizen*, S. Lamprecht (ed.) (New York: Everyman's Library).

Ignatieff, M. (1978) *A Just Measure of Pain: The Penitentiary in the Industrial Revolution, 1750–1850* (New York: Pantheon).

Ignatieff, M. (1983) State, Civil Society and Total Institutions: A Critique of Recent Social Histories of Punishment in S. Cohen and A. Scull (ed.), *Social Control and the State* (Oxford: Blackwell).

Lukes, T. and Scull, A. (1983) *Durkheim and the Law* (Oxford: Basil Blackwell).

Lyotard, J. H. F. (1984) *The Postmodern Condition: A Report on Knowledge* (Manchester: Manchester University Press).

MacIntyre, A. (1985) *After Virtue: A Study of Moral Theory* (2nd edn. London)

Mathiesen, T. (1990) *Prison on Trial* (London: Sage).

Melossi, D. and Pavarini, M. (1981) *The Prison and the Factory: Origins of the Penitentiary System* (London: Macmillan).

Mill, J. (1818) 'Prisons and Prison Reform', *Encyclopedia Britannica*, 7th edn.

Morris, L. (1994) *Dangerous Classes: The Underclass and Social Citizenship* (London: Routledge).

Morris, T. (1976) *Deviance and Control: The Secular Heresy* (London: Hutchinson).

Morrison, W. (1995) *Theoretical Criminology: From Modernity to Post-Modernism* (London: Cavendish).

Murray, C. (1984) *Losing Ground: American Social Policy, 1950–1980* (New York: Basic Books)

Murray, C. (1990) The British Underclass, *The Public Interest*, 99 4–28.

Norrie, A. (1993) *Crime, Reason and History: A Critical Introduction to Criminal Law* (London: Weidenfeld and Nicolson).

Rusche, G. and Kirchheimer, O. (1968) *Punishment and Social Structure* (New York: Russell and Russell)

Sellin, J. T. (1976) *Slavery and the Penal System* (New York: Elsevier).

Stern, V. (1989) *Bricks of Shame: British Prisons* (Harmondsworth: Penguin)

Taylor, I.; Walton P.; and Young, J. (1973) *The New Criminology: For a Social Theory of Deviance* (London: Routledge and Kegan Paul).

Weber, M. (1978) *Economy and Society*, G. Ruth and C. Wittic (eds) (Berkeley: University of California Press).

Wilson, J. Q. (1975, rev. edn 1983) *Thinking About Crime* (New York: Basic Books).

Wilson, J. Q. and Herrnstein, R. J. (1985) *Crime and Human Nature: The Definitive Study of the Causes of Crime* (New York: Simon and Schuster).

6 The Changing Functions of Imprisonment

Claude Faugeron

INTRODUCTION

Since the Second World War the organization and the use of custody has changed significantly in many western countries. This chapter presents a framework for analyzing these changes. Although the mode of analysis draws primarily on the French situation it is applicable, I believe, with certain qualifications, to most Western countries.

There are two specific features of imprisonment in western democratic states which we must distinguish at the outset. Both features are rooted in the developments within penal policy which began at the end of the nineteenth century and have accelerated markedly since the Second World War. They refer on the one hand to custodial practices and on the other to the codification of penalties.

TWO BASIC CHARACTERISTICS OF PENAL PRACTICE

The prison system tends to monopolize all forms of confinement. As other forms of institutionalization decrease in most western countries the prison becomes increasingly identified as the central and dominant form of confinement. Administrative forms of confinement, political detention, the confinement of illegal immigrants and the incarceration of the mentally ill are all becoming circumscribed and subject to stricter forms of regulation. These forms of confinement are ordinarily limited to relatively short-term detention, and are governed by special legal regulations and normally involve the specification of detainees rights.

Against the background of the changing use of confinement, we are encouraged to address the issue of the role of medium and long-term penal confinement both before and after trial. As the list of behaviours leading to such penalties becomes more extensive in western legal codes we might reasonably expect that the number of people detained in prisons is likely to grow.

Penal custody, which remains relatively easy to use, is now able to deal with a range of problematic situations, including public order issues. As well as accommodating populations involved with problems of order, the prison is also utilized to tackle more enduring problems associated with drug use and persistent petty criminals. As the crisis in the labour market intensifies the prison is increasingly being used to deal with and absorb the growing social tensions in many western countries. In many respects the present situation is reminiscent of the regulation of vagrancy in the last century (Schapper, 1983).

At the same time as corporal punishment and the death penalty are being abolished, the use of imprisonment has risen in most countries to the highest point on the scale of coercive penalties. As prison moves into this elevated position a range of alternatives to custody are being developed. The day fine, suspended sentence, probation and community service orders are constantly being developed and expanded at the lower end of the process. These non-custodial sanctions are designed to slow down the flow of offenders into the prison. These developments have not been without a certain amount of success, at least in relation to the early stages of delinquency. Unfortunately, however, the various alternatives to incarceration which have been developed have not succeeded in reducing the prison population as a whole. In some cases they have, paradoxically, served to increase the number of people in prison by drawing more people into the correctional system. As Kuhn (1993) has shown from the analysis of Swiss data these measures can produce unanticipated consequences in the form of increasing the length of sentence. In the United Kingdom, Bottomley (1989) has also shown that the increase in the use of community-based sanctions has not had any real impact on prison overcrowding because judges tend to raise rather than reduce the length of custodial sentences. The only measure which has had a significant effect on the number of people in prison in Britain appears to be parole.

At the other end of the spectrum the abolition of the death penalty for some, has resulted in an upward trend in the length of sentences imposed for serious crimes. In some countries there has been the increased use of mandatory prison sentences for violent crimes. In periods of tension, or in situations in which the media is able to hype up the problem of crime, judges are generally less willing to take risks or to exercise leniency. Instead they impose longer and more severe punishments.

Within these general movements it is possible to distinguish two major patterns of imprisonment which have become increasingly pronounced in recent years.

TWO PATTERNS OF IMPRISONMENT

The first noticeable change in the use of imprisonment is its role in managing public order problems. Imprisonment for this purpose can be of variable length. Short-term confinement can avert trouble, deflect tensions and provide the public with reassurance. Long-term confinement, on the other hand, serves to incapacitate and to absorb violent offenders. The relative growth of the remand population is evidence of the former strategy, while the growth in the numbers of 'lifers' and long-term prisoners is evidence of the latter tendency.

The second change involves a transformation of the nature of the penalty inflicted. That is, there has been a major shift in the moral and political purpose of penal sanctions. Some examples of similar shifts in the mobilization of sanctions were evident in the experimental stages in the use of the prison, when the idea of individual reform was introduced through the combination of discipline which was already evident in the workhouse and the morality which was established through new codes of legislation. Penal codification allowed the implementation of this new morality in a measured form. The combination of these two requirements was not possible until the end of the modern era (Spierenburg, 1991).

Although these two processes coexist and overlap there has been an ongoing attempt to modify them through a general policy of bifurcation. That is, there has been a marked tendency for prison administrators to differentiate between the use of short- and long-term penalties for different types of offenders. In some countries there have been efforts to remove the use of short-term incarceration and even automatically to suspend or defer prison sentences below a certain length. Paradoxically, however, these efforts serve to undermine the public order functions of imprisonment. Thus in times of uncertainty and of growing social tension there is a reversion back to the use of short-term confinement as a response to perceived public order problems.

In relation to the second tendency there has been an increase in the length of sentences given for certain crimes, both for electoral reasons (McGarell and Castellano, 1991) and more generally for the state to demonstrate its willingness to protect citizens and to respond to their demands. Indeed, as far as France is concerned, there has, in recent years, been the introduction of new penalties for crimes involving interpersonal violence, such as rape, child abuse, and terrorism, which the media focus on extensively, as well as those areas where the government wants to demonstrate that it can be firm, such as drug dealing and reckless driving (Faugeron, 1994).

Therefore the logic underlying the use of custody in the present period is on the one hand a change in the nature of the penal sanction itself, and on the other, maintenance through the use of remand or incapacitation. If we follow through this line of reasoning we can identify the historical replication of developments which first became evident in the nineteenth century – developments which involved a changing relation between the state and civil society. The object of regulation was predominantly that of vagrancy and it was in response to this problem that the modern prison was mobilized to contain the transient and volatile populations. As in the nineteenth century the penal sanction lent legitimacy to the use of confinement for problem populations.

I fear that some historians will commit the sin of anachronism. Indeed when they describe the monasteries, the workhouses, the hospitals, the factories and so on, as the forerunners of the training prison, they describe technical patterns of confinement. But they move too quickly from these developments to patterns of penal confinement, thus forgetting that the implementation of prison sentences was linked to a political use (in France against the opponents to the newborn Republic) and to social and educational policies (for instance, policies promoted by the philanthropic movement). As we know, penality is a legal means to use confinement for political purposes, essentially against 'the idle' poor, beggars and vagrants and more recently for hooligans, drug-addicts and foreigners. What used to be obvious as regards what Foucault (1977) had called 'the great confinement' has become less obvious when penality, backed by judicial ideology, has come to include public order confinement. And confinement techniques have been confused with punishing techniques, with the latter being used as a model for the former. Paradoxically, however, it is through prison penalty or, to express it in a different way, through the use of prison for penal purposes, that the state manifests its authority. Because of its position on the scale of penalties and because it is legitimized by penal law, the prison has become the sole means of punishment which reflects the states coercive authority. Through the use of confinement it is increasingly required to take charge of everything that threatens public order.

Having explored some of the general dimensions of confinement in the present period, it is necessary to focus more specifically upon the operation of the prison. In order to do this there is a need to fashion some analytic tools which will help us to develop a detailed understanding of the role of the activities of various penal agents and emerging penal strategies and practices.

DEVELOPING DESCRIPTIVE CATEGORIES OF CONFINEMENT

One approach to the analysis of imprisonment has been developed from the sociology of organizations (Etzioni, 1975; Lemire, 1990). The categories derived from this approach are, however, not sufficient for an adequate understanding of the functioning of incarceration. Indeed, these categories were established in the context of the evaluation of administrative services rendered to particular clients. However, it is much more difficult to assess the level of satisfaction which the clients have of the prison. Yet who is the client to be satisfied in this case? It is unlikely to be the inmate, and in many cases it would not be the victim. It could be considered to be something called 'public opinion', in whose name laws are made and sentences passed, but according to opinion polls they are not satisfied with imprisonment. Some authors have suggested that the true clients of the penal system are the police and the judiciary. This may be the case but there is also a need to include the political and governmental interests in this list. Most noticeably, their interest in maintaining public order through the infliction of punishment in the name of maintaining peace and security.

In our democratic societies these same arguments need to demonstrate that they are able to respect individual freedom and maintain each citizen's rights. These two objectives are in conflict, and it is the resulting tensions that dictates penal policy and the use of custody. Thus the two parameters which must be taken into account when analyzing specific forms of confinement is the nature of state power and its legitimacy. With regard to the former, the state intervenes to determine the moment of incarceration and the duration of the custodial period through the operation of the judiciary. The ultimate authority to make these decisions cannot be allowed to be publicly challenged. The second parameter involves the issue of legitimacy. Each act of confinement and judicial decision must be legitimized for fear of appearing arbitrary, especially in relation to the twin notions of citizen protection and the maintenance of the physical and moral integrity of the person under arrest. These two parameters, in combination, will serve to define the range of managerial strategies and the practices of prison staff.

In order to develop our analysis of the changing nature and functioning of the prison it is necessary to look in more detail at the functions of incarceration. There are four functions which any system of penal confinement must necessarily display.

The Custodial Function

The primary function of custody is to define the limits between restraint and freedom, and the autonomy which an individual has the right to claim in society. This limit carries a strong social message. It marks out the state's 'hold' on the individual and the contours of state power. The state is responsible for custody and it is for this reason that allowing an escape is the most serious professional mistake that prison staff can make (Coyle, 1992). In an important sense, this function of custody has not changed a great deal since the introduction of the prison, except for the introduction of more sophisticated security equipment.

The Restorative Function

Except for those exceptional cases in which the death penalty is ordered, most democratic societies claim that the objective of incarceration is to rehabilitate offenders and eventually return them to civil life. This restorative function proceeds directly from the custodial function. For if one incarcerates, at some time or other, one will have to de-incarcerate. The prison rules in each country as well as agreements such as the European Convention for the Prevention of Torture establish guidelines for how this restorative objective should be achieved. However, the restorative function is not without its problems and controversies (Martinson, 1979).

Nevertheless, a great deal of the legitimacy of the prison is dependant upon the achievement of this objective (Faugeron and Le Boulaire, 1992). Since the nineteenth century this restorative function has given rise to endless debate about the possibility of effective treatment or rehabilitation within the coercive environment. More recently as it has become evident that the prison population is mainly comprised of individuals with low educational levels, a range of social, economic and personal problems, as well as problems linked to various forms of addiction, the type of interventions which are developed have to be tailored towards these disadvantaged populations.

The Controlling Function

As soon as a number of people are gathered in the same place, and especially when these people are locked up, it is necessary to regulate them. This involves establishing a regulatory relationship between the prison staff and the inmates. At root, this relationship is essentially coercive, although there is necessarily some reciprocity in order that the necessary day to day tasks are efficiently carried out. In consequence this essentially coercive relationship is mediated by a number of administrative and therapeutic approaches which ensure that a plurality of adaptations operate in different prisons. There always remains a precarious balance, however, between coercion and treatment (Morris, 1974).

In relation to prisoners a number of typologies have been developed in order to classify inmates' behaviour and to assess the effects of imprisonment. They are normally ordered along two main dimensions: adaptation–unadaptation and submission–rebellion. However, as these classifications do not mention the social relationship within the inmate subculture, they overlook some of the complexities of the situation and thereby limit the possible effectiveness of the various controlling strategies employed. In most cases, the rules governing the organization of prisoners come from the inmates' background. These social and subcultural processes are routinely adapted to the environment within particular custodial establishments. It is only by acknowledging and, if necessary, engaging with these rules that some kind of daily balance can be achieved (see Chauvenet, et al., 1993). Similarly, it is only through an understanding of these processes that prison disturbances can be effectively prevented and forms of collective and individual self-discipline can be established in prison.

We cannot fully comprehend how the precarious balance of order within the prison is achieved unless we also understand something of the rules which regulate the staff as well as the relations between staff. Whether they are salaried workers, or voluntary workers, specialists or non-specialists, wage earners or private contractors, the relationship between these different staff members is significant. However, few studies since the 1950s have carried out research on the different logics of intervention pursued by different staff groups. As a result prison warders are often depicted as the 'bad guys' who do the job of repressing, while the other personnel are the 'good guys' who help with the rehabilitation of the inmates.

Recently, these stereotypes have been weakened by the gradual disappearance of theories linked to therapeutic aspirations in favour of less ambitious goals merely designed not to compensate for, rather than compound the inmates' social handicaps. Sociological studies of the relationship between the various types of staff would progress if the social characteristics of each social group was more clearly acknowledged. Instead, current research is going astray by reducing the interaction and the tensions between these groups into a mere opposition between symbolic and ideological interests. This form of analysis is clearly inadequate.

What is required is an approach which takes into consideration the class and power relations between these different staff groups.

The Maintenance Function

The confinement of large groups of people within the prison has required the provision of a range of services including accommodation, food, washing and laundry facilities, and the provision of resources. In addition, albeit gradually, prison has come to provide welfare services and leisure activities. The introduction of these additional services has helped to improve the management of inmate populations and maintain control. While these improvements have reflected changed expectations in the wider society, they have been conditioned in the past by the criteria of 'less eligibility' (see Sparks in this volume). There is some evidence, however, that the gap between the lifestyle of prisoners is less evident today, in a number of different countries (Rusche, 1980; Melossi, 1992).

Nowadays, when there is a significant delay, it is likely to be due to poor adjustment to the evolution of lifestyles outside the prison, because of budgetary constraints, administrative red tape, difficulties in equipping the buildings, overpopulation and so on. These constraints usually weigh heavily on the organization of most public establishments such as hospitals, schools, army barracks and police buildings. Delays and the disruption of services within prisons, however, can have particularly adverse effects. Indeed, professionals have often suggested that the maintenance of ordinary services is essential to keep the peace inside the prison – the problem of food being, it seems, one of the main priorities.

All confinement devices rest on a complex web of connections. Two poles of exchanges can be identified: those which rest on financial flows and which allow economic exchanges; and those consisting of a complex and subtle set of exchanges of services and information, as well as various allowances and benefits. This indicates the extent to which the maintenance function has grown and become more complex in the course of time. Recently we have seen an upward trend in the importation of methods adapted from external public and private organizations.

THE CHANGING RELATION BETWEEN THE FUNCTIONS OF IMPRISONMENT

There is a sense in which these core functions have remained largely unchanged and continually reinforce each other. The maintenance function, for example, conditions the custodial and restorative functions and particularly the controlling function. Because the maintenance function determines the technical choices with relation to the training and the development of warders, it affects the custodial function. Similarly, the range of services and expenditure which is available will influence the restorative function. Generally, the shifting balance which is noticeable when there is a change from one type of government to another can lead to an upheaval in the system of control relations and a shift in the nature of power relations. This is sometimes difficult for certain categories of prisoners to accept.

Much of the uneasiness among prison staff can be ascribed to the growing prison bureaucracy and the increased number of services which are given to inmates (Chauvenet, et al., 1993). In such a context, educational and vocational training policies essential to the staff responsible for custody and control have been replaced by a growing number of rules and paperwork which try to codify every action of daily life. At the same time, the tasks have become hazier and the increasing number of professionals and volunteers coming from outside have increased competition for the control of the powerful posts in prison.

It is interesting to note that when scholars or professionals mention the specific tasks in the prison system, they refer mainly to custody and control. This is not, however, what Lord Justice Woolf (1991) meant when he ascribed the riots in British prisons in 1990 to an imbalance between security and control on the one hand and justice on the other hand. If we take a closer look at what he meant by the term 'justice', it is in fact a number of services which should be offered to the inmates and run by them, according to a sharing of responsibilities among themselves, the prison administration and the prison environment. It comes back to presenting a pattern combining the four functional prison categories, whose ultimate goal would be control (or at least the avoidance of serious disorder) and which would be based on giving more responsibility to prisoners and greater fairness in the treatment of prisoners.

At this point I would like to take two examples of the relation between the four general functions which have been outlined above: the health sector and the labour sector.

The Health Sector

In analyzing the medicalization process within the prison we have to be careful to avoid simplistic conclusions. For example, some research studies have shown a high level of consumption of drugs in prisons. This phenomenon has been interpreted as a mechanism by which prison doctors and prison administrators control inmates (the chemical straitjacket), even though complementary studies have shown that the level of consumption is often a function of the specific characteristics and demands of the incarcerated population.

Indeed, there have been, there are, and there still will be, some attempts at organizing if not collusive, at least complementary connections between the prison administration and medicine. But in the beginning the logic for a medical presence in prison, just like alms and charity, was part of the maintenance function. It helped to facilitate the daily activities of the inmates and particularly their contribution to the prison-factories of the nineteenth century (Petit, 1990). The picture became more complex when, with the hygienists and later on with the alienists, specialized knowledge was established which aimed at transforming the prison into a privileged site where these theories could be applied. If hygienists and alienists became interested in the prison, it was because they believed that their particular skills were of some importance to it, as body and soul would be cared for in a joint effort to fight for public welfare (Lecuyer, 1977). This involved the struggle against contamination on the one hand and caring for mental and moral health on the other. In the course of discussions on solitary confinement, social hygiene has become a partner to forensic medicine. The same is true for newly-born psychiatry which soon joined up with the new discipline of criminology through the establishment of social defence.

However, the emergence of disciplines and their struggle in the field of knowledge and power should be dissociated from the reality of the rudimentary medical practices which circulated in prison. It was only when medicine started to organize itself as an autonomous knowledge from the nineteenth century onwards that prison medicine showed its presence, but more as a discourse on method than as a practice (Leonard, 1984). Public health did not become truly concerned with prison until health policies were first worked out for civil society. Some devices were then transferred to the inmates' particular case, particularly in periods of 'crisis'. It was in such a crisis in post-war France, that systematic check-ups to detect epidemics were introduced, files kept on each inmate's medical record and, by 1945, dental and nursing care was made generally available (Faugeron and Le Boulaire, 1992).

Devices only found outside the prison can be used if the exceptional characteristic of the situation requires an immediate solution. It is the case today with AIDS. In other instances, when the objective is to fall in line with existing external services, specific devices which are first poorly set up, often from analogy, become normalized. That is how things started in France. A network of prison hospitals was introduced, which specialized in general medicine and with their staff's status poorly copied from the public hospital, while doctors who did not belong to the prison staff were still in charge of medical care. Only in 1983 did the Health Department become accountable for health in prison. It was only when faced with sanitary difficulties in French prisons in 1993, that the head of the Prison Department took into consideration the complete transfer of medical responsibilities to public health services as well as health benefits for the inmates.

As far as psychiatric services are concerned, after an unsuccessful attempt at organizing them in the mid-1940s, they were then organized more rapidly than prison medical services, and according to the external pattern, by incorporating prison psychiatry to the 'normal' system of psychiatric organization. In the last ten years, we have witnessed the conjunction of penal, moral and pathological fields, for example in relation to drug-addiction. An assemblage of social and psychological discourses and practices have emerged. Considering how far behind France is in developing solutions to drug-addiction, it is the prison system which has now become a resource for medicine and psychiatry.

Custody, control and rehabilitation have historically been part of the implementation of the medical and psychiatric apparatus. But it is the maintenance function which has been the main factor in normalizing the health sector. Faced with an increasing number of drug-addicts, the spreading of AIDS, tuberculosis and hepatitis, and its obligation to keep the mentally ill in custody, the prison administration does not have any other choice but to ask external services for help.

The Labour Sector

The prison management's ability to provide decent services is linked to the prison economy itself. Indeed, the necessary conditions to produce or provide resources is one of the basic functions of prison management. Just as in all organizations, these resources refer to financial inputs as well as to the use of human resources. Even if the objective is only to make sure that the vital functions of the captives are kept up, the question of resources still remains. Thus the prison managers should be able to create or find resources whether they are allocated by the government or come from external contributions or are produced by the inmates themselves.

Since the beginning of the nineteenth century, the relationship between the different methods for producing or providing resources has become extremely complex through the introduction of an increasing variety of 'partners'. Yet, as soon as the penal characteristic of the prison is put forward, the question of its financing by the state becomes more problematic. Indeed, the prison is caught in a game of public morality which weighs heavily on the types of resources allocated to it. It plays a part in the resourcing of penal policies, although it is not granted control over its own goals nor over the populations it is landed with. Thus, on the one hand, it is in a position of needing to provide resources in order to meet demands not always in tune, and sometimes even conflicting with its own logic. Moreover, it does not always have, for reasons of moral constraints, the possibility to choose the most suitable resources. Paradoxically, in a field which seems to be most suitable for the implementation of public policies, one of the major moral constraints weighing heavily on the penal administration has long been the reliance on public financing.

The solution which has long prevailed to guarantee the prison its financial autonomy has been the use of prison labour, either by assigning the inmates tasks within the scope of its operation, or by hoping to generate profit by means of its productive activity. This second solution presents the advantage that it follows the same process of legitimization as external labour. So to economic necessity is added moral justification (Rothman, 1971). During detention, the strong moral legitimacy of work allows the transfer of values referring to external labour directly to the prison. So from rational thinking based on practical necessities and in a context of direct exploitation of slave-like labour, a legitimization of prison labour has developed through its corrective, educational, exemplary effects and more particularly through utilitarian justifications.

Nevertheless, the evolution of productive types of prison labour has not always followed external developments because of the peculiar characteristics of the prison labour market. Though the incarcerated labour force is defined by its low cost, its availability and its proximity, it is also characterized by its low qualification level, its high turnover and its lack of incentive. Moreover, the productive apparatus of prison labour is not easily adaptable to new technologies. In spite of the utopias of the beginning of our industrial era, the prison has never been transformed durably into production units able to generate enough income to guarantee its autonomy. For the most part, the organization of labour inside the prison remains very archaic. All this has driven the prison system into seeking its main funding from public budgets.

However, it is the establishment of work programmes which has given an impetus to and justified the implementation of devices associated with the evolution of working benefits: social welfare, vocational training, unemployment benefits, and so on. Moreover, the issue of penal work is evaluated less and less in terms of economic inflow, but more and more in terms of the ability to provide the inmates with an income, allowing them to buy consumer goods. Because they have become consumers, the inmates today have a more complex relationship to prison labour. At the same time, their relation to confinement has changed, as their claims have been legitimized through their entitlements to extended social welfare and to what Pires (1991) has called 'indebted rights'. The labour issue was markedly transformed when the inmate went from being coerced into working to being entitled to working rights, and later to vocational training and social support. Nowadays it is no longer a matter of disciplining the body and soul, but of ensuring that the inmates keep their means to consume: a right to which every citizen is entitled.

In a similar way to the health sector, the organization of labour within the prison, which is now linked to consumption, has compelled the prison administration to resort to various external partners. The latter have brought along with them their own logic which had to be more or less accepted. Yet recent prison monographs have shown that the logics of medicine and of labour have led to a preoccupation with security and to increased bureaucratization.

CONCLUSION

I have presented a typology of functional categories of confinement (custody, restoration, control and maintenance) and I have examined the way in which they interact within two prison sectors, health and labour. Obviously, interacting patterns are conditioned by specific national and historic circumstances. Nevertheless, there is no simple solution or clear-cut method for dealing with these issues. Therefore, it is necessary to resort to an incongruous assemblage of strategies and resources. My examples have shown that the maintenance function includes two different types of duties: managing populations by providing them with a minimum level of conditions and services, and the management of emergency situations.

Health and labour can be considered two key sectors for the implementation of prison policies which include education and vocational training. The way they have historically evolved from practical necessities has produced a kind of make-shift development legitimized by penal theory. In the case of France, what looks like some rather successful improvization is due largely to the power of judges in influencing the prison administration.

However, the importation of the external logics of the marketplace has modified prison management irreversibly, thus making it more complicated and exceedingly bureaucratized. This is all the more difficult because the custody function still weighs heavily upon the prison mangers. Indeed, this custody function remains the only symbol of state authority in countries where most of the other types of incarceration have disappeared.

We are at a crossroads. Nowadays, the restorative function is less driven by the functions of penalty and increasingly legitimized by notions of individual free will. Indeed, we are still dealing with another process of legitimization but, without doubt, it attempts to be more respectful of the individual's autonomy than previous ones. Moreover, although the growth in the prison population has had a number of drawbacks there has been at least one positive result in France. It has forced the prison administration to become familiar with new styles of management and to increase external resources, while expanding the range of welfare services. Unfortunately, this increase is also responsible for the unavoidable gap between needs and the increase of external resources, thus making the prison appear less capable of achieving the restorative function properly. France, like a number of other countries has resorted to the private sector in an attempt to overcome this problem (see Beyens and Snacken in this volume).

France and Belgium have been confronted with problems arising from the increased use of remand. Remand, when used to control petty crimes and minor forms of drug use shows the role of imprisonment in protecting social order. In relation to this development two responses are possible. On the one hand, an attempt can be made to improve the rights of the remand population while on the other efforts can be made to develop policies which will reduce their number. At the other end of the spectrum, the increase in long-term penalties and the number of 'lifers' carries the possibility of imploding the prison system. From this vantage point one can but agree with Sessar when he writes:

> Maybe our thoughts about prisons were wrong altogether. Therefore, beyond our concern about how to reduce the problem of overcrowding we should turn our scientific attention to the timeless question of whether prisons can (still) be legitimised ... After the replacement of capital punishment by life imprisonment, after the introduction of probation and suspended sentences, after the victory of non-custodial sanctions over prison sanctions, the next step will be the prohibition of life imprisonment which has already been achieved in Brazil, in Portugal, in Spain, and in Norway, and the reduction or the abolition of imprisonment for juveniles. (Sessar, 1994: 114)

In many countries, the reduction of legitimization, coupled with the difficulties experienced by prison officers which have been brought into the open by their unions, will perhaps allow some consideration of the prison as a public service as well as a moralizing enterprise. In this way the relationship between services and resources could be optimized according to strategic patterns of intervention rather than as a form of crisis management.

References and Bibliography

Barak-Glantz, I. L. (1983) 'The Anatomy of Another Prison Riot', in *The Prison Journal*, vol. 53: 2–23.

Bernat de Celis, J. (1988) *Peines Prononcées, Peines Subies (La Mise à Exécution des Peines D'emprisonnement Correctional: Practiques du Parquet de Paris)* (Paris: CESDIP).

Bernat de Celis, J. (1988) 'La difficulté de faire exécuter les peines d'emprisonnement correctionnel à Paris', in *Revue de Science Criminelle et de Droit Comparé*, 3: 469–73.

Bottomley, K. A. (1989) 'The Problems of Imprisonment', in R. Hood (ed.) *Crime and Criminal Policy in Europe. Proceedings of an European Colloquium* (Oxford: Centre for Criminalogical Research): 227–8.

Bourdieu, P. (1992) *Résponses* (Paris: Le Seuil).

Brodeur, J. P. (1991) 'Policer l'apparence', in *Revue Canadienne de Criminologie*, pp. 285–332.

Chauvenet, A.; Benguigui, G.; and Orlic, F. (1993) 'Les surveillants de prison: le prix de la sécurité', in *Revue Française de Sociologie*, XXXIV: 345–66.

Clemmer, D. (1940) *The Prison Community* (New York: Holt).

Collective (1960) *Theoretical Studies in Social Organisation of the Prison* (New York: Social Science Research Council).

Collective (1980) *Rapport sur La Décriminalisation* (Strasbourg: Council of Europe).

Coyle, A. (1992) 'The Responsible Prisoners: Rehabilitation Revisited', in *The Howard Journal*, XXXI, 1: 1–7.

Cressey, D. R. (1959) 'Contradictory Directives in Complex Organisations: The Case of the Prison', in *Administrative Science Quarterly*, IV, 1: 1–19.

Ditchfield, J. (1990) *Control in Prisons: A Review of the Literature* (London: HMSO, Home Office Research Study 118).

Downes, D. (1988) *Contrasts in Tolerance, Post-War Penal Policy in The Netherlands and England and Wales* (Oxford: Oxford University Press).

Etzioni, A. (1975) *A Comparative Analysis of Complex Organisations* (Chicago, Rand McNally).

Evans, P. (1980) *Prison Crisis* (London: George Allen & Unwin).

Foucault, M. (1977) *Discipline and Punish* (Harmondsworth: Penguin).

Faugeron, C. (1989) 'Prisons in France: An Irresistible Increasing of the Detained Population?' in R. Hood (ed.), *Crime and Crime Policy in Europe. Proceedings of a European Colloquim* (Oxford Centre for Criminological Research): 230–41.

Faugeron, C. (1991a) 'De la Libération á la guerre d'Algérie: l'espoir d'une réforme pénitentiaire', in J. G. Petit, N. Castan, C. Faugeron, M. Pierre and A. Zysberg, *Histoire des Galères Bagnes et Prisons en France* (Toulouse: Privat): 281–308.

Faugeron, C. (1991b) 'Les prisons de la Vème République: à la recherche d'une politique', in J. G. Petit, N. Castan, C. Faugeron, M. Pierre and A. Zysberg, *Histoire des Galères Bagnes et Prisons en France* (Toulouse: Privat): 309–34.

Faugeron, C. (1991c) 'Prisons in France: Stalemate or Evolution?', in D. van Zyl Smit and F. Dunkel (eds), *Imprisonment Today and Tomorrow. International Perspectives on Prisoners' Rights and Prison Conditions* (Deventer: Kluwer), 1: 249–78.

Faugeron, C. (1994) 'The problem of "Dangerous" Offenders and Long-Term Prisoners in France', in J. Vagg (ed.), (unpublished) *Prevention and Punishment: Corrections, Dangerousness and Long-Term Prisoners. An International Perspective.*

Faugeron, C. and Houchon, G. (1987) 'Prison and the Penal System: From Penology to a Sociology of Penal Policies', in *International Journal of the Sociology of Law*, 15: 393–422.

Faugeron, C. and Le Boulaire, J. M. (1988) 'La Création du service social des prisons et l'evolution de la réforme pénitentiaire en France de 1945 à 1958', in *Déviance et Société*, XII, 4: 317–59.

Faugeron, C. and Le Boulaire, J. M. (1992) 'Quelques remarques à propos de la récidive', in *Kriminologisches Bulletin de Criminologie*, 1: 12–31.

Faugeron, C. and Tournier, P. (1991) 'La crise des prisons françaises', in *Coll, La Justice* (Paris: Cahiers Français, La Documentation Française): 128–36.

Feest, J. (1990) *Interventions visant à éviter l'entrée dans le systéme pénal ou à interrompe ce processus. Rapport présenté à la XIXéme Conférence de rescherches criminologiques* (Strasbourg: Council of Europe).

Foucault, M. (1977) Discipline and Punish (Harmondsworth: Penguin).

Frisching, A. de (1992) 'Le maintien de l'ordre et de la sécurité dans le prisons, ainsi que des liens entre l'univers carcéral et la sociéte', in *Bulletin d'Information Pénologique*, 17: 4–10.

Garland, D. (1980) *Punishment and Modern Society: A Study in Social Theory* (Chicago, University of Chicago Press).

Goethals, J. (1980) 'Les effets psycho-sociaux des longues peines d'emprisonnement', in *Déviance et Société*, IV, 1: 81–101.

Gonin, D. (1991) *La santé incarcérée. Médecine et conditions de vie en prison* (Paris: L'Archipel).

Igas-Igsj (1993) *L'emprisonnement Prolongé des Détenus Difficiles et Dangereux* (Paris: Ministére de la Justice).

Ignatieff, M. (1979) *A Just Measure of Pain. The Penitentiary in the Industrial Revolution 1750–1850* (Harmondsworth: Penguin).

Irwin, J. (1980) *Prisons in Turmoil* (Boston: Little, Brown).

Jacobs, J. B. (1976) 'Prison Violence and Formal Organisation', in A. K. Cohen, G. F. Cole and R. G. Bailey, *Prison Violence* (Lexington, MA: Lexington Books): 79–88.

Joutsen, M. (1993) 'Legitimations and the Limits of the Criminal Justice System', in *European Journal on Criminal Policy and Research*, I, 1: 9–26.

Kuhn, A. (1993) *Punitivité, Politique Criminelle et Surpeuplement Carcéral* (Berne: Haupt).

Lecuyer, B. P. (1977) 'Médecins et observateurs sociaux: les Annales d'Hygiène publique et de médecine légale', in *Pour une Histoire de la Statistique*, (Paris: INSEE): 445–75.

Lemire, G. (1990) *Anatomie de la Prison* (Montreal: Presses de l'Université de Montréal).

Leonard, J. (1984a) 'L'historien et le philosophe. A propos de surveiller et punir: naissance de la prison', in M. Perrot, *L'impossible Prison* (Paris: Seuil): 9–39.

Leonard, J. (1988b) 'Les médecins des prisons', in J. G. Petit (ed.), *La Prison, Le Bagne et L'histoire* (Paris, Geneva: Ed. des Méridiens, M&H): 141–9.

McGarell, E. F. and Castellano, T. C. (1991) 'An Integrative Conflict Model of the Criminal Law Formation Process', in *Journal of Research in Crime and Delinquency*, XXVIII, 2: 174–96.

Martinson, R. (1979) 'Restraint and Incapacitation: An Analytical Introduction', in Wolfgang, M. E. *Prisons: Present and Possible* (Lexington, MA: Lexington Books): 55–88.

Melossi, D. (1992) 'L'hégémonie et les vocabulaires de la motivation pénale: la gestion discursive des crises', in *Criminologie*, XXV, 2: 93–114.

Melossi, D. (1993) 'Gazette of Morality and Social Whip: Punishment, Hegemony and the Case of the USA, 1970–1992', in *Social and Legal Studies: An International Journal*, II, 3: 259–80.

Morris, N. (1974) The Future of Imprisonment (Chicago: University of Chicago Press).

Perrot, M. (1980) '1848. Révolution et prisons', in M. Perrot, (ed.), *L'impossible Prison* (Paris: Seuil): 277–312.

Petit, J. G. (1990) *Ces Peines Obscures. La Prison Pénale en France (1789–1870)* (Paris: Fayard).

Petit, J. G.; Castan, N.; Faugeron, C.; Pierre, M.; and Zysberg, A. (1991) *Histoire des Galères, Bagnes et Prisons en France* (Toulouse: Privat).

Pires, A. (1990) 'La devoir de punir: le rétributivisme face aux sanctions communautaires', in *Revue Canadienne de Criminologie*: 441–60.

Pires, A. (1991a) 'La Réforme pénale et la réciprocité des droits', in *Criminologie*, XXIV, 1: 77–104,

Pires, A. (1991b) 'Ethiques et réformes du droit criminel: au-delà des philosophies de la peine', in *Ethica*, III, 2: 47–78.

Reyaud, J. D. (1989) *Les Régles du Jeu. L'action Collective et la Régulation Sociale* (Paris: Armand Colin).

Rothman, D. J. (1971) *'The Discovery of the Asylum: Social Order and Disorder'*, in *The New Republic* (Boston: Little, Brown).

Rusche, G. (1980a) 'Marché du travail et régime des peines: contribution à la sociologie de la justice pénale', in *Déviance et Société*, IV, 3: 215–28.

Rusche, G. (1980b) 'Prison Revolts or Social Justice: Lessons from America', in *Crime and Social Justice*, 1980, 13: 41–4.

Rusche, G. & Kirchheimer, O. (1968) *Punishment and Social Structure* (New York: Russel and Russel).

Sessar, K. (1994) 'Overcrowding – Not the only Crisis in the Custodial System', *European Journal on Criminal Policy and Research*, 24: 107–16.

Schapper, B. (1983) 'La récidive, une obsession créatrice au XiXème siècle', in *Le Récidivisme* (Paris: Presses Universitaries de France): 25–64.

Sim, J. (1990) *Medical Power in Prisons. The Prison Medical Service in England 1774–1989* (Milton Keynes: Open University Press).

Spierenburg, P. (1991) *The Prison Experience. Disciplinary Institutions and Their Inmates in Early Modern Europe* (New Brunswick and London: Rutgers University Press).

Thomas, J. E. and Williams, T. A. (1977) 'Change and Conflict in the Evolution of Prison System: Old Dilemmas, Emergent Problems and Future Strategies', in *International Journal of Criminology and Penology*, V, 4: 349–65.

Woolf Lord Justice (1991) *Prison Disturbances April 1990. Report of an Inquiry by the RT Hon. Lord Justice Woolf and His Honour Judge Stephen Tumim*, Cmnd 1456 (London: HMSO).

7 Ethnic Minorities in British Prisons: Some Research Implications

Marian FitzGerald and Peter Marshall

BACKGROUND

For decades American criminology has concerned itself with the links between ethnicity and crime; and similar preoccupations have much more recently been apparent in the European literature. Concerns in Britain about ethnic minorities as suspects and offenders have tended to centre on black people – that is, those of Caribbean and African origin – rather than Asians, and they have been documented mainly by reference to prison statistics. Until recently[1] these have been the only available national source of criminal justice data on ethnic minorities. They have consistently shown a significant over-representation of black prisoners relative to the black population resident in England and Wales and this is especially marked in the case of women.

At a popular and political level, but also in academic work, four main lines of argument are deployed by way of explanation. The first is that ethnic differences in the prison figures broadly reflect ethnic differences in patterns and levels of offending. The second tends to be diametrically opposed to the first and holds that the differences are at variance with the real pattern, but instead reflect differential treatment of the various ethnic groups by the criminal justice system. Thirdly, there is an argument that the figures reflect socio-economic rather than ethnic differences (an explanation which implicitly assumes differential patterns of offending by different socio-economic groups). And fourthly, there is the possibility that the explanation lies in some combination of the previous three. There are, however, major and unresolved questions in this argument about the weight of the different factors, the reasons for and the interaction between them (Jefferson, 1988; Reiner, 1989; FitzGerald, 1993a; Smith, 1993).

Against this background, we take a new look at the ethnic make-up of prison populations by reference to three recent data sets which have not previously been brought together for this purpose. The chapter begins by examining the level and pattern of minority ethnic representation in the prison population using data based on the new classification adopted by the Prison Service in 1992 which allows for more refined analyses than the system which had operated from 1985 onwards. It then uses material from the 1991 Census to compare the main ethnic groups in terms of key characteristics where the prison population as a whole is known to differ from the general population. Finally, it uses the National Prison Survey (NPS) to compare prisoners of different ethnic origins with each other in terms of their social and economic characteristics.

The chapter then discusses the links between these three elements in the context of the wider debate about 'race'[2] and crime. It concludes by suggesting an approach to analyzing ethnic differences in official criminal statistics which avoids some of the pitfalls in the interpretations of 'racial disproportionality' which predominate in the American literature.

THE ETHNIC MAKE-UP OF THE PRISON POPULATION OF ENGLAND AND WALES

Under the system of ethnic monitoring adopted by the Prison Service in 1985 prisoners were allocated by prison officers on reception to categories which, in their published form, were grouped as follows: White; West Indian; Guyanese; African; Indian; Pakistani; Bangladeshi; Chinese; Arab; Mixed origins; Other; not recorded (including refusals). Detailed analyses of these data appeared in a Home Office Statistical Bulletin in 1986 (HOSB 17/86) and again in 1994 (HOSB 21/94); and the annually published *Prison Statistics* have routinely included tables showing the ethnic breakdown of the prison population (for males and females separately) by the following variables: type of prisoner (remand, sentenced or non-criminal); sentence length (up to 18 months, 18 months to 4 years, over 4 years); age (whether young offender or adult); offence type. These data have perennially confirmed four sets of findings in respect of the white, black (West Indian, Guyanese, African) and South Asian (Indian, Pakistani and Bangladeshi) groups.[3] The first two sets of findings concern over-representation as such. The other two are of interest in their own right and may also be relevant to understanding this over-representation. (see Table 7.1).

First, compared to the available data for the population at large, black people (that is, the West Indian, Guyanese, African group) have always been over-represented in ethnic data on receptions into prisons; and their level of over-representation in the prison population at any given time is greater still. This is particularly true of black women. The proportion of

Table 7.1 Population in Prison Service establishments on 30 June 1991: by ethnic origin, type of prisoner and sex

England and Wales
Males

Number of persons

Type of prisoner	Ethnic origin					All persons in Prison Service establishments
	White	West Indian Guyanese African	Indian Pakistani Bangladeshi	Chinese Arab Mixed origin	Other, not recorded (including refusals)	
Population of Prison Service establishments	36 081	4470	1296	885	478	43 210
All remand prisoners	7394	965	226	285	86	8876
Untried criminal prisoners						
Aged 14 to 20	1681	143	46	48	16	1934
Aged 21 and over	4147	664	150	124	55	5140
Convicted unsentenced prisoners	1566	158	30	33	15	1802
All sentenced prisoners	28 580	3379	996	636	375	33 966
All sentenced young offenders[1]	4993	384	143	135	28	5683
Up to 18 months[2]	2757	126	66	70	13	3032
Over 18 months (inc. life)	2236	258	77	65	15	2651
All sentenced adults	23 587	2995	853	501	347	28 283
Up to 18 months[2]	6706	477	163	94	32	7472
Over 18 months up to 4 years	7663	910	190	137	92	8992
Over 4 years (inc. life)	9218	1608	500	270	223	11819
Non-criminal prisoners	107	126	74	44	17	368

1. Includes persons detained under Section 53 of the Children and Young Persons Act 1993 and custody for life cases.
2. Includes persons committed in default of payment of a fine, compensation order or costs.

Table 7.1 Continued

England and Wales
Females

Type of prisoner	Ethnic origin					Number of persons in Prison Service establishments
	White	West Indian Guyanese African	Indian Pakistani Bangladeshi	Chinese Arab Mixed origin	Other, not recorded (including refusals)	All persons in Prison Service establishments
Population of Prison Service establishments	1049	253	27	67	49	1544
All remand prisoners	280	69	4	23	11	387
Untried criminal prisoners						
Aged 14 to 20	46	5	–	5	1	57
Aged 21 and over	149	55	3	13	9	229
Convicted unsentenced prisoners	85	9	1	5	1	101
All sentenced prisoners	767	278	23	42	38	1148
All sentenced young offenders[1]	84	16	–	7	3	110
Up to 18 months[2]	43	3	–	1	–	47
Over 18 months (inc. life)	41	13	–	6	3	63
All sentenced adults	683	262	23	35	35	1038
Up to 18 months[2]	298	48	2	10	2	360
Over 18 months up to 3 years	138	25	2	7	5	177
Over 3 years (inc. life)	247	189	19	18	28	501
Non-criminal prisoners	2	5	–	2	–	9

1. Includes persons detained under Section 53 of the Children and Young Persons Act 1993 and custody for life cases.
2. Includes persons committed in default of payment of a fine, compensation order or costs.
Source: Prison statistics.

black people in the population at large has remained about 1 per cent; but black men accounted for about 8 per cent of the prison population in 1985, rising to 11 per cent in 1993. The corresponding figures for black women were 12 per cent in 1985 and 20 per cent in 1993. The South Asian group, on the other hand (the Indians, Pakistanis and Bangladeshis) have not been significantly over-represented, although there has been a slight increase in the proportion of male South Asian prisoners recently.

Secondly, the prisons data have consistently shown that the level of over-representation of black men in the remand population was even greater than their over-representation in the sentenced population.

However, two other findings are potentially relevant to the extent of over-representation in both the sentenced and the remand population. The prisons data have consistently shown that the proportions of different ethnic groups varies between offence categories and that minority groups are serving longer sentences than whites. The statistical bulletins referred to above have shown that differences in sentence length and remand are accounted for largely – although not entirely – by differences in offence, compounded (in terms of sentence length) by additional relevant factors such as previous convictions and court of sentence. The slightly higher rate of over-representation in the prison population compared with receptions is accounted for by the fact that, once received into prisons, ethnic minorities are kept there for longer than whites and this increases the proportion of resident prisoners they will make up at any given time.

Since October 1992, prisoners have, on reception, been asked to classify *themselves* using categories which equate to those used in the national population Census of 1991. The picture which emerges is broadly in line with that described above; but due to these changes in classification and further improvements in the collection and storage of other data, it is considerably illuminated because the minority ethnic groups can now be further subdivided in two ways. The black group can be broken down into those of Caribbean, African and 'Other' black origins, while the South Asians can be identified separately as Indian, Pakistani or Bangladeshi in origin. Further, the coverage and quality of the nationality data has improved so that it is now possible to identify more reliably the proportion within these groups who are foreign nationals and, thereby, to get a better impression of the proportion who may normally be British residents.

The ethnic profile of the male and female prison populations using this new system of classification is shown in Table 7.2 which gives the figures at June 1993. It shows that the black groups continue to be strongly over-represented, but that the gender difference in this over-representation is most marked in the Black African group. Among the South Asian groups, there is

Table 7.2   Prison population of England and Wales at June 1993 by
gender and ethnic origin

	Male	Female	(England and Wales pop.)
		(Percentages)	*(Census 1991)*
White	83.8	74.1	(94.1)
Black Caribbean	6.7	8.1	(1.0)
Black African	2.0	6.3	(0.4)
Black Other	2.1	5.3	(0.4)
Indian	1.5	0.9	(1.7)
Pakistani	1.5	0.3	(0.9)
Bangladeshi	0.2	0.1	(0.3)
Chinese	0.1	0.1	(0.3)
Asian Other	0.6	0.4	(0.4)
Other	1.5	4.4	(0.6)

in fact over-representation among males of Pakistani origin which had previously been obscured in the aggregated data, although the over-representation is not of the same order of magnitude as among the black groups.

However, a further breakdown by nationality shows that female prisoners of all minority ethnic origins are less likely than male prisoners to have UK nationality (see Table 7.3). This is particularly striking in the African group, but is also marked among prisoners of Caribbean origin.

Nationality does not *de facto* define which prisoners are normally resident in Great Britain.[4] However, these figures serve as a useful reminder that comparisons of figures for the prison population with those for the resident population should only be regarded as approximate because of the presence of foreign prisoners. In particular, caution should be exercised for this reason in making inferences about over-representation in the female prison population. There have been widespread assertions of 'double discrimination against black women' (Chigwada 1989; Ritchey Mann 1989), but it is worth noting that black men with UK nationality form 8.2 per cent of the prison population and the figure for black women is almost identical at 8.5 per cent.

KEY ETHNIC DIFFERENCES IN THE GENERAL POPULATION

The 1991 Census for Great Britain allows inter-ethnic comparisons on several of the key indicators where the NPS shows the prison population

Table 7.3   Prisoners with UK nationality by ethnic origin (June 1993)

| | *(rounded percentages)* | |
	Male	*Female*
White	96	95
Black Caribbean	81	40
Black African	49	13
Black Other	86	69
Indian	47	40
Pakistani	61	40
Bangladeshi	43	*
Chinese	31	*
Asian Other	57	57
Other	49	51

*Numbers too small to be reliably included.

to differ markedly from the population at large. These are summarized in Table 7.4 which highlights the fact that, in the population at large, differences on these measures are often *as* great between the minority groups as they are between these groups and the average for the majority 'white' population. Where there are important gender differences, figures are given for males only since the discussion of ethnic differences in the NPS which follows refers only to male prisoners.

All minority groups are, on average, younger than whites; but the age profile of the Black Caribbean group is most similar to that of the majority population, while the Black Other, Pakistani and Bangladeshi groups are the youngest of all, with between 40 and 50 per cent aged under 15 in 1991. The Black, Pakistani and Bangladeshi groups have very high levels of male unemployment; but for those who are actually in work, it is Pakistani and Bangladeshi men who are by far the most likely to occupy semi- and unskilled manual jobs. In terms of education, the Labour Force Surveys for 1989 to 1991 additionally show that the composite Pakistani/Bangladeshi group is least likely to have any educational qualifications. Figures for males of working age with no educational qualifications were 49 per cent for this group, compared with 35 per cent for Black males, 29 per cent for Indians and 27 per cent for whites.

While the Census does not cover the same range of information on family background as the NPS, there is some overlap and, again, a number of striking differences between groups (see Table 7.5). The

Table 7.4   Key differences between ethnic groups (United Kingdom, 1991) (i)

	Aged under 16	Unemployed (M)	Semi/unskilled manual (M)
		(percentage within groups)	
White	19	11	19
Black Caribbean	22	24	29
Black African	29	29	–
Black Other	51	26	–
Indian	30	13	20
Pakistani	43	29	
Bangladeshi	47	31	28
Chinese	23	11	–
Asian Other	24	14	–
Other	42	20	–

Table 7.5   Key differences between ethnic groups (United Kingdom, 1991) (ii)

	'Large family' households with dependent children	Lone-parent households
White	5.0	4.0
Black Caribbean	5.9	16.4
Black African	7.7	16.0
Black Other	3.9	21.6
Indian	21.2	3.1
Pakistani	27.3	4.8
Bangladeshi	32.8	4.4
Chinese	12.3	4.4
Asian Other	11.6	5.5
Other	6.5	8.7

South Asian groups are the most likely to live in large families (that is, families with three or more adults and one or more dependent children). The Black groups, on the other hand, are less likely to be married, are more likely to live in households headed by a single parent and have the highest proportions of adults below pensionable age living alone.

ETHNIC MINORITIES IN THE NATIONAL PRISON SURVEY 1991

The National Prison Survey was undertaken on behalf of the Home Office in 1991. It randomly sampled 10 per cent of all male and 20 per cent of all female prisoners in England and Wales, with the exception of juveniles and Immigration Act detainees, and had three principal objectives:

> The first was to obtain systematic information about the background of prisoners ... The second was to learn about prison régimes and life in prison as seen through the eyes of the prisoners themselves ... Finally, it was hoped that by comparing prisoners' childhood circumstances and background and their current living arrangements and family circumstances with the crimes they have committed, the sentences they have received and their attitudes to crime and punishment, some light might be shed on the roots of their criminality. (Walmsley, Howard and White, 1992: vi)

Respondents were asked their ethnic origin using the Census categories, so the data potentially offers valuable insights into the 'race' and crime debate.

In meeting its first objective, the report of the survey concluded that 'the prison population is very different in structure from the general population'. For, in addition to confirming differences in its ethnic and gender make-up, the NPS report documents differences in terms of age, education, employment status and economic activity, marital status and childhood circumstances.

The NPS found that the prison population as a whole was younger than the population at large. They were much more likely to have a background in semi- or unskilled work, although only half had been working immediately before they were imprisoned; and male prisoners were more likely to have no qualifications than men in the population at large. The proportion who were married when they came into prison was much lower than in the population at large, although the proportion cohabiting was much higher. They were more likely to have spent some time in local authority care; and a relatively high proportion had spent most of their childhood with just one parent.

Setting the ethnic differences shown by the Census in this context, one would predict that the Black Caribbean and African groups would tend to be over-represented in the prison population. On several indicators, one would also expect to find disproportionate numbers of Pakistani and Bangladeshi prisoners. The effect is offset, however, by the younger average age of the Pakistani and Bangladeshi groups (which means a smaller proportion have, as yet, reached the peak age for offending) and also by their high rate of marriage, which is associated with lower rates of imprisonment. The prison statistics cited earlier are *broadly* in line with these anticipated findings, although it has been noted that they are already showing some over-representation of Pakistanis. However, the comparisons made here say nothing about the precise extent of the over-representation one would predict. We already know (see above) that there are some ethnic differences in criminal characteristics, such as previous convictions and offence categories; but the NPS is unique in providing information on the economic and social characteristics of the different ethnic groups in the prison population. That is, ideally, it should enable us to explore how far these *converge* in the prison population by contrast with their divergence in the population at large.

In practice, however, there are limitations. Thus, for meaningful analyses, all prisoners must be disaggregated by gender. Minority prisoners must further be divided into the different ethnic groups and, if possible, comparisons with whites should be limited to those normally resident in the UK. Disaggregation by gender effectively restricts comparisons to males since the number of female prisoners is too small for inter-ethnic comparisons on most questions, especially when – as a crude device for restricting comparisons to UK residents – all those who said that they had recently arrived in the country before imprisonment were eliminated from the analysis. Even for male prisoners, the resulting numbers are relatively modest and have required re-aggregation of the Indian, Pakistani and Bangladeshi prisoners[5] into a single 'Indian Subcontinent' (South Asian) category which – for the reasons cited earlier – is less than ideal.

The sample used in the analyses which follow, therefore, comprises only male sentenced prisoners, excluding those who had recently arrived in the country. It is made up of 2404 whites, 184 Black Caribbeans and 86 South Asians. Because of small numbers, we have resisted the temptation to include the 62 Africans and the 49 'Black Others' (although the latter might arguably have been combined with the Black Caribbeans); nor is any reference made to the remaining 100 prisoners who comprised in order of magnitude: 'Others'; those whose ethnicity was not recorded; and 'Other Asians'. The discussion focuses only on the part of the survey data which allows us to make inter-ethnic comparisons of the key economic and social characteristics of this group. Table 7.6 summarizes the economic characteristics (including educational factors which may be thought of as related) and Table 7.7 the social characteristics.

In comparing the profiles of the different groups, however, two important differences must be borne in mind. One is that although we have tried to confine the sample to prisoners who are likely normally to be resident in Britain, a significant number of minority ethnic prisoners were born abroad. This is particularly true of our Asian sample where the proportion was 65 per cent – over twice the rate for the Black Caribbean group (30 per cent)[6]. (Only 3 per cent of the white sample was born outside the UK or Eire.) The second is that the age range in the samples differed. Although well over half of white and Black Caribbean prisoners were under 30 years old, 17 per cent of whites were aged 40 or more, compared with 7 per cent (15) of the Black Caribbean sample. The Asians again differed markedly, with 22 per cent (19) over 40 and slightly less than half under 30.

Table 7.6 suggests that, in terms of their economic characteristics, many of the ethnic differences found in the population at large have diminished, disappeared or in some instances reversed in the prison population. There are no significant differences in the extent to which white, Black Caribbean and Asian prisoners were in paid work immediately before coming into prison or were unemployed. Both minority groups had left school later than whites and were overall as likely to hold one of the three basic school leaving qualifications (CSE, 'O' level or GCSE).

Some of the differences in the domestic circumstances of the three ethnic groups immediately before entering prison appear to reflect variations in the population at large. The Black Caribbean group were most likely to have been single (although whites were at least as likely to have been living alone before coming into prison). The Asians were most likely

Table 7.6   Economic and educational characteristics of male prisoners by ethnic group

	White	*Black Caribbean*	*Asian*
Employment prior to imprisonment			
In paid job	55	57	63
Unemployed (and seeking work)	23	26	22
Total unemployed	31	35	27
Education			
Left school after age 16	6	11	19
CSEs	20	31	34
'O' levels	18	15	19
GCSEs	6	9	7

to have been married and, although they were no more likely to *have* children, a much higher proportion were living with them.

Of particular interest, though, is the light thrown by these data on the earlier experiences of the sample – those which may be thought of as formative and, in that sense, influential on the development of their criminal careers. The broader patterns shown by the Census are reflected in the much higher proportion of Black Caribbeans who grew up with only one parent and the very marked contrast with the Asian group. However, the black group were no more likely than whites to have spent part of their childhood in care; and both they and the Asian group were much less likely than whites to have been persistent truants from school.

Data from the questions on criminality in respondents' families need to be interpreted with caution for two reasons. One is the proportion of ethnic minority prisoners whose parents, at least, may live elsewhere in the world or may have done so at the age when criminal convictions are

Table 7.7   Social and family characteristics of prisoners by ethnic group

	White	Black Caribbean	Asian
Marital status before prison			
Married	19	8	52
Cohabiting	31	42	11
Single	39	46	30
Children			
Has children	52	60	56
Living with children before prison (as % of those with children)	64	60	83
Own childhood			
Lived with one parent at some time	29	43	8
Mostly with one parent	16	30	7
At some time in care	27	28	7
Mostly truanted from school	32	17	12
Criminal involvement of other family members (where known)			
Parent(s) with criminal conviction(s)	17	6	2
Sibling(s) with criminal conviction(s)	33	30	14
Parent(s) ever imprisoned	12	4	2
Sibling(s) ever imprisoned	26	25	13

most likely. It cannot be assumed that the term 'convicted of a criminal offence' means the same – whether in strictly legal terms or in the minds of respondents – as it would if they had been resident in the UK. The second consideration is the higher proportion of Black Caribbeans brought up mainly with one parent and who, for that simple reason, may not be as fully informed about criminality in that generation as are whites or Asians. It is, none the less, striking that comparable proportions of whites and Black Caribbeans have siblings who have criminal records and who have been imprisoned, although the figures for Black Caribbean parents are very significantly lower. (The figures for Asians are very much lower both for parents and for siblings; but the combined considerations of the proportions born abroad, the difference in their age profile and the relatively small numbers involved suggest that even greater caution should be exercised in drawing inferences from them.)

SUMMARY AND DISCUSSION

The data assembled here make for a more refined understandings of the scale and nature of minority ethnic over-representation in British prisons. Certainly, they highlight the importance of distinguishing within ethnic groups between members of British ethnic minorities and the proportion – which is very substantial in the case of women – who are not normally resident in Britain at all. They confirm that, even if allowance is made for this, the over-representation of black ethnic minorities is very marked by comparison with their presence in the general population. But they indicate that there is no effective difference in the proportion of black British male and female prisoners; and they point to a degree of over-representation of Pakistanis within the 'Asian' group which had largely gone unremarked previously.

In terms of the wider debate about 'race' and crime, the evidence assembled here appears to add weight to the socio-economic explanations. But this is not to say that the other two explanations may not also play a role and, in this concluding section, we draw out some of the wider implications of these findings. For the most part, comparisons are confined to the black and white groups in view of the relatively small numbers in the Asian group (which preclude the necessary disaggregation) and the high percentage of these who were born abroad.

Although some important differences remain, there is a significant covergence in the social and economic characteristics of the black and white samples of male prisoners relative to the population at large. This should come as no surprise since the information available on those caught up in the criminal justice process has long suggested a correlation between certain economic and social characteristics and involvement in crime. Superficially, however, this evidence of ethnic convergence from the NPS might be adduced to undermine the 'discrimination' argument. The contention of this chapter is that the socio-economic versus discrimination debate rests on – if not a false – at least a strongly overstated dichotemization which is only sustainable on the basis of a very crude understanding of both discrimination and the links between crime and socio-economic factors.

In the UK, a number of studies covering aspects of the criminal justice process have tried to collect information on a full range of respondents' characteristics – from the demographic, social and economic (including ethnicity) to relevant legal factors (such as offence, plea, previous convictions, mode of trial, etc.). Some studies have been methodologically flawed and many have been limited by very small sample sizes. However, when analyzed with statistical rigour, the largest and fullest of the data sets have tended to show that *prima facie* ethnic differences often diminish markedly once all other relevant factors are taken into account.

By far the most important of these studies is that undertaken in 1989 by Roger Hood (1992) of decisions taken at the point of sentencing in cases which had reached the Crown Court at five centres in the West Midlands.[7] Broadly, this found that among a proportion of black defendants appearing before the court, the rate at which those found guilty received custodial sentences and the length of those sentences was higher than it was for whites. Although on the basis of this study Hood estimates that about 80 per cent of black over-representation in prisons is due to the proportion appearing at the Crown Court and the nature and circumstances of their offences, he explicitly recognizes the questions which remain about the factors which have produced this situation. He acknowledges (and, indeed, produces evidence which suggests) the possibility of discrimination at earlier stages in the criminal justice process; but much of the significance of the study lies in its ability to demonstrate how apparently 'race neutral' factors may have contributed to ethnically different outcomes and the questions which this raises, in turn, about indirect discrimination. This aspect of the study and some of its implications are discussed more fully elsewhere (FitzGerald 1993b). However, a good example which is worth citing here concerns Hood's findings on the bail decision.

Hood confirms other studies in showing that whether the defendant has been remanded in custody is itself an important factor in explaining ethnic differences at the sentencing stage. What is of particular interest, though, is that he also identifies the reasons for ethnic differences at this critical earlier stage. Important among these is the fact that black defendants are more likely than whites to be remanded in custody simply because they are more likely than whites to be unemployed. Yet, even when all the relevant social and legal factors are taken into account, the rate at which black defendants appear for sentencing from custody is much higher than for whites.

So the factors which drive up the remand rate for black defendants go beyond their offending histories and the characteristics of the offences with which they are charged: they appear to include elements of both direct and indirect discrimination. What is particularly striking is that the amount of unexplained difference in the bail/remand decision was at least twice as large as the difference found at the point of sentencing. That is, there is a strong inference of discrimination in the decision to bail or remand. Yet this decision is one of the apparently 'race neutral' or strictly legal factors which 'explains' ethnic disparities at the sentencing stage, minimizing any possible inference of discrimination at this point.

Certainly Hood and the cumulative evidence of other UK studies provide empirical support for the arguments of a number of more theoretical commentators who have highlighted the need for more sophisticated understandings of the process at work. Robert Reiner, for example, refers to the 'Holy Grail ... of pure racism' (Reiner, 1992), while Tony Jefferson captures the problem thus:

> ... the currently dominant approach to investigating ethnicity and criminalization centred on attempting to uncover by ever more sophisticated techniques the purely 'racial' dimension is a bit like sieving flour with ever finer meshes: eventually there is too little getting through to enable anything to be made ... or ... to construct a very meaningful account. (Jefferson, 1993: 39)

Understood in these terms, the clear link between the skewed socioeconomic profile of certain minority ethnic groups and their involvement in the criminal justice process serves also to illuminate the nature of the correlation between social and economic factors and crime. A crude understanding of this correlation is unwarrantedly deterministic for two main reasons. The first is that the particular social and economic factors which have been shown to be most strongly correlated with offending do not *de facto* create criminals: only a small minority of young men who are unemployed and come from single-parent families become involved in crime, get caught, convicted and go on to re-offend (and get caught, etc.). The second is that a very simplistic association between social and economic factors with offending *as such* obscures the impact of these factors at key stages of the criminal justice process. This process (see Figure 8.1) may be conceived of as a series of filters at each of which those who actually commit offences of any type may be filtered out or drawn in more deeply. A range of studies of self-reported offending (see Bowling 1990, for an overview) indicate that the profile of those who have at any time been involved in an activity which could – if reported, be detected and prosecuted – have brought them into this process approximates more closely to the population at large than is suggested by studies of 'at risk' groups or those already caught up in the process.

That is, the criminal justice process itself may strongly compound the effects of particular social and economic factors in ways which have not been fully explored. Some of these ways, however, have already been illustrated by the studies of ethnic minorities in the criminal justice system. Reference has already been made to Hood's findings in respect of the bail decision; and other studies have shown, for example, the adverse effect of coming from a single-parent family on the likelihood of being filtered out of the process by receiving a caution. Patchy as the UK literature may be relative to the body of statistics and research findings generated in the USA over a much longer period, it is beginning to suggest that, cumulatively, decisions made on apparently social and economic grounds at any single point in the process may have a significant differential *ethnic* impact.

In this sense, the findings of socio-economic convergence here do not so much call into question the argument that there may be discrimination against ethnic minorities. Rather, they bring to mind again Elizabeth Burney's classic description of ethnic minorities as 'the barium meal' in the system (Burney, 1967). Yet there is a danger of forgetting that, while such factors adversely affect a larger *proportion* of particular minority groups, the absolute *numbers* of people in the majority population who share the same disadvantages is very much larger.

This may seem a purely academic point, or one which is calculated to play down concerns about minorities' collectively worse experience of the system. In the context of increasing international interest in these issues, however – and in particular in view of the pitfalls of comparisons – it is essential to view ethnic differences in this broader framework. For there is an obvious danger (of which there are already numerous examples) that unthinking parallels will be drawn between official crime statistics comparing *black* groups with the majority population in different countries. The main frame of reference here is the US literature but this tendency seems likely now to extend to comparisons with other European

155

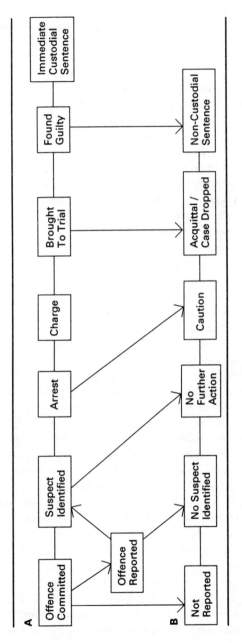

Figure 7.1 Criminal justice process from offence to imprisonment

countries (such as Holland, France and Italy). Such comparisons fail to recognize important differences in the provenance, culture(s) and size of the groups in question – to say nothing of their social, political and migration histories or of national differences in the social and political contexts in which they are identified as being (or having) a problem in relation to the criminal justice system. Such comparisons also tend to ignore the fact that 'problem' minorities identified in several other countries are not black. (Indeed, French discourse is at least as likely to problematize North Africans in terms of religion rather than colour and to bracket them – as 'Muslims' – with Turks in Germany.)

The logical inference of such comparisons based on phenotypical similarities is a determinism more sinister than the socio-economic determinism referred to previously, for it has connotations of biological racism. It is only by understanding what *else* these – and other minorities – have in common that we can avoid this danger and, at the same time, develop a more realistic understanding of the international phenomenon of ethnic differences in crime statistics.

In conclusion, therefore, this chapter has sketched the outline of an approach to interpreting such ethnic differences. The aims of such an approach would be three-fold and inter-related: First, it should allow for all three lines of explanation referred to in the introduction and to improve understandings of how each operates and of the balance and interactions between them. Secondly, it should avoid some of the pitfalls of the American approach to 'racial disproportionality'. This approach, in essence, has tended to suggest that ethnic differences in official data simply reflect actual ethnic differences in rates and patterns of offending, but that these differences do not themselves call for further explanation. (For a flavour of this approach and a recent overview of the literature see Blumstein, 1993, and Tonry, 1994). Finally, to provide a framework within which policymakers and criminal justice practitioners can reflect on the extent to which existing policies and practice may intensify or reduce apparently ethnic differences in crime statistics – both directly and indirectly. In discussing the model, brief reference is made as relevant to both the UK studies and the American 'racial disproportionality' literature.

The findings described in previous sections of this paper strongly suggest that the first line of an approach to interpreting ethnic differences in criminal statistics must be to examine the socio-economic characteristics of the groups in question relative to the majority population and to each other. Inferences of possible differential criminality and/or discrimination can adequately be explored only once like is being compared with like – that is after account has been taken of all relevant factors other than ethnicity. In practice, the available criminal justice data are rarely sufficiently comprehensive to be analyzed in this way. However, with adequate ethnic data on the population at large (such as are now available from the British Census), it should be possible to model expected levels for different groups.

The American literature – despite the richness of the available ethnic data – appears to be particularly negligent in this regard. Blumstein, for example, concedes that the incarceration of blacks may also be due to factors outside the criminal justice system and continues:

> These other factors could well include racial discrimination in many other aspects of black people's lives, but must also include the many factors that contribute to the limited opportunities available to them in the American economy and society. (Blumstein, 1993: 759)

However, the implications of this caveat are not followed through in the way suggested above. The impression which remains is one of black criminality *per se* and that, even if the reasons for this are complex, they are not directly relevant to the analysis and are, in any case, somehow peculiar to black people.

The second stage of the approach to analyzing ethnic differences in criminal statistics is then to explore the potential for both direct and indirect discrimination in the criminal justice process. The proportion of offences committed which are reported in the first place and/or which lead to detection, arrest and successful prosecution is very small. Certainly there is considerable scope for differential outcomes for different groups at each stage of the process illustrated in Figure 7.1. The UK evidence is relatively scarce on the critical question of whether offences committed by certain minorities are more likely to be reported, although on balance this seems probable (see FitzGerald and Hale, forthcoming). However, the results of a recent UK study of self-reported offending among young people (Bowling, Graham and Ross 1994) do not reflect the ethnic differences documented in initial contact and subsequent processing by the criminal justice system.

Importantly, this gap between self-reported offending and subsequent ethnic differences is confirmed not only in parallel studies in other European countries (Junger-Tas *et al.*, 1994) but in earlier US studies (see for example, Hindelang, 1978). The 'racial disproportionality' literature, however, tends to play down the findings of self-report studies and, instead, to attach greater weight to victims' descriptions of offenders without fully acknowledging two major limitations which, in turn, attach to these. The first is the question of accuracy of victim recall (to say nothing of suggestibility) and the other is that – whether reliably or not – a large proportion of victims of crime will not be able to say anything about the offender involved. Indeed, it was for these reasons that the Metropolitan police decided several years ago to cease collating this information for statistical purposes.

There is further evidence (most recently confirmed by Hood) that black people may disproportionately be brought into the criminal justice system as a result of proactive policing. Once in the system, reference has also been made to the ways in which the socio-economic factors which influence decisions may filter certain groups more inexorably into the process which can lead ultimately to imprisonment. But attention should also be paid to the potentially significant effects of the exercise of discretion. To varying degrees, discretion may – quite legitimately – influence, for example: decisions to stop, to arrest and to prosecute; the offence charged; the bail decision; the court of trial; and the type and severity of the sentence, including the length of custody. One telling illustration of the way in which this may affect black defendants is in Hood's finding that the disparity in length of custody was much more marked for offences in the middle range of seriousness which *de facto* allow much more scope for the exercise of discretion. Similarly his apparently anomalous finding of no significant inter-ethnic difference in sentence length for younger men appears to be explained by the relatively lower scope for the exercise of discretion in sentencing juveniles and young offenders.

Although the American studies referred to place considerable emphasis on the overall correlation between ethnically-based arrest data (which are not nationally available in Britain) and the prison figures, two further points are worth drawing out here. One is that they imply the possibility of proactive policing. Blumstein, in something of a throwaway line, concedes:

> We know that there are important racial disparities in arrest for minor crimes ... because of police patrol practises ... and that there are disparities also in general patterns in the exercise of police discretion to arrest.   (1993: 748)

And in relation to drugs offences, Tonry explicitly states:

> ...both the national policy decision to launch a war on drugs and local police decisions to focus on street trafficking foreseeably increased black arrests, prosecutions, convictions and incarcerations.   (1994: 108)

This almost echoes Hood who comments:

Black offenders [in his sample] were also disproportionately involved in the supply of drugs, usually cannabis, and *these convictions regularly arose from police activity rather than from a complaint by citizens* ... [I]t is incontrovertible that the continued legal proscription of cannabis and the insistence that trading in it, even on a small ... scale, is an offence which should always be committed to the Crown Court for trial, is a substantial factor influencing the number of black persons in the prison population. (1992: 180–1; emphasis added)

But secondly, the correspondence found by Blumstein between arrest and imprisonment is 'almost identical' for murder and robbery, both of which, as very serious offences, do not allow much scope for discretion. However:

For the less serious crime types, the fraction of blacks actually in prison tends to be larger than the fraction of blacks at arrest. For these crimes, there is more scope for discretion at the various stages of decision-making within the criminal justice system ... *Of course, the room for discretion also offers the opportunity for the introduction of racial discrimination.* (Blumstein, 1993: 746; emphasis added)

This tends to support the contention of Jefferson and Reiner cited earlier. It does not preclude the possibility of direct discrimination – and Hood strongly points to a margin of about seven percentage points of unexplained difference which can only be explained in this way; but it suggests both that such discrimination may not always be conscious and that it may occur within the bounds of legitimate decision-making.

A final point to make in terms of differential decision-making within the criminal justice system is the problems of inference from large-scale aggregated data. For there are marked variations in decision-making within the system as between both areas and individuals. Thus Hood found no *systematic* bias across the decisions he studied: the majority of cases were tried at one of the five centres and appeared to be treated equitably. By the same token, however, average differences across all the cases necessarily muted marked differences in one or two centres and by a minority of sentencers. Again, this point is not explicitly acknowledged in the American literature referred to here. The possibility is implicit in Blumstein's reference to considerable state-specific differences, but is not pursued. Instead, he chooses tentatively to explore explanations for this variation based on general differences in state sentencing policies or in hypothetical differences between the blacks in question (including, on the one hand, differences in 'compliance and socialization into local mores' and 'aggressiveness and weaker local roots' on the other).

Neither an approach to understanding ethnic differences in crime statistics based on socio-economic considerations nor the potential for discrimination within the criminal justice process precludes a third source of explanation in different levels and patterns of offending by different groups, that is offending rates over and above those which may directly be explained by their socio-economic characteristics. For different groups may react differently to apparently similar circumstances and may collectively respond differently to similar experiences. The factors which influence their processes of adaptation to the norms and expectations of wider society and to the attitudes and behaviour towards them of elements in that society may vary (individually and in their configuration) from one group to another and may include factors which are locally and historically specific. One striking finding of the considerable literature which documents the process of ethnic adaptation in its widest sense is that different strategies may be pursued by the same groups in different circumstances (see, for example, Yinger, 1986). But important ethnographic studies have also documented the differences in criminal involvement of men from apparently similar socio-economic backgrounds in different ethnic communities and have offered insights into the reasons for these (see, for example, Sullivan, 1989).

That is, subcultural theory may have a lot to offer in this area *but it is not the place to start*. Certainly, in terms of public policy, there are many important questions to be addressed in the first two areas. Inasmuch as explanations for differential criminal involvement are related to the structural position of different ethnic groups, they will raise questions about race relations, anti-discrimination and equal opportunity policies, as well as the impact on different groups of economic and social policies more generally. Inasmuch as they relate to the operation of the criminal justice system, they raise three main questions about the process of decision-making. These concern the influence of socio-economic factors, the amount of variation, and the latitude for discretion.

Only when these questions are satisfactorily answered and their implications for the development of policy and practice understood is it appropriate to turn the searchlight on to ethnic-specific explanations for any remaining differences. The approach which is taken to inter-group differences is likely to prove very illuminating if it recognizes diversity between and within groups and if it avoids reification – that is, if it treats ethnicity as an ongoing process rather than a fixed quality. If it does not, it will fall into labelling. And if it does that, its effect on the development of policy and practice may be to compound existing problems rather than to offer any hope of their solution.

Notes

1. Since April 1993 all police forces have been required to record the ethnic origin of those they stop and search.
2. The use of the term 'race' has no biological significance except inasmuch as the groups referred to in this discussion are visibly different primarily in terms of skin colour. Rather it reflects social, academic and legal usage to describe groups who because of these visible differences may popularly be thought of as inherently different and may be treated differently on the basis of these perceptions.
3. Comparisons are made here only between the white, black and South Asian groups because the other categories are too heterogeneous to be meaningful for the purposes of discussion.
4. Nationality can be acquired in a variety of ways. The most important is by birth in the UK, although many of the post-war immigrant generation held British citizenship under the 1948 Nationality Act (whose provisions obtained until the new Act of 1981). Non-citizens who have formally been accepted for settlement in the UK may either acquire British nationality through the process of naturalization or they may remain resident (and be counted in surveys and Censuses as part of the population) while retaining their original nationality
5. Within the South Asian group, Indians accounted for 39.5 per cent, Pakistanis 55.8 per cent and Bangladeshis the remaining 4.7 per cent.
6. According to the 1991 Census, 42 per cent of Black Caribbeans were born outside the UK, compared with 58 per cent of the population of Indian origin, 49 per cent of Pakistanis and 63 per cent of Bangladeshis.
7. The study covered all 889 black and all 536 Asian males sentenced at these five Crown Court centres in the year, along with a matched sample of 1,443 whites and conducted a parallel analysis of the much smaller numbers of cases involving women. No significant ethnic differences were found in the latter.

References

Blumstein, A. (1993) 'Racial Disproportionality of U.S. Prison Populations Revisited', in *University of Colorado Law Review,* vol. 64. 743–60.

Bowling, B (1990) 'Conceptual and Methodological Problems in Measuring "Race" Differences in Delinquency', in *British Journal of Criminology,* vol. 30, no. 4. 483–92.

Bowling, B.; Graham, J.; and Ross, A. (1994) 'Self-Reported Offending Among 14–21-year-olds in England and Wales', in J. Junger-Tas, G. J. Terlouw and M. Klein (eds), *Delinquent Behaviour Among Young People in the Western World: First Results of the International Self-Report Delinquency Study* (Amsterdam: Kluger).

Burney, E. (1967) *Housing on Trial: A Study of Immigrants and Local Government* (Oxford University Press).

Chigwada, R. (1989) 'The Criminalization and Imprisonment of Black Women', in *Probation Journal* (September): 101–5.

FitzGerald, M. (1993a) *Ethnic Minorities and the Criminal Justice System*, in Research Study No. 20, the Royal Commission on Criminal Justice (London: HMSO).

FitzGerald, M. (1993b) 'Racial Discrimination in the Criminal Justice System', in *Research Bulletin No. 34* (London: Home Office Research and Statistics Department).

Hindelang, M. (1978) 'Race and Involvement in Common Law Personal Crimes', in *American Sociological Review*, vol. 43: 93–109.

Home Office (1986) *The Ethnic Origins of Prisoners: The Prison Population on 30 June 1985 and Persons Received, July 1984–March 1985*, Home Office Statistical Bulletin 17/86.

Home Office (1994) *The Ethnic Origins of Prisoners*, Home Office Statistical Bulletin 21/94.

Hood, R. (1992) *Race and Sentencing* (Oxford: Clarendon Press).

Jefferson, T. (1988) 'Race, crime and Policing', in *International Journal of the Sociology of Law*, No. 16: 521–39.

Jefferson, T. (1993) 'The Racism of Criminalization: Policing and the Reproduction of the Criminal Other', in L. Gelsthorpe (ed.), *Minority Ethnic Groups in the Criminal Justice System* (Cambridge: Institute of Criminology).

Junger-Tas, J, Terlouw, G. J. and Klein, M. (1994) Delinquent Behaviour Among Young People in the Western World: First Results of The International Self Report Delinquency Study (Kluger: Amsterdam).

Reiner, R. (1989) 'Race and Criminal Justice', in *New Community*, vol. 16, no. 1: 5–21.

Reiner, R. (1992) 'Race, Crime and Justice: Models of Interpretation'. Paper presented at the Cropwood Conference on Minority Ethnic Groups in the Criminal Justice System (Cambridge).

Ritchey Mann, C. (1989) 'Minority and Female: A Criminal Justice Double Bind', in *Social Justice*, vol. 16, no. 4: 95–112.

Smith, D. (1993) 'Race, Crime and Criminal Justice', in M. Maguire, R. Morgan and R. Reiner, *The Oxford Handbook of Criminology* (Oxford University Press).

Sullivan M. (1989) *'Getting paid': Youth, Crime and Work in the Inner City*, (Ithaca and London: Cornell University Press).

Tonry, M. (1994) 'Racial Disproportion in U.S. prisons', in *British Journal of Criminology*, vol. 34, Special Issue: 97–115.

Walmsley, R.; Howard, L.; and White, S. (1992) *The National Prison Survey 1991: Main Findings*, Home Office Research Study No. 128 (London: HMSO).

Yinger, M. (1986) Intersecting strands in the thoerisation of race and ethnic relations in J. Rex and D. Mason (eds), *Theories of Race and Race Relations* (Cambridge University Press).

status, sex, age, health and the criminal history of the inmates kept in each of them: i) general (a and b type), ii) special and iii) therapeutic custodial institutions. Prison statistics adopt their own terminology dividing prisons in: i) restorative (14 institutions), ii) correctional closed (6 institutions) and rural (3 institutions), iii) therapeutic and detention (3 institutions) and iv) juvenile correctional (2 institutions). Moreover, there exists three juvenile educational institutions.

Almost all Greek prisons are custodial institutions receiving all kinds of inmates. Segregation of specific groups is exceptional and there are no special maximum security facilities, although certain prison regimes or units are more strict and severe than others. There are no special facilities for drug addicts either. A significant number of these prisoners are kept in the same institution with the mentally ill in a 'mental health centre'. Furthermore, in practically all institutions accommodation is inadequate, and sanitation and exercise facilities are rudimentary. The same is also true of medical care. The prison system seems to adopt a self-sufficiency model for health services. Nevertheless, prison administrators applying the Greek Code of Basic Rules for the Treatment of Detainees resort to local hospitals, or to visiting doctors for their support and services (Koulouris, 1990).

According to (unpublished) prison administrators' annual reports, most problems are attributed to overcrowding and the lack of resources. It is pointed out that living conditions are degrading, while most buildings are old and decaying. The number of custodial, medical and welfare personnel is insufficient, the quality and quantity of food is inadequate and order and security are fragile. The construction of new prisons, as well as the expansion of existing facilities, an increase of personnel, and the modernization of security measures are some of the proposed remedies which have been suggested in recent reports and which are gradually materializing.

In the relevant literature it is suggested that, besides legislative amendments, pre-trial detention is over-used with between one third and one half of the total prison population made up of pre-trial detainees. According to impressionistic estimates, emerging from court practices and journalists' reports parole appears to be generally under-used, while drug-related crimes are held to contribute significantly to the increase in the prison population (the proportion of persons imprisoned for drug-related crimes climbed from 19.4 per cent in 1980 to 31 per cent in 1990) (Courakis, 1991; Paroskevopoulos, 1991; Grivas, 1991).

It is also widely known that there are two safety valves operating at the 'front end' of the prison system which keep the proportion of convicted persons who end up in prison relatively low (see Table 8.1). The first is the conversion of custodial sentences to pecuniary ones in cases where the period of imprisonment is less than two years. The second is the suspension of custodial sentences which are longer than two and up to three years. Other alternatives to imprisonment (probation, community service) have also been introduced, but their implementation has been delayed, mostly due to financial restrictions.

In addition there are some qualitative changes which should be noted. Research which was carried out in a male prison in 1990 in Athens, called Korydallos, revealed that drug offenders were the largest group (32 per cent), then came property offenders (30 per cent), followed by homicide – attempted or actual – (17 per cent). A considerable number of detainees were convicted for white collar or economic crime: embezzlement, fraud, violations of the law involving cheque fraud and forgery (26 per cent) (unpublished).

Among those detained pending trial, the frequency of violations of drug laws was even higher, while a few were detained for rape, and for sexual abuse of adults or minors. Furthermore, the percentage of foreigners detained in this particular prison was approximately 16 per cent. By mid-1993 this had increased to 17.7 per cent. Nationally, in 1983 the proportion of foreigners stood at 11.6 per cent. By 1993, it had risen to 22.7 per cent of the total prison population (Figure 8.1). The rate of growth in the Greek prisons over this period involved a 13.5 per cent increase for men, and 52.8 per cent increase in the number of women. Significantly, this

Table 8.1 Crimes, convictions and the prison population in Greece, 1985–92

Year	Crimes committed (police statistics)	Convicted persons (court statistics)	Prisoners (prison statistics)	Detainees awaiting trial
1985	291 335	108 011	6198	2916
1986	294 300	123 958	6420	3398
1987	303 182	140 403	6970	3566
1988	311 179	132 925	6921	3501
1989	287 177	108 983	6748	4015
1990	330 803	109 190	7588	4247
1991	358 998	112 203	7992	4603
1992	379 652	107 564	8649	5593

involved a 0.1 per cent increase in the proportion of Greek nationals and a 126.2 per cent increase in the number of foreigners.

The general and unprecedented increase in the number of foreigners imprisoned undoubtedly aggravated the existing level of prison overcrowding. The occupancy rate increased from 106.9 per cent on 1 September 1987 (3803 prisoners to 3558 prison places), to 181.24 per cent in late 1993 (7054 prisoners to 3892 prison places). Anyway, it is feared that prison overcrowding and the changing ethnic mix threatens to undermine human rights in prison. Clearly, being a detainee and a foreigner is an unfortunate combination (Spinellis, 1993).

A closer look at the non-indigenous prison population reveals at least two things. First, that the statistics which are generally available from the Ministry of Justice are insufficient to comprehend fully this new dimension of the problem. Thus, our research involved the construction of tables and at our suggestion the Ministry of Justice requested that the administrators of all Greek prisons fill in these tables every two months. Secondly, from the responses which we received, it was evident that the number of foreigners held in all but one Greek prison (Alikarnassos) in May 1993 was 1544. This constituted almost a quarter of the total prison population.

Of the 1544 foreign prisoners detained in Greek prisons at that time, 977 had been convicted and 567 were awaiting trial. Of the convicted population, drug-related cases were the most common, followed by crimes against property, as Figure 8.2 indicates.

Of the 567 detainees awaiting trial, 341 are charged with property crimes. Almost 20 per cent of cases involved drug trafficking and the

Figure 8.1   Change in the proportion of foreign prisoners in Greece 1983–93

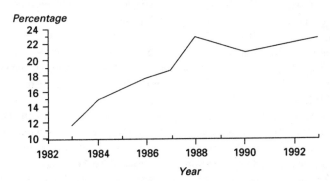

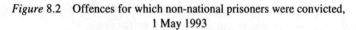

Figure 8.2   Offences for which non-national prisoners were convicted,
1 May 1993

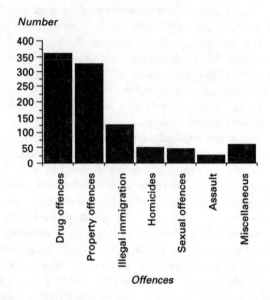

remainder were charged with various offences ranging from homicide to sexual offences (see Figure 8.2).

The 1544 foreign detainees were drawn from 81 countries. The majority came from Albania, but as Table 8.2 indicates a considerable number also came from Turkey and Romania.

The prisons with the largest number of foreign prisoners were those located in Athens. The male prison Korydallos held 246 foreign prisoners, while Larissa held 215, Patras 200 and Thessaloniki 114.

The level of over-representation of certain foreign groups in Greek prisons should be assessed with caution. Note, for example, that more Albanians enter Greece than nationals from other countries. Albanians in particular appear more visible and more vulnerable, since there is a high level of illegal immigration by this group.

A two-fold problem of eligibility emerges at this point. A considerable proportion of illegal immigrants are charged and convicted on exclusively administrative grounds. Others are incarcerated for property crimes which are often committed under the pressures created by their illegal status. We therefore suggest that for some, their presence in Greek prisons is problematic particularly in terms of their offences. The disproportionate rate of imprisonment of foreigners in Greek prisons raises critical issues about

Figure 8.3 Offences with which remand prisoners were charged, June 1993

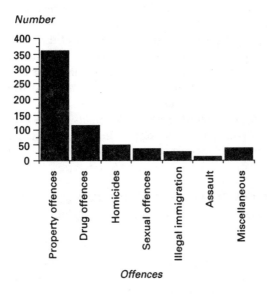

Table 8.2 Country of origin of non-national prisoners detained in Greek prisons, as of 1 May 1993

Country	Number	Country	Number	Country	Number
Albania	489	Poland	44	Italy	28
Turkey	134	Syria	43	Bulgaria	26
Romania	116	Lebanon	38	India	25
Former		Iraq	38	Iran	21
USSR	67	Ex-Yugoslavia	37	Other	340
Tanzania	64	Germany	34	Total	1544

the underlying rationality and humanity of the criminal justice system and also about its possible discriminatory and racist nature (Sim, 1993; Blagg and Smith, 1989).

The increasing levels of mobility throughout Europe has resulted in growing numbers of working-class and marginalized people coming into contact with the Greek criminal justice system. Thus the growth of foreign nationals in Greek prisons can be seen to be the result of a number of factors, most aggravating of which seem to be property and drug offences.

In conclusion, it may be pointed out that it is possible, to detect a new generation of detainees belonging to various ethnic groups, and some of these are more at risk for violation of their fundamental human rights than others. Theoretically, foreign detainees can be placed on a continuum representing the degree of potential violations of their human rights. At one extreme there are nationals of traditional western countries (Europeans, Americans, Canadians and Australians) and at the other extreme nationals from ex-socialist regimes, the Middle East and the Third World.

Currently, there are a number of measures which are available and which have been designed to protect the rights of non-national prisoners not only in Greece but in the rest of Europe as well. These measures operate in direct and indirect ways and involve four levels of protection.

THE FOUR LEVELS OF PROTECTION OF DETAINEES' HUMAN RIGHTS IN GREECE: THE LAW IN THE BOOKS

The history of sanctions can be divided into five identifiable periods or 'generations'. According to the Dutch penologist Tak (1992), deprivation of liberty belongs to the second generation of sanctions. The death penalty, corporal punishment, forced labour and being sentenced to the galleys constitute the first generation. Suspension of sentence, probation and fines, especially as alternatives to short-term imprisonment, constitute the third. The fourth generation of sanctions is associated with community-based penalties, especially community service, victim–offender mediation, compensation orders and the like. Monitoring, and the restriction of liberty by means of electronic devices can be seen as representing a fifth generation.

It was only during the 1960s that the second generation of sanctions – imprisonment – was related to the legal discourse on human rights. In the landmark decision of Koch vs. FRG, the European Court of Human Rights held that imprisonment for a crime does not deny a detainee the guarantee of the rights and freedoms defined in the Convention. Taking into consideration the emergence of a new generation of detainees and the acute overcrowding in Greek prisons the crucial question that we must address is: To what extent does the existing legal framework in Greece guarantee the protection of human rights of detainees in general, and of non-nationals in particular?

In theory, a 'shield' with various layers of protective legislative provisions covers those detained in Greek custodial institutions. The first outer layer comprises provisions of the Greek Constitution (GC) which refers to the human rights of i) Greeks and ii) any person living within the Greek territory. Needless to say, the most fundamental right of every human being, is the respect of his/her dignity (art. 2, par. 1 and art. 5, par. 1 of the GC).

The second layer of protection is provided by the European Convention of Human Rights (ECHR) and its First, Fourth, Sixth, Seventh and Eighth Protocols which Greece has signed and/or ratified. According to art. 28, par. 1 of the GC all ratified international norms constitute an integral part of domestic Greek law, prevailing over any contrary provision of laws (other than the GC). The European Convention of Human Rights and the Greek Constitution are, however, silent on the rights of detainees. Yet, the European Court of Human Rights, as pointed out, guarantees the application of rights to detained individuals as well.

The third and more direct layer protecting persons serving custodial sanctions is formed by the Greek Prison Rules or the so-called 'Code of Basic Rules for the Treatment of Detainees' (CBRTD). This Code, enacted in 1989, became effective on 1 January 1990, and contains fifteen chapters, 123 articles and aims to safeguard the human dignity of detained persons on the one hand, and maintain the orderly functioning of custodial institutions on the other, by regulating the rights and duties of both the detainees and the prison staff. However, the enforcement of certain provisions of this Code (for example, those providing for semi-detention facilities, or for adequately remunerated prison work and with social security) were suspended until the end of 1994 by subsequent laws (most recently Law 2041/1992, art. 12) due to lack of economic resources. Detainees in Greece under the prevailing legislative norms thus enjoy three sets of rights, stemming from the Greek Constitution, the European Court of Human Rights and the Code of Basic Rules for the Treatment of Detainees.

A closer look at the protected human rights by the CBRTD reveals the adherence to the view of Constitutional Law theorists according to which persons deprived of their liberty upon a lawful sanction during the execution of their sentence enjoy all human rights except that of personal liberty.

The basic detainees' rights are safeguarded by Article 5 of the CBRTD. This grants the right to make written or oral complaints to the prison administration and the Ministry of Justice first and then to the (never-established) Court of Execution of Sentences. The right to communicate in writing with any public authority and the prison administration is coupled with the corresponding duty to expedite the communication without delay and without inspecting its content. There is also a right to satisfy the prisoners' religious needs and customs.

Furthermore, prisoners have the right to be represented by counsel in disciplinary hearings. In Greek prisons, in principle, there are no prohibitions against receiving books, newspapers or food from home. However, it is within the discretion of the prison administration to impose restrictions on such kinds of external, informal support. Prisoners are allowed to buy food and other goods from the prison canteen. Detained persons may also be visited under certain circumstances by a physician or a psychiatrist of their choice. Finally, the GC and the Greek Code of Penal Procedure give detainees the right to compensation in the case of unlawful detention. This right is, however, exercised rarely and has only been upheld once in the post-war period.

The final and most recent form of protection relates to the European Convention for the Prevention of Torture and Inhuman and Degrading Treatment or Punishment signed and ratified by Greece in 1991 (Law 1949/1991). Among others, the so-called 'anti-torture Convention' in Article 1 provides for a European Committee which through inspection may prevent or correct breaches of human rights in the context of imprisonment. The Committee has visited Greece and the Minister of Justice admitted to the Greek Parliament in March 1994 that incidents of torture are cited in the Committee's report.

THE RIGHTS OF FOREIGN PRISONERS IN GREEK PRISONS: LAW IN ACTION

During the 1980s and 1990s there has been a surge of national and international legislation designed to safeguard prisoners' rights. Yet prisoners are still suffering. According to a Memorandum written in 1981 by a group of foreign prisoners in Korydallos, foreign detainees are still subject to various forms of (economic) exploitation, degrading living conditions, lack of adequate medical services, delays and loss of correspondence, and improper treatment by prison staff.

Our research data revealed that in spring 1993 the prison population in Greece included people from over 80 different countries. This obviously creates major problems of communication between the prison staff and foreign inmates. Also, communication between non-Greek-speaking foreigners and public prosecutors is rarely direct. Only in exceptional cases do prison officers, public prosecutors inspecting prisons, social workers and inmates know enough English or French to carry on a discussion. Many of the former, however, mentioned the assistance of informal 'interpreters' (other inmates acting as mediators and translators). As in other parts of the prison system (for instance, medical care), pragmatic responses are often activated to cover perceived needs due to lack of resources.

Another area of investigation was the distribution of information about prison rules and regulations. Some respondents said that prisoners are given the required information and that this was one of the obligations of the prison staff. Others expressed the view that there is no possibility of informing inmates, due to lack of time and foreign-language skills. Still others said that only foreigners who ask for such information actually get it.

With respect to the prisoners' right to submit written complaints and petitions, most respondents felt that these were too frequent. The content of these documents varied greatly, but the matters which were the central concerns of the inmates involved legal issues as well as personal and family problems. Applications and complaints are addressed to embassies and consulates, the Ministry of Justice, prison administrators, public prosecutors, social workers, lawyers, courts, and prison guards. However, the extent to which all of these efforts result in any action remains an open question for a number of reasons. First, foreign prisoners are not treated equally by their various national representatives. Some do not have active representatives at all. Some respondents mentioned that citizens from Western European countries and North America are more likely to receive the support they need. Yet little reference was made to the remaining population of foreign prisoners whose rights were often overlooked.

A further area investigated concerned the religious needs and customs of prisoners. Respondents revealed that those prisoners who do not belong to the Eastern Orthodox Christian Church seem to have very limited opportunities to perform their religious duties properly, with the exception of followers of the Roman Catholic Church. Consequently, the exercise of their right is dependent upon their own personal resources and initiatives.

With respect to the health problems of foreign prisoners, respondents suggested that these are dealt with 'regularly', in exactly the same way as Greek detainees. That is, they would receive the same limited facilities which were available to Greek prisoners.

Many foreign prisoners seem to face acute economic problems which can normally be solved through the intervention of their embassies or consulates. It was apparent, however, that within the prison system a new breed of paupers is emerging (among them a significant number of foreign inmates coming from ex-socialist countries) who are unable to buy necessities from the prison canteen.

Foreign prisoners rarely take advantage of any transfer agreements which would allow them to serve their sentence in their own country. In some cases this is because conditions in Greek prisons are preferable to those in their homeland. Also, in some prisons foreign inmates are able to form human relationships and develop informal systems of mutual support.

Sometimes Greeks (and other detainees of different nationalities) attempt to exploit or attack other inmates. Exploitation of foreign prisoners has been observed on a number of occasions. Perpetrators of such behaviour include lawyers, embassy representatives and prison staff. Some respondents reported that these irregular and illegal acts are formally controlled by a number of disciplinary measures and regulations, but that they are rarely implemented.

Certain recommendations were provided by the respondents in the course of answering the questionnaire. The first was the establishment of a service exclusively dealing with foreign prisoners. Secondly, it was suggested that prisoners should be given immediate information from their embassies and consulates and receive regular communication from them. Thirdly, that foreign prisoners should have direct access to specially trained public prosecutors. Fourthly, that there should be an overall improvement in the co-ordination and provision of services. Fifthly, that a selection of the prison staff should be trained in foreign languages or be drawn from a wider range of ethnic groups. Finally, that more effort should be made to allow foreign prisoners to serve their sentence in their own country.

CONCLUSION

In sum, prison overcrowding, depression, pessimism, lack of confidence and difficulties of communication between prisoners and staff are among the most immediate problems confronting foreign prisoners. The gap between prison legislation and reality and the lack of social support were also seen as major problems. Clearly, the available forms of protection offered by the international and national legal agreements do not adequately safeguard the fundamental rights of these detainees. The available domestic and international mechanisms guaranteeing the enforcement of these rights involve complex bureaucratic procedures, to which the average foreign prisoner has no easy access. As a consequence there is a great discrepancy between law in the books and law in action. Furthermore, the provisions of the European Convention of Human Rights do not specifically concern detained individuals, and therefore these provisions, when applied to the protection of prisoners, remain vague and are only able to offer guidelines for the provision of minimum standards.

The situation which has been outlined is a challenge for the guardians of human rights. Thus, the above mentioned research team, without claiming to perform the role of guardian, has prepared a Manual for Migrants and Refugees which has been translated by the Marangopoulos Foundation of Human Rights into English and Albanian, and will be translated into other languages in due course (Spinellis *et al.*, 1993).

Human Rights education is an indispensable condition if we wish to deal with judges, public prosecutors, police officers, social workers and other welfare personnel as well as prison staff and citizens concerned about this issue. All in all, a fifth 'shield' of protection is needed. The development of attitudes of tolerance and non-discrimination should be given particular emphasis.

The Bar Associations in Greece through co-operation with the Council of Europe Directorate of Human Rights could provide training opportunities both in Greece and Strasbourg for young lawyers in the area of protection of human rights especially addressed to persons deprived of their freedom. The Ministry of Justice could also make provision for training prison personnel in human rights and in giving them some background knowledge of the languages of ethnic groups most frequently represented in custodial institutions. The social institutions involved in these problems as well as the mass media and the public should be encouraged to avoid xenophobia and racism.

The concentration of foreign prisoners in separate institutions, as practised in countries like Germany could serve to improve training facilities (such as language courses) but must be examined with some caution since it could produce new penal ghettos (van Zyl Smit and Dunkel 1991).

A set of measures could also be taken, as far as international agreements and co-operation is concerned. A new Protocol might be added to the European Convention of Human Rights which could effectively deal with the fundamental rights of persons deprived of their liberty or suffering from restrictions to it imposed by penal legislation. Even a single additional provision could be enough: 'All human rights are valid in the case of persons deprived of their freedom with the exception of rights withdrawn by the court decision.'

Other reforms could be added to this list. But essentially what is required is the 'political will' which has been conspicuously absent in matters relating to imprisonment. At the same time there is a growing need for justice. As Berthold Brecht put it: 'The same way we need everyday bread, we need everyday justice. Yes, we need justice many times a day.' And this justice requires that the guardians of human rights critically monitor not only the institution of imprisonment but also other types of sanctions in order to ensure that they are implemented in a fair and humane way.

Note

1.   The team consisted of: C. D. Spinellis, Professor and Director of the Centre for Penal and Criminological Research; S. Dermati, attorney and post-graduate student; N. Koulouris, post-graduate fellow; H. Tavoul, doctoral candidate; S. Vidali, doctoral candidate; at a later stage, P. Symiyanni, economist and post-graduate law student; E. Zaliropoulou, post-graduate student; and K. Angelopoulou, holder of State fellowship, doctoral candidate.

References

Bartollas, C. (1990) 'The Prison: Disorder Personified', in J. Murphy and I. Dison (eds), *Are Prisons any Better?* (Newbury Park: Sage): 16–20.
Basic Statistics of the Community (1993) (Luxembourg: Eurostat.).
Bianchi, H. and van Swaaningen, R. (eds) (1986) *Abolitionism* (Amsterdam: Free University Press).
Blagg, H. and Smith, D. (1989) 'Managing the Crisis', in H. Blagg and D. Smith (eds), *Crime, Penal Policy and Social Work* (Harlow: Longman): 33–5.
Brecht, B. (1983) *76 Poems* (Athens, in Greek): 92.
Bueno Arus, F. (1992) 'General Report', in *Human Rights and Penal Detention*, Proceedings of the Seventh International Penal and Penitentiary Foundation, Switzerland.
Corbett, R. and Marx, G. (1992) 'Emerging Technofallacies in the Electronic Monitoring Movement', in J. Byrne; A. Lurigio; and J. Petersilia (eds), *Smart Sentencing* (Newbury Park: Sage).
Courakis, N. (1991) 'Pre-trial Detention: Dysfunctions of an Institution', in A. Sakkoulas (ed.), *Criminological Horizons* (Athens: Komotini).

Farsedakis, I. (1991) 'Deprivation of Liberty and Protection of Human Rights at the Pre-trial Stage', in *The Social Reaction to Crime and Its Limits* (Athens: Nomiki Bibliothiki): 216–17.

Gottfredson, S. D. and McConville, S. (eds) (1987) *America's Correctional Crisis?* (New York: Greenwood).

Grivas, C. (1991) *Drugs: The Cost of Repression* (Thessalonika: Ekdotiki).

Hudson, B. (1993) *Penal Policy and Social Justice* (London: Macmillan).

Human Rights Education in Schools: Concepts, Attitudes and Skills (1984) (Strasbourg; Council of Europe).

Karydis, V. (1992) 'The Fear of Crime in Athens and the Construction of the "Dangerous Albanian" Stereotype', in *Chroniques*, 5.

Koulouris, N. (1990) 'General and Mental Hospitals for Prisoners in Korydallos (Athens)', A. Sakkoulas (ed.), *Criminological Horizons* (Athens: Komotini).

Manitakis, A. (1989) 'The Constitutional Rights of Detainees and Their Judicial Protection', in *Penal Chronicles*: 161, et seq.

Mathiesen, T. (1990) *Prison on Trial* (London: Sage).

Matthews, R. (1994) *Prisoners Abroad: An Evaluation of the Role of the Consular Service* (Centre for Criminology, Middlesex University).

Overcrowded Time: Why Prisons Are so Crowded and What Can Be Done (1982) (New York: The Edna McConnel Clark Foundation): 5.

Paroskevopoulos, N. (1991) 'Thoughts on Causes and Demands of Prisoners' Revolt', in *Law and Politics*, 19–20: 37.

Player, E. (1994) 'Women's Prisons after Woolf', in E. Player and M. Jenkins (eds), *Prisons After Woolf* (London: Routledge).

Prison Information Bulletin, (1990/92) Council of Europe, 15 and 16,

Prison Overcrowding (1991) NACRO Briefing, National Association for the Care and Resettlement of Offenders (London).

The Prison Population in 1991 (1992) Home Office Statistical Bulletin 8.

'Protest Memorandum of Foreign Detainees in Greek Prisons' (1987) in *Crime and Society*: 145.

Rolston, B. and Tomlinson, M. (eds) (1986) *The Expansion of European Prison Systems*, Working Papers in European Criminology, no. 7, The European Group for the Study of Deviance and Social Control (Belfast): 113ff.

Sim, J. (1993) 'Reforming the Penal Wasteland? A Critical Review of the Woolf Report', in E. Player and M. Jenkins (eds), *Prisons After Woolf* (London: Routledge).

Spinellis, C. D., *et al.* (1993) 'Protection of Human Rights of Recent Migrant Groups in Greece, with Emphasis on Those Deprived of Their Freedom' (Athens: unpublished).

Spinellis, C. D. (1992) 'Human Rights in Greek Prisons' Proceedings of the Seventh International Penal and Penitentiary Foundation, Switzerland.

Spinellis, C. D.; Couzakis, N. E.; and Koulouris, N. K. (1995) *Correctional Legislation* (Athens: Nomiki Bibliothiki).

Statistical Yearbook of Greece: 1989 (1992) Athens.

Tak, P. J. P. (1992) 'The Generations of Sanctions', in Proceedings of the Seventh International International Penal and Penitentiary Foundation, Switzerland: 191–3.

Thomas, J. E. (1994) 'Woolf and Prison Staff', in E. Player and M. Jenkins (eds), *Prisons After Woolf* (London: Routledge)

Tomasevski K. (1994) *Foreigners in Prison* (Helsinki: European Institute for Crime Prevention and Control).

van Zyl Smit, D. and Dunkel, F. (eds) (1991) *Imprisonment Today and Tomorrow* (Deventer: Kluwer).

9 Is There a Feminist Future for Women's Prisons?

Margaret Shaw[1]

INTRODUCTION

My motivation for writing this chapter was the opportunity to reflect on the huge changes in public attitudes and policies towards women which have developed over the past few years in Canada. At various levels of government this has resulted in the embracing of feminist ideas *in practice* and most strikingly in relation to women's imprisonment.

In some countries, such as Britain, while there has been a high level of analysis and discussion and some significant theoretical contributions to the understanding of women's imprisonment, this does not appear to have had much impact on policies relating to women offenders. In other countries, feminist approaches have influenced certain policies and programmes for women in prison (Carlen, 1990). Australia, for example, was one of the first countries where feminist approaches helped shape public enquiries into women's imprisonment (e.g. New South Wales Task Force, 1985) and a number of states in the USA such as Minnesota, Wisconsin, New York, District of Columbia and North Carolina have undertaken studies or introduced prison-based programmes for women influenced by feminist analysis of women's offending (see Immarigeon and Chesney-Lind, 1992; Kendall, 1993b).

It is arguable, however, that nowhere else has feminism made such marked inroads into official discourse than in Canada. Not only has there been a number of changes in the way women are perceived in society, but these changed conceptions have resulted in changes in law and practice relating to women. Specifically they have resulted in the acceptance and implementation of the recommendations of a federal Task Force based on feminist principles. Moreover, on-going policies and programmes relating to women offenders both inside and outside prison, and which are feminist in their conception, have also been established.

This natural experiment in feminist intervention raises a basic question. Can feminism make a difference to the way women are dealt with in the criminal justice system and particularly the prison, when so many other approaches have failed? Moreover, is feminism subject to the same

179

problems as other approaches to the transformation of the prison, such as therapeutic communities or liberal reforms? This chapter examines recent developments in Canada relating to women in conflict with the law; the specific changes which are taking place which reflect a feminist philosophy; and the impact of these changes in terms of what can go wrong and right.

THE CANADIAN EXPERIENCE

There have been major changes in public attitudes towards issues affecting women in Canada over the past twenty years. This has been largely the product of effective lobbying by women's organizations. These changes have been mapped elsewhere (Rock, 1986; Currie and Kline, 1991; Snider, 1991; Currie, 1992) but they include the development of the Shelter movement for battered women, the growth of the victims' movement, and much greater awareness of the extent of violence against women and children. They have been accompanied by a flood of academic research and policy analysis. A recent book on gender bias in the law contains a 37-page 'selected' bibliography on Canadian sources (Brockman and Chunn, 1993). Commenting on the power of women's organizations in Canada in relation to the victims' movement in the 1970s and 1980s, Rock wrote:

> So widespread did their presence seem to be ... moulding the develop-
> ment of policies in Ontario, the arguments that directed victimology,
> and the policies of domestic crisis intervention ... Women had been
> awarded an entrenched place in the institutional structure of Ottawa,
> being required to monitor new proposals and ideas for their bearing on
> the status of women. (1986: 210)

This shift in attitudes towards women has resulted in legislative changes such as that which replaced rape with the much broader offence of sexual assault in 1983. It has also influenced more specific decisions such as that relating to Angelique Lavallee in 1990, who was acquitted of murdering her partner, after a plea of self-defence was accepted on the basis of prior battering (Comack, 1993; Noonan, 1993). The enactment of legislation in 1993 against 'stalking' created the offence of criminal harassment and was designed to deter predators, usually ex-husbands or partners, who stalk and intimidate women (similar legislation can also be found on the statute books in 31 American states).

Apart from these legislative landmarks, there have been a large number of official investigations and surveys which underline the Canadian government's awareness of the importance of the issues affecting women.

In 1993, for example, there was the publication of the report of the Panel on Family Violence, funded at a cost of $10 million by the Federal Department of Health and Welfare (Canadian Panel on Violence Against Women, 1993). This involved an 18-month investigation of violence against women in domestic situations with extensive testimony from women across the provinces and territories.

In 1990 the Federal Department of Justice, together with provincial and territorial justice ministers, was responsible for setting up and funding a major investigation of gender equality in the justice system. The working group examined five overlapping issues: women's access to the justice system; the response of the justice system to violence against women; gender bias in the courts; the response of the justice system to women in conflict with the law; substantive law bias against women, and the situation of women working in the justice system. The working groups report was published in July 1993 (Department of Justice, 1993) and apart from its detailed analysis of systematic and overt biases in the justice system, it made numerous recommendations. These included training and appointment of judges and others working in the system; a reconsideration of policies relating to the sentencing of women and men; the development of public legal education to improve women's access to the courts; better victim and witness services; and the introduction of measures aimed at the elimination of violence against women in the community.

Finally, in November 1993, the first results from a nationwide survey of violence against women, funded at a cost of $1.9 million by the Department of Health and Welfare were published (Statistics Canada, 1993). This telephone-based survey of victimization was the first of its kind in the world, and involved interviews with 12 300 women of eighteen years of age or older. It reported that one in every two women in Canada had experienced violence in the form of physical or sexual abuse which would constitute a criminal offence since the age of sixteen.

Apart from such developments in relation to women, there have been a large number of provincial and federal investigations in to the treatment of Aboriginals by the justice system (Solicitor General, 1988; Osnaburgh/ Windigo Tribal Council, 1989; Hamilton and Sinclair, 1991; Linn, 1992) as well as the development of alternative justice systems (Laprairie, 1992; Hollow Water First Nation, 1993). The significance of these developments for the current discussion is that apart from their demonstration of the systemic and overt discrimination against Aboriginal peoples by the justice system, and their social and economic oppression by the majority white society, they have raised discussion about the treatment of minorities in general by the justice system.

Increased government funding for research and policy development in relation to family violence, as well as women in conflict with the law has also been evident in recent years. Major funding for a women in conflict with the law initiative was made available by the ministry of the Solicitor General from 1984 to 1989 and a number of federal ministries have funded projects and research under the Family Violence Initiative (1990–95).

Finally, as if this was not sufficient indication of the high level which women currently occupy on the public agenda, there has been extensive media involvement. Documentaries about women in prison and as victims of violence have included two films on Aboriginal women in the justice system (*To Free the Spirit*, 1991; *Getting Out*, 1993); a film on women's experience of imprisonment (*A Double Tour*, 1994); and two films on women's responses to violence (*Life with Billy*, 1993; *When Women Kill*, 1994). This has been against a continuing background of the exposure by the media of the sexual abuse of children in institutions (portrayed, for example, in a controversial film, *The Boy's of St Vincent*) as well as on-going investigations into the sexual and physical abuse of girls by staff in the Grand View Training School in Ontario in the 1970s. Compensation of sums up to $60 000 was recently awarded to each of 150 women involved.

From the discussion above, there would appear to have been an acceptance in Canada on the part of the public as well as the government that women are subject to violence in society, which has led to formal changes in legislation and policy. It has also created a climate which legitimates change in relation to women to an extent which does not seem possible in many other countries.

CHANGE AFFECTING WOMEN IN PRISON

How has this affected women in prison? The most obvious and recent developments have stemmed from the decision to re-investigate the imprisonment of federally sentenced women (those serving sentences of two years or more). The total population of such women in Canada amounts to approximately 400 with around 140 women receiving a federal sentence each year. Of these, on average around 200 will be in prison at any one time, the rest on parole.

There has been a number of investigations into women's imprisonment in Canada (Berzins and Hayes, 1987; Biron, 1992; Hannah-Moffat, 1994). There has also been a growing recognition of the particular problems faced by Aboriginal women who are over-represented in the prison system. The Task Force on Federally Sentenced Women, appointed by the

Solicitor General in 1989, was unusual in combining both voluntary sector and government members as well as representatives of Aboriginal and minority groups and women who had themselves been in prison. Many of the members of the Task Force worked from a feminist perspective which took the experiences of women as the starting point for its critique. These members rejected the notion that women's needs were similar to those of men, and that equality of provision should be the primary provision. They also rejected the idea that traditional correctional approaches which were based on the needs and activities of the male population were appropriate. There was an emphasis on the extensiveness of violence in women's lives, on the powerful social and economic controls exerted over them, and on the need for a 'women-centred' approach in developing new facilities, regimes and programmes. The Task Force was careful, however, to use the term women-centred rather than feminist.

The outcome was the report *Creating Choices* (1990) which recommended extensive changes to the imprisonment of the federal population including the construction of five new regional facilities and a healing lodge for Aboriginal women, in place of the single penitentiary for women in Kingston, Ontario. The new facilities were to be situated close to major centres of population in the regions, and near to existing networks of support services for women. A community release strategy was also to be developed.

The report set out a series of five feminist principles on which all future developments were to be based. These were empowerment; the provision of meaningful choices; treating women with respect and dignity; providing a physically and emotionally supportive environment; and finally the sharing of responsibility for women's welfare between institutional staff, community members, and with the women themselves.

i) *Empowerment.* Empowerment was to be achieved through the development of programmes to raise the self-esteem of women, giving them greater control over their own lives. It was to be seen by the Task Force as a way of enabling them to overcome their traditional dependency and the inequalities they have experienced in terms of violence, poverty and racism.

ii) *Meaningful Choices.* Empowerment was in turn seen as dependent upon the provision of programmes and facilities which represented meaningful choices for the women and which gave them realistic opportunities to develop their potential. These were to include choices which related to their experiences and skills, and their cultural or spiritual backgrounds, and not to some pre-determined set of programmes into which they could be slotted.

iii) *Respect and Dignity.* The principle of respect and dignity was based on the assumption that people can only gain a sense of self-respect and respect for others if they are themselves treated with respect. Religious and cultural differences in particular must be recognized and responded to, while the adoption of arbitrary rules or the use of procedures which induce a feeling of hopelessness and dependency among women are to be avoided.

iv) *Supportive Environment.* All these principles were in turn seen as requiring a supportive environment with access to good nutrition, fresh air, light, space and privacy, as well as supportive relationships. All these were seen as essential to promoting physical and emotional health and personal development.

v) *Shared Responsibility.* Finally, the principle of shared responsibility stressed the need for the community and voluntary organizations, along with the women themselves, to accept responsibility for their care and development, and not for this to be seen as the exclusive responsibility of the correctional system.

The report based much of its approach on the experiences of women in the justice system, and argued not just for new buildings, but for fundamental changes in the way the new facilities should be run and staffed (Shaw, 1993). The new regional facilities were to be situated in several acres of land, providing natural light, fresh air, colour, space and privacy, with cottage-style houses accommodating six to ten women each. There were to be independent living areas, and facilities for women to live with small children and for family visits. Staffing levels were to vary according to the needs of the women, but there was to be an emphasis on high levels of staffing and support where necessary, rather than on physical security measures.

A central core area would provide educational, recreational, day care and spiritual facilities, as well as flexible space for programmes. All staff were to be carefully selected for their sensitivity to the circumstances of federally sentenced women and given mandatory training in counselling, communication and negotiation skills. This training would be designed to help them develop a broader understanding of the backgrounds and experiences of the women concerned as well as increasing their awareness of racism and sexism.

Programmes were to be holistic. That is they were to work together to deal with the 'inter-related nature of a woman's experience' (*Creating Choices*: 105) and reflect the wishes and needs of individual women. They were to be provided primarily by community groups and agencies, or local authorities outside the correctional system in the case of educational or health services. It was envisaged that each facility would provide core programming which would include individual and group counselling (for example, for family violence, incest survivors, living skills, stress reduction and relaxation). Health care, mental health services, addiction programmes, education, vocational training, recreational and spiritual and cultural programmes were all to be provided.

The circular Healing Lodge was to be developed, staffed and run by Aboriginal peoples, and linked to a nearby native community and an Elder Council. It would provide for Aboriginal ceremonies, teachings and workshops, as well as providing a range of programmes based on the needs and experiences of Aboriginal women.

The second part of the Task Force plan was the development of a range of community-based resources for women which would provide them with continuity of programmes and support on their return to the community. These were to include halfway houses, satellite and supported accommodation, residential addiction centres for women and community release centres. The recommendations were accepted by the government and $50 million was allocated for their implementation. The new facilities are expected to be in operation by 1995.

Creating Choices in turn inspired the provincial government of Nova Scotia to set up its own Task Force on women's imprisonment, with voluntary sector and government members. Their report *Blueprint for Change* (1991) adopted the same five feminist principles and argued for the virtual ending of imprisonment at the provincial level in Nova Scotia (i.e. all those women serving sentences under two years). The number of women receiving provincial sentences in Nova Scotia is small, reflecting the size of the province as a whole. There are approximately 100–130 a year sent to prison, with an average prison population in the Halifax Correctional Centre of 24 women. These women were to be housed instead in four small community residences for 5–12 women, and located around the province. These residences, like the proposed federal facilities, would provide a supportive environment focusing on the women's needs and based on feminist principles. The recommendations of this report were also accepted by the provincial government and are in the process of implementation.

Ontario, one of the largest provinces in Canada, admitting some 3500 women to prison a year, and with an average female prison population of 365 (Ministry of Correctional Services, 1992) subsequently established a Task Force on Women and Corrections in 1993. Their remit was to develop 'a long-term policy to address the special needs and experiences of women in the provincial correctional system and action plans to address the policy direction' (Women's Issues Task Force, 1993). Their report is likely to stress the development of a more coherent community-based approach and a reduction in the use of incarceration for women convicted of non-violent offences, as well as stressing a 'women-centred' approach as their interim report suggests:

> That the Ministry commit itself to defining and taking a women centred and culturally sensitive approach to programme development based on the principles of empowerment, respect and dignity and on the needs and experiences of female clients. (Task Force Discussion Paper, October 1993: 13)

THE DEVELOPMENT OF FEMINIST INTERVENTION PROGRAMMES

Apart from recommended strategies, there are a number of active programmes in Canada based on feminist principles which have received government funding (Kendall, 1993a, Scarth and McLean, 1994; Atkinson and McLean, 1994; Pollack, 1994). These include a range of feminist therapeutic programmes at the Women's Federal Penitentiary Kingston (P4W), at one or two provincial prisons, and community-based projects.

Therapeutic programmes or services at P4W have been evaluated by Kendall (1993a). They include over 25 services ranging from individual counselling with feminist psychologists, therapeutic groups, peer-based support groups and staff training groups, dealing with sexual abuse and trauma, substance abuse, self-injury and suicide, as well as cultural support groups (e.g., black, Aboriginal, francophone). These programmes have been developed over the past five or more years, but particularly since the publication of *Creating Choices* which identified the need for such services. Some are run by community groups such as the Elizabeth Fry Society, others by psychologists and counsellors on contract to the Correctional Service.

The basis of these programmes is their focus on enabling women to understand their situation within a broader social context, and to take control over their lives. Feminist therapy, for example, which is provided on an individual basis by psychologists at P4W to deal with issues of trauma and abuse uses, as Kendall puts it 'essentially a philosophy of treatment, rather than a technique of treatment' (Kendall, 1993b: 5). It sees people within their social, economic and political environment, and attempts to enable women to understand their situation, to give them the tools to take control of their own lives. It contrasts with more traditional forms of therapy which tend to focus more narrowly on the individual or their immediate network of relationships. It also distances itself from those forms of therapy which emphasize the professional status of the therapist, the distance between the therapist and the client, and in which power over all treatment decisions lies with the therapist.

Another programme, the Peer Support Team, is designed to train women inmates to help others in distress, and comprises a six-week training session for potential peer counsellors. The training covers issues of sexual abuse, domestic violence, anger, sexism, racism, homophobia, self-injury and suicide. After receiving this training peer counsellors provide individual support to women in the population who are suicidal or likely to injure themselves (Pollack, 1994).

Other examples of programmes based on feminist principles include one run by prison officers for women survivors of family violence at a women's provincial prison (Portage Correctional Institution, Manitoba) (Mooney, 1993). This is a two-part programme combining educational and information sessions to raise awareness of abuse issues and the resources available inside and outside the prison, and a support group meeting twice weekly for a month. There is a stress on creating a feeling of safety and confidentiality, the use of peer support, and the development of alternative coping mechanisms.

Two programmes at another women's provincial prison in Saskatchewan, Pine Grove Correctional Centre, include what amounts to a 'Women's Studies for Jail's initiative focusing on well-ness and life-skills, including, socialization, parenting and health, and an intensive six-week Healing Circle for Aboriginal women. Almost all women at this prison are Aboriginal, and their experience of physical and sexual abuse is even greater than among other groups.

Finally, a pioneer project in Nova Scotia, the Coverdale Community Chaplaincy Project (Coverdale Courtwork Services, 1993) offers counselling and therapy based on pastoral counselling, spiritual and feminist principles to women in prison and those in the community. Women are referred from the courts, by probation or parole officers, from emergency shelters and other community sources. Like the programmes at P4W, it uses a framework of feminist principles which stress giving women choices and enabling them to taken decisions and control, reducing the power differences between the therapist and the client, the sharing of experience, allowing women to identify their own agenda, to work at their own pace, a commitment to absolute confidentiality and, more broadly, to social change. This project offers individual sessions to women with histories of abuse on a weekly basis initially, and combines support and counselling with more intensive therapy. Those in prison can continue sessions on their release into the community.

Since many of these programmes are of recent origin, their long-term effects have not been assessed, but the evaluation of programmes at P4W (Kendall, 1993a; Pollack, 1994), in Manitoba (Mooney, 1993) and Nova Scotia (Shaw, 1994) all indicate that the women completing the programmes express greater self-confidence, more understanding of their own situation, and feel more control over their lives. Those receiving individual counselling and therapy expressed a high degree of satisfaction with the type of approach used, and the scope it gave them to make their own decisions.

THE IMPACT OF CHANGES: WHAT CAN GO WRONG?

It will be clear from the above that current policies relating to women offenders in Canada follow a 'special needs' model. This focuses on an increasing specialization of programmes and policies for women which are distinct from those available for men. It rests on the assumption that women become involved in offending for reasons which are somewhat different from men, that they respond emotionally and physically to sentencing and incarceration differently from men, that their needs in terms of treatment or services are not the same, and highlights their experience as victims.

These assumptions are to some extent extensions of the traditional view of women prisoners as primary care-givers, or as having, as some would argue, greater mental health problems than men (Maden, Swinton and Gunn, 1994). They have developed in part as an attempt to move away from a liberal-feminist position which argued for *equality* of provision for women offenders, a position which, as Carlen has pointed out, uses men as the standard for programme provision, and one which is in any case inadequate (Carlen, 1990).

Not all observers share this view of women as 'different' as being a productive one. Carlen (1994), for example, argues that little understanding of or impact on the power of the prison to punish will be gained by studying women's prisons separately from men's. Currie (1992) points to the limitations of seeing the problems of women's imprisonment in causal terms as a consequence of their victimization. Bruckert (forthcoming) points to the limitations of focusing on the programme needs of women prisoners, as *Creating Choices* does, reinforcing the view that it is 'the individual who remains the object of reform' and argues as does

Hannah Moffat (1994) that women's portrayal as victims and mothers is in fact a traditional one which differs little from the views of nineteenth century reformers.

Some of these issues are discussed below in considering the impact of change in the correctional system, which appears to be vulnerable at a number of points: the development of plans for change; the acceptance or rejection of plans and recommendations by government; and the implementation of recommendations. Within the prison, new initiatives or programmes are vulnerable to weakening or subversion by the management or control functions of the prison as an institution. Such modifications of the impact of new policies are either consciously or unconsciously set in motion as government attempts to balance political and financial interests, as well as the concerns of employees, unions and public opinion. What else can 'go wrong'? The seeds of future problems may also be sown by 'radical' initiatives themselves, in using too narrow an analysis of the problems, or by diverting attention away from wider and more fundamental issues and developments.

PRESSURE GROUPS AND INCORPORATION

For pressure groups and grassroots organizations, a major fear in engaging with government is of becoming 'incorporated' and weakened, of loosing their critical edge and credibility. From a government point of view, having the willing co-operation of a well-known pressure group can provide legitimacy, by showing sensitivity and concern for the issues involved.

The history of pressure groups associated with criminal justice is replete with examples of the dangers of co-option. In Canada, the Elizabeth Fry Society provides a number of examples of local organizations which have fought against incorporation and those which have embraced government as a 'partner' (Stewart, 1993). In England, Ryan's comparative study of the long established Howard League for Penal Reform and the short-lived militant pressure group Radical Alternatives to Prison provides a clear picture of the dangers of working too closely with government:

> ... it would be foolish to ignore the fact that such a close relationship has, on occasions, turned out to be inward looking and conservative, unable to accommodate new ideas at the expense of old assumptions. (Ryan, 1978: 151)

Such a fear of incorporation was a major concern to the Canadian Association of Elizabeth Fry Societies (CAEFS) in their decision to join with the federal government in the 1989 Task Force on Federally Sentenced Women. In recent years the organization had seen itself as committed to the abolition of imprisonment for women. As the Executive Director of the organization is quoted as saying:

> It really tried our souls to be designing a prison system when we don't believe women should be in prison.   (Kershaw and Lasovich, 1991: 234)

The sense of achievement and progress felt by the members of the Task Force in developing its women-centred vision was perhaps tempered by the knowledge that the recommendations would result in the creation of five new prisons for women, albeit rather different from the existing penitentiary. In the aftermath of the implementation of the Task Force recommendations, CAEFS withdrew its support for the government

IMPLEMENTATION: THE SEPARATE STRUGGLE

In many cases, Task Forces and advisory group recommendations may be received with interest, even enthusiasm, by government and the public, but fail to spark action to implement them. Even when recommendations are accepted, the extent to which they are implemented as planned is problematic (Hannah-Moffat, 1994). Rock (1986) in his analysis of the development of victims' legislation in Canada provides an extensive account of the transformation of the concerns of women's groups about battered women into the 'Justice for Victims of Crime' initiative as it was moulded into government timetables and interests.

In relation to a Task Force report on women's prisons in New South Wales, for example, it was evident that only those parts of the report which were acceptable to the government were acted upon (Browne and Quinn, 1985). New buildings were developed, but management practices and traditional staffing methods were left untouched. As Browne and Quinn (1985) concluded:

> It seems trite to point out that reform recommendations, even when strongly and unanimously supported by government are not self-enforcing ... the process of debate, the discourse and the content of such reports are fields of political struggle in themselves and can be evaluated as such independently of the linked but separate struggle over implementation.

Such a prediction proved to be the case in the implementation of the Federal Task Force. While accepting the main recommendations of the report *Creating Choices* the government rejected those on the process of implementation. In the eyes of the voluntary sector, it effectively excluded those outside government from this process (Shaw, 1993). The voluntary sector and notably CAEFS, who had a role on an external Advisory Committee to oversee the implementation, felt they were not consulted or informed about crucial decisions until they were a *fait accompli*. This included the selection of sites for the new institutions, which in some cases failed to conform to the criteria established by the Task Force, and the appointment of wardens, and led to the eventual withdrawal of support for the federal initiative by CAEFS.

Furthermore, the government failed to provide funds for the development of community services which *Creating Choices* had seen as a crucial aspect of the new regional facilities. The number of new facilities has also reduced to four plus the Healing Lodge, with the decision to utilize a newly constructed but traditional women's prison in British Columbia. Subsequent changes have included decisions to change the plans for the facilities themselves, with the development of more secure accommodation, plans for the erection of eight-foot high fences and electronic monitoring, and in at least one centre, the elimination of certain key components, such as a day-care centre, or a gymnasium.

These decisions have been made by the government on a variety of grounds (Hannah-Moffat, 1994) including: cost; considerable public pressure from local citizens living near the proposed sites; considerations of employment and job creation; and perhaps, in the aftermath of the withdrawal of CAEFS, location away from existing organizations who might prove too critical.

In the case of the Nova Scotia report *Blueprint for Change*, current plans envisage the construction of four new community residences, but to be built and run by private companies. Privatization, with its accompanying emphasis on profit margins, and no guarantees of community commitment or the maintenance of feminist principles, is clearly a long way from the blueprint envisaged by the members of that Task Force.

FEMINISM IN THE PRISON

After some six years of development of feminist programmes in the women's federal penitentiary, it would seem, as was suggested earlier, that the women have found them very beneficial. They have felt they have gained in self-confidence, and in their ability to understand and cope with their own situation and experiences (Shaw *et al.*, 1991; Atkinson and McLean, 1994; Kendall, 1993a; Pollack, 1994).

So what can go wrong inside the prison? The experience of those who have developed such services suggests that the pressures of the institution to maintain its management and control functions – what the prison is really there for – together with shortage of funding, staff shortages or turnover can all work to circumvent or obstruct such programmes (McLean and Darke, 1991; McLean, 1993). While some staff at P4W, for example, saw the value of feminist counselling being offered at the prison, there were suggestions that it increased the volatility of women's behaviour in the institution, and led to increases in suicides and self-injury (Kendall, 1994a). Short-term contract funding has also made some programmes vulnerable.

The development of any treatment programme may give the illusion of fulfilling the other purpose of imprisonment in encouraging reform and reintegration into the community (Correctional Service Canada, 1990). As Norval Morris argued twenty years ago in *The Future of Imprisonment* (1974), the fundamental problem with the notion of treatment in the prison is that it should not be coerced. Treatment should neither be a reason for sentencing a person to prison, nor should participation in treatment pro-grammes be a condition of release. Treatment programmes in general are more likely to be effective if they are taken up voluntarily.

Yet requiring or expecting participation in treatment programmes, rather than allowing choice, is still a feature of a penitentiary system which in recent years has focused much more sharply on the classification of offender risk and their assessed treatment needs (Logan and Gaes, 1993). This has been accompanied by the development of targeted prison treatment programmes in the federal system (for example the cognitive/behavioural skills programme developed by Ross and Fabiano, 1985). The development of these programmes has taken place against a background of debate about the revival of rehabilitation as a viable and a legitimate activity (Gendreau and Ross, 1987; Doob and Brodeur, 1989; Andrews, et al., 1990; Lab and Whitehead, 1990). Nowhere in this debate, however, at least from the proponents of rehabilitation, does the question of indi-vidual choice appear, or any discussion of the consequences of coercing change.

Moreover, the structure of the institution, and the stresses it poses on all those living and working inside, remove it from the realities of living in the community. Even were there is choice in programme participation, without consequential effects on management and release decisions, the coercive nature of the setting remains. As Kathy Kendall (1994a) points out in her study of programmes developed inside P4W, there is a basic paradox between the position of being a prisoner, and the tenets of feminism. The former removes personal autonomy and control over movement and daily functioning, the latter stresses the ability to be self-reliant, to take autonomous action, to exercise choice in your life. The principles of a feminist philosophy, therefore, *increase* the dissonance between a programme of 'treatment' which attempts to change or reform, but which takes place within an institutional setting.

If it is accepted that it is not possible for women to develop a real sense of self-determination within the existing institutional setting, the question arises of whether it will be possible in the new facilities for women to experience the feminist principles of empowerment, meaningful choices, shared responsibility, and the provision of a supportive environment (Shaw, 1993; Hannah-Moffat, 1994). Certainly the new facilities will give them greater control over daily routines such as cooking and eating, but there will still be considerable restrictions on movement. And with small populations of women (the five facilities will vary in size, accommodating between 21 and 76 women), a wide range of choices of programmes or job training seems unlikely. Some women will be allowed out to take programmes in the community, but the location of three of the facilities in rural settings does not promise an abundance of available programmes.

KNOWING THE ANSWERS

A further danger, however, lies with the tendency for proponents of an approach to 'over-sell' their case, or to assume they know the answers. In theoretical terms, it may involve the imposition of one viewpoint to the exclusion of others, and to promote what Carlen (1994) has referred to as 'conceptual imperialism'. Feminism seems no exception to this problem (Hannah-Moffat, 1994; Bruckert, forthcoming). In the case of the Federal Task Force, while the range of views of federally sentenced women themselves may have been downplayed in an attempt to imprint strong feminist principles on the future plans. There was also a tendency to portray women principally as victims of physical and sexual abuse and without any self-esteem or personal strengths (Shaw, 1992; Kendall, 1993b). Even using the now more common term 'survivors' to refer to women who have experienced abuse does not counteract the problem.

As Kendall points out (1993b), as do Scarth and McLean (1994), abuse is not seen as the only issue in the women's lives by those developing therapeutic programmes at P4W. Nevertheless, the danger remains of perpetuating a picture of women as acted upon, as having individual and personal problems requiring personal therapy, as being mentally or psychologically maladjusted. It locates the problem within the individual. Reflecting on the place of feminist therapy in the prison, Kendall (1994b) suggests that not only the coercive nature of the prison, but also the dishonourable history of medicine, psychology and psychiatry with their tendency to pathologize and depoliticize women should warn us about the dangers of too enthusiastic an adoption of such programmes within the prison.

This dilemma lies at the heart of all individual treatment programmes, but it is particularly at odds with the basic premise of feminist philosophy which sees women and their experiences within the much broader context of their environment, politically, economically and socially (Kendall, 1993b). Individual therapists may offer a service which is true to its feminist roots, and which does contextualize behaviour or experience more broadly, but it may be perceived within the management context of the prison as just another form of individual therapy indicating individual maladjustment. And not all the women themselves may perceive their own needs in feminist terms. They may have experienced abuse in their lives, but may not wish to 'deal with it' or see it as central to their lives.

A second consequence of 'over-selling' a particular viewpoint is that by ignoring, or placing little stress on other aspects of women's situation, there is room for other groups with different concerns to intervene. *Creating Choices*, for example, placed little emphasis on the issue of violence by women themselves. The precise need for secure facilities, and what they should look like, how they should be run, was left open. Traditional analyses of violence and its containment have greater opportunity to be developed, particularly in response to isolated violent incidents, in the absence of a more clearly articulated discussion in the report. Feminists should be prepared to confront issues with which they feel uncomfortable.

FEMINISM OUTSIDE THE PRISON

Feminist treatment programmes, like other types of treatment programmes, may stand a better chance of providing realistic opportunities for women if they are based in the community rather than the institution. If they are true to their principles in allowing and enabling women to make choice about the progress of their lives, and the issues dealt with in treatment sessions; if they provide continuing support rather than a rigid or fixed programme, they may have a greater chance of helping women deal with difficult day-to-day situations, and of enabling them to develop a long-term ability to survive without drugs or alcohol, in relationships which are non-abusive, without being re-convicted.

The Coverdale Community Chaplaincy project in Nova Scotia referred to earlier would appear to be true to its feminist principles in allowing women entering the project to make their own choices and develop their own programme (Shaw, forthcoming). Yet such programmes may still be vulnerable to local views on legitimate programmes for offenders. They are likely to be very vulnerable to funding problems, and to the dangers of over-extending their energies and resources, and hence to 'burn-out'. Consequently they may not last very long.

UNINTENDED CONSEQUENCES

Unintended consequences can, almost inevitably, be foreseen (Hannah-Moffat, 1994). Indeed, a number of unintended outcomes of engagement with the government were foreseen by CAEFS. These included the possibility that the use of federal sentences of imprisonment for women would increase with the establishment of the new facilities, since women would no longer have to be sent so far from their homes, and because their 'special needs' would be provided for. There is also the possibility that controls over women will be extended by the eventual development not only of new facilities, but of more community programmes (Shaw, 1993).

Another factor (recognized by CAEFS as well) has been that the new federal plans have diverted attention away from the more fundamental issues of the use of imprisonment for women in Canada. At the provincial level a far greater number of women (some 13 500 in 1991) receive sentences of under two years. Even the daily population of women in provincial jails and detention centres in the province of Ontario at around 400 exceeds the total federal population (Shaw, 1994). Attention has been diverted away from *rethinking* the use of imprisonment for many women in the first place, when the majority of women in Canada serve sentences of six months or less, and as many as 40 per cent serve sentences of less than fourteen days.

Hannah-Moffat (1994) suggests that feminist engagement with the reform of federal women's imprisonment has ultimately amounted to an endorsement of existing theories of punishment, and an expansion of women's prisons, rather than challenging the use of the prison itself. The planned capacity well exceeds the current population of women in prison. Kendall (1994b) similarly argues that in embracing feminism, the correctional system has legitimated the role of prison.

In a trenchant critique based on a discourse analysis of the Task Force report Bruckert (forthcoming) argues that *Creating Choices* uses feminist language self-consciously but cannot disguise the traditional correctional framework of the report. As she puts it, 'a discourse is created which employs feminized control talk and a veneer of progressive feminism', but 'facilities' are still prisons, and 'enhanced security cottages' still maximum security units, and women are portrayed traditionally as mothers and victims in need of 'healing' rather than treatment, and economic and social differences downplayed.

> In *Creating Choices* the initial promise of feminist policy is never realised and the recommendations never transcend dominant corrections frameworks. Having determined that women are special and require a unique approach, the Task Force ... recommends a modified version of androcentric corrections – resurrecting the rhetoric if not the terminology of rehabilitation... (Bruckert, forthcoming: 24)

None of these problems are new, and many were predictable. It is easy, after the fact, to criticize those who were prepared to engage with government, and those who had a feminist vision of a different world for women offenders. The new prisons will, however, provide physically better conditions than the current institutions and feminist inspired programmes have had some impact on the lives of some women in conflict with the law.

WHERE NOW?

At the beginning of this chapter it was suggested that feminism has been embraced by the correctional system in Canada to an extent not found in many other countries. This should not be interpreted to mean that all women in prison have been affected by these developments. The majority remain outside the remit of the federal government in provincial prisons, and within the federal correctional system, as this paper suggests, there is still considerable scope for transforming the feminist intentions of the Task Force to 'fit into' a more established carceral framework.

None of the four new prisons nor the Healing Lodge has yet been built although plans for some are well advanced, and most are due to begin operations in 1995. It remains to be seen how far the correctional system will be able to develop a supportive environment, how far the staff will utilize communication and mediation skills in place of the existing rule enforcement and punishment practices, how far women will be able to exercise choice in their use of programmes, and how far community groups will be able to work with the new institutions in an innovative way.

It also seems clear that feminism is no more able to avoid the problems faced in trying to change the prison than other approaches. It can be argued, nevertheless, that the more overt and explicit language of feminist intervention used in North America sets off a range of reactions and expectations which do contain the seeds of a better way of working. Far from solving the problem of women's imprisonment and providing a comfortable new regime with which both those inside and out can feel reasonably content for the next decades, feminism has forced a reassessment of the use of prison, and the Task Force report has highlighted rather than resolved a number of the problems to be tackled. These include the development of non-custodial services for women offenders, reassessing the stress on women as victims, and a broader approach to facilitating change which recognizes the basic needs of those trying to live marginal lives. And outside the prison and released from correctional consequences, feminist-based programmes can also be empowering for women who are released from prison.

Note

1.   I am grateful to Kathy Kendall and Kelly Hannah-Moffat who share many of the ideas in this chapter.

References

Adelberg, E. and Currie, C. (eds) (1987) *Too Few to Count: Canadian Women in Conflict with the Law* (Vancouver: Press Gang Publishers).
Andrews, D. A.; Zinger, I.; Hoge, R. D.; Bonta, J.; Gendreau, P.; and Cullen, F. T. (1990) 'Does Correctional Treatment Work? A Clinically Relevant and Psychologically Informed Meta-Analysis,' *Criminology*, 28 (3): 369–404.
Atkinson, J. and McLean, H. (1994) 'Women and Fraud: Results of a Programme at the Prison for Women', *Forum on Corrections Research*, 6 (1) (Ottawa: Correctional Service Canada).
Berzins, L. and Hayes, B. (1987) The diaries of two change agents in Adelberg, E. and Currie, C. (eds), *Too Few to Count* (Vancouver: Press Gang Publishers).
Biron, L. L. (1992) 'Les femmes et l'incarcération. Le temps n'arrange rien', *Criminologie*, xxv (1): 119–34.

Blueprint for Change (1992) Report of the Solicitor General's Special Committee on Provincially Incarcerated Women, Province of Nova Scotia (April).

Brockman, J. and Chunn, D. (eds) (1993) *Investigating Gender Bias: Laws, Courts and the Legal Profession* (Toronto: Thompson Educational Publishing).

Browne, D. and Quinn, M. (1985). 'Women in Prison: Review of the New South Wales Task Force Report', *Legal Service Bulletin* (December).

Bruckert, C. (forthcoming) *The Construction of Feminized Correctional Discourse: the Report of the Task Force on Federally Sentenced Women* (University of Ottawa).

Canadian Panel on Violence Against Women (1993) *Final Report. Changing the Landscape: Ending Violence – Achieving Equality* (Ottawa: Supply and Services Canada).

Carlen, P. (1990) *Alternatives to Women's Imprisonment* (Milton Keynes: Open University Press).

Carlen, P. (1994) Why Study Women's Imprisonment? Or anyone else's, *British Journal of Criminology*, 34 Special Issue pp. 131–140.

Clark, L. M. G. (1989–90) 'Feminist Perspectives on Violence Against Women and Children: Psychological, Social Service, and Criminal Justice Concerns', *Canadian Journal of Women and the Law*, 3: 420–31.

Comack, E. (1993) 'Feminist Engagement with the Law: The Legal Recognition of the Battered Women Syndrome', in *The CRIAW Papers* (Ottawa: Canadian Research Institute for the Advancement of Women).

Cooper, S. (1987) 'The Evolution of the Federal Women's Prison', in E. Adelberg and C. Currie, *Too Few to Count* (Vancouver: Press Gang Publishers).

Correctional Service Canada (1990) *Mission Statement of the Correctional Service Canada* (Ottawa: Correctional Service Canada).

Coverdale Courtwork Services (1993) *Coverdale Community Chaplaincy Proposal* (June) (Halifax: Nova Scotia).

Creating Choices (1990). Report of the Task Force on Federally Sentenced Women (Ottawa: Correctional Service Canada).

Currie, D. (1992) 'Feminism and realism in the Canadian context', in J. Lowman and B. D. Maclean (eds), *Realist Criminology: Crime Control and Policing in the 1990's* (Toronto: University of Toronto Press).

Currie, D. and Kline, M. (1991). 'Challenging privilege: Women, Knowledge and Feminist Struggles', *Journal of Human Justice*, 2 (2): 1–36.

Department of Justice (1993) *Gender Equality in the Canadian Justice System. Summary Document and Proposals for Action* (Ottawa).

Doob, A. N. and Brodeur, J.-P. (1989) 'Rehabilitating the Debate on Rehabilitation', *Canadian Journal of Criminology*, 31 (2) pp. 179–192.

Gendreau, P. and Ross, R. R. (1987) Revivification of Rehabilitation: Evidence from the 1980s *Justice Quartely*, 4: (1987) 349–407.

Hamilton, A. C. and Sinclair, C. M. (1991) *Report of the Aboriginal Justice Enquiry of Manitoba* (Province of Manitoba).

Hannah–Moffat, K. (1994) 'Unintended Consequences of Feminism and Prison-Reform', *Forum on Corrections Research* 6 (1) (Ottawa: Correctional Service Canada).

Hollow Water First Nation (1993) *Community Holistic Circle Healing*, Aboriginal Peoples Collection 6 CA (Ottawa: Ministry of Solicitor General).

Immarigeon, R. and Chesney-Lind, M. (1992) *Women's Prisons: Overcrowded and Overused* (San Francisco: National Council on Crime and Delinquency).

Kendall, K. (1993a) *Programme Evaluation of Therapeutic Services at the Prison for Women* (Ottawa: Correctional Service Canada).

Kendall, K. (1993b) *Companion Volume I. Programme Evaluation of Therapeutic Services at the Prison for Women* (Ottawa: Correctional Service Canada).

Kendall, K. (1994a) 'Creating Real Choices: A Programme Evaluation of Therapeutic Services at the Prison for Women', *Forum on Corrections Research*, 6 (1) (Ottawa: Correctional Service Canada).

Kendall, K. (1994b) 'Therapy Behind Prison Walls: A Contradiction in Terms?', paper presented at Prisons 2000: An International Conference on the Present State and Future of Imprisonment, University of Leicester (April).

Kershaw, A. and Lasovich, M. (1991) *Rock-a-Bye Baby: A Death Behind Bars* (Toronto: McClelland & Stewart).

Lab, S. P. and Whitehead, J. T. (1990) 'From "nothing works" to "the appropriate works": the latest stop on the search for the secular grail', *Criminology*, 28 (3): 405–17.

Laprairie, C. (1992) 'Aboriginal Crime and Justice: Explaining the Present, Exploring the Future', *Canadian Journal of Criminology*, 34 (3–4): 281–97.

Linn, Judge P. (1992) *Report of the Saskatchewan Indian Justice Review Committee* (Saskatchewan Dept. of Justice; Government of Canada; Federation of Saskatchewan Indians).

Logan, C. and Gaes, G. G. (1993) 'Meta-Analysis and the Rehabilitation of Punishment', *Justice Quarterly*, 10 (2): 245–63.

Maden, A.; Swinton, M; and Gunn, J. (1994) 'A Criminological and Psychiatric Survey of Women Serving a Prison Sentence', *British Journal of Criminology*, 34 (2): 172–91.

McLean, H. and Darke, J. (1991) Paper Presented at Symposium on Women in Conflict with the Law, Toronto (18 September).

McLean, H. (1993). Paper presented at the panel on Women in Conflict with the Law, Canadian Congress on Criminal Justice, Quebec City (12–15 October).

Ministry of Correctional Services (1992) Annual Report (Toronto: Ontario).

Mooney, G. (1993) *Abuse Hurts: a Programme for Incarcerated Adult Women Survivors of Family Violence*, paper presented at the 4th North American Conference on the Family and Corrections, Quebec City (10–12 October).

Morris, N. (1974) *The Future of Imprisonment* (Chicago: University of Chicago Press).

New South Wales (1985) *Report of the New South Wales Task Force on Women in Prison* (New South Wales: Ministry of Correctional Services).

Noonan, S. (1993) 'Strategies of Survival: Moving Beyond the Battered Women Syndrome', In E. Adelberg and C. Currie (eds), *In Conflict with the Law: Women and the Canadian Justice System* (Vancouver: Press Gang Publishers).

Osnaburgh/Windigo Tribal Council Justice Review Committee (1990) Report prepared for the Attorney General (Ontario) and Minister Responsible for Native Affairs, the Solicitor General (Ontario) (July).

Pollack, S. (1994) 'Opening the Window on a Very Dark Day: a Programme Evaluation of a Peer-Support Team at the Kingston Prison for Women', unpublished Masters thesis (Ottawa: Carlton University School of Social Work).

Rock, P. (1986) *A View from the Shadows: The Ministry of the Solicitor General of Canada and the Justice for Victims of Crime Initiative* (Oxford: Clarendon Press).

Ross, R. R. and Fabiano, E. A. (1985) *Time to Think: A Cognitive Model of Delinquency Prevention and Offender Rehabilitation* (Johnson City, Tenn.: Institute of Sciences and Arts).

Ryan, M. (1978) *The Acceptable Pressure Group* (Farnborough: Saxon House).

Scarth, K. and McLean, H. (1994) 'The Psychological Assessment of Women in Prison', *Forum on Corrections Research*, 6 (1) (Ottawa: Correctional Service Canada).

Shaw, M. (1992) 'Issues of Power and Control: Women in Prison and Their Defenders', *British Journal of Criminology*, 32 (4): 438–52.

Shaw, M. (1993) Reforming Federal Women's Imprisonment in E. Adelberg and C. Currie (eds), *In Conflict with the Law: Women and the Canadian Justice System* (Vancouver: Press Gang Publishers).

Shaw, M. (1994) 'Women in Prison: A Literature Review', *Forum on Corrections Research*, 6 (1) (Ottawa: Correctional Service Canada).

Shaw, M. (forthcoming) *Evaluation of the Coverdale Community Chaplaincy Project* (Ottawa: Ministry of the Solicitor General).

Shaw, M.; with Rodgers, K.; Blanchette, J.; Hattem, T.; Thomas, L. S.; and Tamarack, L. (1991) *Survey of Federally Sentenced Women: Report to the Task Force on Federally Sentenced Women on the Prison Survey*, User Report No. 1991–4 (Ottawa: Ministry of the Solicitor General).

Snider, L. (1991) 'The Potential of the Criminal Justice System to Promote Feminist Concerns', in E. Comack and S. Brickey (eds), *The Social Basis of Law: Critical Readings in the Sociology of Law* (2nd edn) (Halifax: Garamond).

Solicitor General (1988) *Final Report: Task Force on Aboriginal Peoples in Federal Corrections* (Ottawa).

Statistics Canada (1993) *The Daily*, Catalogue No. 11–001E, Ottawa (18 November).

Stewart, L. (1993) *Women Volunteer to Go to Prison: a History of the Elizabeth Fry Society of B.C. 1939–1989* (Victoria: Orca Book Publishers).

Women's Issues Task Force (1993) Discussion Paper, Ministry of Attorney General and Correctional Services, Ontario (October).

10 Women's Imprisonment in England at the End of the Twentieth Century: Legitimacy, Realities and Utopias

Pat Carlen and Chris Tchaikovsky

INTRODUCTION

In 1991 the Woolf Inquiry reported to the British government on the underlying causes of the riots which had occurred at six prisons in England and Wales in 1990. Women's prisons had been excluded from the terms of reference of the judicial inquiry, even though there had been a serious disturbance at the women's section of Risley Remand Centre a few months earlier. Three years later, Elaine Player (1994) wrote about the implications of Woolf for women's prisons. Disappointingly, this was primarily an exercise in administrative penology. Player not only failed to put the issues of women's imprisonment in any theoretical context whatsoever, but also omitted to mention: the 'gender-wise' theorizing about women's prisons engaged in by feminists over the past couple of decades (see Howe, 1994, for an up-to-date bibliography); and the 'women-wise' brand of penal politics doggedly fashioned by the radical campaigning group Women in Prison since its founding by women ex-prisoners in 1983.

This present chapter, in an attempt to engage once more with some of the issues ignored by Woolf, is directed at describing, analyzing and assessing the relationships between some of the developments in British penality and some of the difficulties confronting prison 'reformers', 'reductionists' and 'abolitionists' during the first ten years of the Women in Prison Campaign. It is thus more concerned with interrogating the *politics* of women's imprisonment than in theorizing women's imprisonment *per se* (though, of course, the two cannot easily be separated).

The chapter is divided into three sections. The first describes the early days and aims of the campaign and assesses the extent to which it can be claimed that those aims have been attained. Section two theorizes the politics of campaigning specifically on the issue of women's imprisonment. Then, in the light of the theoretical issues described in section two, the final section argues for a theoretical perspective on prison campaigning that recognizes present political constraints at the same time as insisting that they could be otherwise. The overall argument is that campaigners who become paralyzed by fears that all reforms must inevitably be incorporated into the state repressive apparatuses tend also to operate with dichotomous conceptions of theorizing and politics that are neither epistemologically sound nor politically useful. None the less, it is also argued that the women's prison lobby should maintain a vigilant stance – by constantly analyzing all posited prison reforms in terms of their often opposed capacities to advance (or not) both social and penal justice for women.

WOMEN IN PRISON CAMPAIGN – THE BEGINNING

Women in Prison (WIP) was founded in 1983 when Chris Tchaikovsky gathered together a group of women anxious about the numbers of disturbed petty offenders held in Holloway and concerned, too, about the standards of safety and care maintained in the prison. From its conception the Group had to consider what is *special* about *women's* imprisonment. After all, there were already plenty of organizations which *claimed* to campaign for better conditions for *all* prisoners, though only one of them, Radical Alternatives to Prison, had seriously campaigned against the rebuilding of Holloway Prison in the early 1970s.

Women in Prison's *raison d'être*, therefore, was initially based on the following claims: first that women's imprisonment is different to men's, and that the special and distinct pains of women's imprisonment have, in the main, been ignored by writers, campaigners and prison administrators; secondly that women in prison suffer from discriminatory practices by administrators that result in their receiving fewer education, work and leisure opportunities than male prisoners serving comparable sentences; thirdly that women prisoners suffer from discriminatory practices by prison officers – as instanced by their being subjected to closer disciplinary surveillance and regulation than male prisoners with similar criminal records; forthly that women in prison do not receive adequate medical care for gynaecological conditions and that their special needs during menstruation, pregnancy and menopause are often not catered for;

fifthly that mothers in prison do not receive adequate support and coun-selling in relation to their children outside prison; sixthly that, because there are relatively few of them, women in custody in Britain were more likely than men to be held in institutions a long way from their homes; and finally that *certain* women are sent to prison on the basis of a judicial logic that sentences them as *flawed women* rather than as lawbreaking citizens.

On the basis of these specific assumptions about the special nature of *women's* imprisonment, WIP's early campaigns centred on: increasing public awareness of the debilitating regimes characteristic of the women's prisons; the plight of women held in extremely close confinement or under brutally harsh disciplinary regimes (for example the inmates of Durham Prison H-Wing, kept under extremes of surveillance because of the one person confined there who had been [wrongly] convicted of a bombing offence; and the behaviourally disturbed women of Holloway's notorious C1 Unit); the daily pains of imprisonment, and especially those specific to women and/or exacerbated by the particular regimes or practices of the different women's prisons; and the difficulties facing women upon their release from prison.

From the outset, WIP was very aware of the disproportionate numbers of women prisoners from ethnic minority groups, and the need for liaison with organizations catering for black and foreign women in prison. Additionally, and in order to pursue strategies directed at achieving both a reduction in the prison population and an amelioration of existing un-satisfactory conditions in *all* prisons, WIP joined with a variety of other penal reform organizations to campaign against the all-pervasive secrecy, non-accountability to the public, censorship, and other undemocratic prac-tices which have characterized the British prison system from the nineteenth century onwards.

In any review of the first ten years of its existence, WIP can certainly claim with justification that its work has been central to the increase in public awareness of the pains of women in penal custody. (Whether or not there has been a concomitant diminution of those pains is, of course, a much thornier question.) Since 1983, many other non-statutory groups have been campaigning or caring for women prisoners – The National Association for the Care and Resettlement of Offenders (NACRO), Women Prisoners' Resource Centre (WPRC), Women in Special Hospitals (WISH), and Hibiscus (for female foreign nationals in prison in Britain). Each has a slightly different task-emphasis, but their very exist-ence constitutes recognition that the category 'woman-prisoner' has no global application to women prisoners' needs, all of which require analy-sis in the contexts of individual women's socio-biographies, as well as in the light of prevailing penal politics. Innumerable policy documents relating to women in the criminal justice and penal systems have also been published (Seear and Player, 1986; Women's National Commission, 1991), and the media nowadays seize on (and feed on) 'women in prison' stories whenever they can. But what has actually been achieved for women in prison?

At the formal, institutional level, quite a bit. For example, since 1991 certain prisoners at Holloway Prison in London have been able to spend two Sundays a month with their children, while at other prisons there have been innovatory education projects and a variety of imaginative experiments to improve the lot of women prisoners. The problem is that many prison reform initiatives remain experimental, are often dependant for their continuation on local conditions, and, most frustrating for prisoners and prison-watchers, are frequently very short-lived. However, WIP (and other campaigning groups) have worked patiently and persistently with prison administrators to provide services to hundreds of women both in prison and upon their release; and it is certainly the case that many of the institutional reforms that have occurred are directly attributable to the work of WIP in publicizing poor prison conditions. In terms of radical and fundamental improvement in women-prisoners' regimes, not a lot. Take, for instance, the outcomes of the 'Holloway C1 Unit' and 'Durham H-Wing' Campaigns.

Holloway's C1 Unit is for women prisoners who manifest a variety of mental and behavioural abnormalities, though from time to time it has been used to house women who have been sent there because they have been seen as constituting a 'prison control' problem, or merely because prison overcrowding meant that there was nowhere else to put them. In 1985, C1 prisoners were kept permanently locked in small cells, received their food and medication through a hatch in the cell-door, and reports of incidents of self-mutilation were horrific (see O'Dwyer *et al.*, 1987). Campaigning by WIP (and others) against conditions in the Unit was followed by the publication of two Reports (Home Office, 1985; Clare and Thompson 1985) recommending far-reaching changes, and on 17 July 1985 the then Home Secretary, Leon Brittan, acknowledged the desirability of re-siting C1 in purpose-built accommodation in a different part of the prison (O'Dwyer *et al.*, 1987: 190). But C1 was not re-sited; and, although the women in C1 unit are no longer locked in their cells all day, there has been no fundamental improvement in the situation of mentally disturbed women in prison, with many still engaging in self-mutilation as imprisonment worsens their already-fragile emotional states (see Leibling, 1992).

Durham Prison's H-Wing had already housed top-security women prisoners for 15 years when in 1989 the Lester and Taylor Report concluded that inmates were treated less favourably than they would have been if they had been male prisoners, and that:

> If H-Wing were to remain as it is, without radical improvement we would recommend that it should be closed as soon as possible. (Lester and Taylor, 1989: 11)

Changes *were* made – in sanitation, association and facilities. But prisoners still complain about the claustrophobia occasioned by confinement to just one wing of a *men's* prison, as well as about the Prison Department's seeming use of the unit as a penal warehouse for prisoners whom they cannot quite decide what to do with, and who, for a variety of reasons, are seen to pose problems of control to prison management.

And elsewhere in the women's prison system? Female prisoners are *still* imprisoned far from their homes, they are *still* subject to more petty restrictions than men, they *still* complain about the quality of the medical treatment they received, and they *still* have fewer educational, work and leisure opportunities than male prisoners. Horror stories (for example in 1993 a women at Styal Prison, at the insistence of prison officers, remained handcuffed both during labour and while giving birth in an outside hospital) *still* regularly surface in the newspapers and are confirmed by the Prison Department. As for the female prison population, in 1981 the average daily population in the women's establishments in England and Wales was 1407 (Home Office, 1982), while in 1993 it was 1560 (Home Office, 1994). Throughout the period the women's prison population has remained at a constant 3–4 per cent of the total prison population.

Yet, despite the massive increase in publicity nowadays given to women's prison issues, it could be argued that women's imprisonment in Britain is as marginalized in serious penal debate as it ever was. For in an era when the 'prison crisis' is seen to centre entirely on the male prisons, their famous Irish Republican Army (IRA) prisoners, and the issues relating to prison privatization, it is easy to see why discussions of *women's* imprisonment post-Woolf have been conducted largely in terms of an 'administrative penology' concerned primarily with managing women on bail, prisoner 'contracts' or 'compacts', skill-training, and the size and siting of custodial facilities (see NACRO, 1991; Player, 1994). There has been little discussion conducted in terms of an 'abolitionist', and 'women-wise' penal politics committed to assessing all penal innovations according to their potential to redress criminal harms without increasing class, racist and gender injustices. This is not to say that issues about how the prisons are run are unimportant. They *are* important. It *is* to insist that *theoretical* work on the administration of women's prisons should always ask: *'Whom are women's prisons for?'* – a question about legitimacy; *'What are women's prisons for?'* – a question about realities; and, *'How can criminal justice for women be Otherwise?'* – a question of utopias.

In order, to explain why we conclude that WIP's campaigning gains – though not their prisoners' welfare achievements – over the past eleven years have been relatively modest, it is apposite to discuss: first some of the changes in social and penal policies that have occurred during that time; secondly some of the penal and gender politics which call for constant theorizing if WIP is to retain its radical edge as a campaigning group against the wrongs of women's imprisonment; and thirdly the implications of these for theorizing both women's imprisonment and the recurring strategy-contradictions with which the WIP Group has been constantly confronted. At first sight, such discussion might appear to wander far away from the declared subject of this chapter; but the detour is a necessary prerequisite to even the slightest understanding of the complex of political, ideological and theoretical conditions within which the battle for penal justice for women in British prisons is still being fought.

WOMEN IN PRISON CAMPAIGN – POLITICS, THEORIES AND CONTRADICTIONS

Politics and the New Punitiveness

During the 1980s the British government's determination to minimalize the role of the welfare state resulted in savage cuts in benefits. These punitive measures fell most heavily upon women and young (especially black) people who, for one reason or another, were already suffering extremes of poverty (see Byrne, 1987; Bull and Wilding, 1983). For the last decade, too, Tory penal 'policy' has backed schemes purportedly designed to save money by reducing the prison population, at the same time as counterproductively indulging in scaremongering rhetoric about a breakdown in law and order to divert attention from the failure of government economic, health and education policies. Such reckless and contradictory tactics (together with the sentencing and penal confusion they caused), played a major part in creating what we are calling the New Punitiveness. It has three interrelated dimensions: the 'New Politics of Community Penality'; the 'New Folk Devils' ('single mothers' and 'unattached male youth'); and, most popular with media moralists, the 'Rise and Rise of the Crime Victim'.

The New Politics of Community Penality

The Women in Prison Group, formed to help ex-prisoners and, through liaison with serving prisoners, to contribute to a climate of change in public opinion about the taken-for-granted efficacy of imprisonment in reducing crime, has always contended that because so few women in prison have committed serious crimes of violence, the female prison population might safely be much reduced, even to the point where it could be seen as the first step in a more general strategy of prison abolitionism (Carlen, 1990). What's more, in 1988 the policy document, *Punishment, Custody and the Community* (Home Office, 1988) proclaimed that the government also wanted to see a reduction in the prison population. But theirs was not an abolitionist policy – it was state transcarceralism. The policy was designed to bring the pains of imprisonment into the 'community' by ensuring that non-custodial penalties were made so punitive that sentencers would have more confidence in awarding them. Concomitantly, more and more people (for example women at home whose errant sons and husbands would be under curfew) would perforce have their homes turned into outposts of the prison estate. Of course, it did not happen. Almost before the relevant legislation was published (Criminal Justice Act 1991) magistrates, judges and media were clamouring against what was rather prematurely portrayed as a 'new leniency'. Vigilante groups were formed and applauded for patrolling the parts that the official police no longer seemed able to reach, and the government set about fashioning new and more punitive legislation (see Criminal Justice Act 1994, which abolishes the 'right to silence' of suspects and introduces new punitive measures against squatters and Travellers).

Allowing 'community' common sense to decide crime issues meshed very well with the Conservative government's populist and increasingly punitive anti-'expert' and anti-professional propaganda. But although the rhetoric of 'punishment in the community' quickly faded, that of 'treatment in the community' (for the mentally ill) did not. During late 1994 the myth of 'community' still serves to justify the almost complete lack of effective care for innumerable mentally disturbed people. Alone, destitute and vulnerable, they repeatedly drift in and out of trouble until, eventually, prison provides the only 'community care' they ever receive.

The New Folk Devils

It was during the period 1988–94, that two new sets of folk devils appeared. 'Single mothers' to be 'deterred' by punitive changes in welfare and housing legislation; the other, 'unattached youth', to become the butts of all kinds of penal fantasies – from hard labour for ten-year-olds, to bringing back both corporal and capital punishments. Here we will just describe the new punitiveness towards women – young mothers living on benefits, and independently of a male.

The 1990s attack on single mothers in Britain was provoked by the mish-mash of anti-poor prejudices that comprise right-wing versions of underclass theory. Basically, the rhetoric goes like this: found in neighbourhoods containing high numbers of fatherless families headed by never-married mothers, the 'underclass' poor are those who, having been reared by permissive mothers and a supportive welfare state, now refuse to work and, instead, engage in predatory, violent and society-threatening crime (Murray, 1990). Implicit in the theory is the old notion that all crime is explicable in terms of family structure and parenting, together with the even older calumny that women are the roots of all evil. As the title of Helena Kennedy's excellent 1992 book puts it, *Eve Was Framed!* None the less, the persistence of these misogynist theories should alert 'women in prison' campaigners to the need to be very careful when making demands for women prisoners in terms of formal equality only.

The Rise and Rise of the Crime Victim

The final strand in the New Punitiveness can be found in the rise and rise of the crime victim. Since the mid-1970s there has been a growing emphasis on the neglect and invisibility of the victim of crime in the administration of justice. The iconography of crime-victim wrongs has been useful both to academics and to politicians of all parties wishing to make a populist appeal on law and order issues. (Even though anyone with a modicum of common sense may always have assumed that it is primarily because crimes *do* have victims that anyone ever cared about crime in the first place!) The most ironical development of the 'crime victim' movement that concerns us here is that, as far as some feminist theorists are concerned, it is nowadays acceptable for women to be seen as 'victims' of male crime, but not as victims of, say, poverty or over-harsh criminal justice or penal systems (cf. Shaw, 1992). In short, the structural causes of women's lawbreaking are often as politically embarrassing to feminists, who wish to represent all women as being 'strong' (and not victims), as they are to the current leadership of both main political parties in Britain who regularly make cheap electoral appeals by concentrating attention on 'respectable women' crime victims.

The results? Increasing fear or crime; daily demands for stiffer sentences as deterrents to potential lawbreakers; and, a steep increase in levels of criminological illiteracy among all sectors of the population. What chance, then, of maintaining concern about what goes on in the women's prisons? Or even of any sensible appraisal of the relationships between crime rates and imprisonment rates, between imprisonment, prison regimes and subsequent re-offending? In such a climate of fear and punitive revenge towards the deviant poor, why bother to continue campaigning on women's prison issues? Moreover, in addition to the mid-1990s difficulties of a changed and more vengeful political climate, the women's prison lobby is also perennially faced with two other questions. One – about how to avoid incorporation into an administrative penology – is a concern shared by all radical prison reform groups; the other – asking whether the pains of women's imprisonment are sufficiently different to those suffered by male prisoners to justify separate theorizing and consideration – is specifically about gender and justice. These issues are discussed in the next part of section two below.

Penal Politics, Gender and Justice

Incorporation and Administrative Criminology
Fear that the power of radical critique will be neutralized if incorporated into the prison's administrative machinery has always provoked debate among prison campaigners as to the extent to which they should become involved in issues relating to the day-to-day running of the prisons. The concern is threefold: first, that they will become part of short-term reformist schemes which often lend a spurious appearance of legitimacy to prison regimes without diminishing their fundamentally debilitating effects; second, that they will become involved in programmes which, though experienced positively by women already in prison, are seen by sentencers to provide justification for sending even more women to prison; and third, that they will endorse innovations which, though they might in principle be radically progressive, are likely in practice to be perverted by punitive sentencing practices or subverted by lack of adequate funding and support. Take, for example, the post-Woolf proposal by the government-funded National Association for the Care and Resettlement of Offenders that women prisoners should serve their sentences in 'community houses':

> In the long term the way to meet the vision of the Woolf Report would be to keep the small numbers of women in their home area, close to court, in houses set aside for the purpose. The women would reside

there during custody and avail themselves of the community's services to supply the elements of their daily regime. This would be essential since it would be uneconomic for the Prison Service to provide full programmes in very small units. Contact with home and family would be maintained by proximity or by joint residence for young children, space permitting. (NACRO, 1991: 19)

This is an imaginative concept and could, in the best (utopian) scenario, lead to the abolition of women's imprisonment as it is known at present. Yet once the proposal is assessed against the *backcloth of contemporary penal politics* in Britain, it is immediately apparent why any radical group of women's prison campaigners should carefully distinguish between the proposal's radical potential and the reformist, and even retrogressive, probabilities of its actual implementation. For in the context of the New Punitiveness, with its emphasis on young unmarried mothers as *the* folk devils of late-twentieth-century 'welfare', it is very likely that the existence of such houses would soon be perceived by sentencers as providing yet another excuse to lock up more and more young women seen to be in need of 'training' as 'mothers'. Similarly, some of the proposals rosier assumptions about women's need for family under all circumstances begin to fade when set against what is known about either domestic violence, or the non-existent 'family lives' of many young women prisoners who have been state-reared in local authority care.

Finally, although the suggestion that, 'Allowing women in this situation to use community facilities would be essential' (NACRO, 1991: 19) is, in itself, an excellent one, it is appropriate to remind enthusiasts for 'community houses' that for the last ten years (at least) it has been the constant complaint of workers attempting to deliver 'alternatives to custody' that their best efforts have been repeatedly subverted by the scarcity of *any* resources in the 'community' and especially those most relevant to women's needs, for example nursery schools, further education grants, satisfying work, move-on accommodation, crisis loans for furniture, and affordable care for elderly relatives, to name but a few. In short, if community houses for women prisoners were to be founded without stringent sentencing controls, and adequate funding and extensive community back-up facilities, they would soon deteriorate into *fin de siècle* workhouses for the welfare state's 'undeserving' and poverty-stricken mothers.

So why continue to take seriously the proposal for community houses for women prisoners? For several reasons. First, because any *intention* to reduce the pains of imprisonment for women is *good in itself*. Secondly, because while prisons exist, in any form, such a good can only be pursued if campaigners continue to engage in democratic discussion and co-operative enterprise with prisoners, prison staff, prison administrators and opinion leaders. Thirdly, because it is essential to keep open to public view the inner workings of the whole carceral machinery, so that its endemic secrecy can be held in check, and its chronic tendency for periodic reversion from progressive to retrogressive practices constantly monitored.

The purpose of giving full recognition to the political conditions which *may* atrophy the radically progressive potential of new penal initiatives is *not* to enable campaigners to take refuge in a 'nothing works' nihilism. Instead, the *intention* in recognizing the contradictions between present realities and utopian desires is to facilitate analysis of the conditions in which present realities might begin to be otherwise. Possibilities for such analysis will be discussed below. But first, a discussion of some problems relating to the theorization of women, gender and penal justice issues.

Women, Gender and Penal Justice

A difficult theoretical question confronting analysis of women's prison issues is: How can penal justice for women be theorized as having distinct conditions and effects which are different to those currently attendant upon penal justice for men? Yet, the problem is not that there is insufficient evidence to support, at the most general level of abstraction, claims that the economic, ideological and political conditions in which women break the law are different to those in which men do (Messerschmidt, 1986; Carlen, 1988); that female prisoners have, both nowadays and previously, been treated differently to their male counterparts (Haln-Rafter, 1985; Carlen, 1983; Dobash *et al.*, 1986; Howe, 1994); and that, overall (and still giving primacy to the very general category 'women'), women are primarily coerced not by the state's criminal justice and penal systems but by innumerable 'anti-social'[1] and informal controls that, for the time being, atrophy women's opportunities for full citizenship (Carlen, 1995). There is abundant evidence to support those claims, and there is no doubt that women's imprisonment *is* different to men's.

Rather, the problem with regard to assessing suggested reforms of the women's prisons is of whether to respond to them with a short-term reformism which, though recognizing the structurally and ideologically disadvantaged position of 'women now', may also imply that the condition of 'women now' should not change; or, whether to hold fast to a long-term abolitionism which would deny that the formal and substantive inequities attendant upon the position of 'women now' are inevitable and forever. Both options have much to recommend them. The first would support the notion of a substantive equality for women prisoners by recognizing that because, *as wives, daughters and mothers*, they are expected to invest more of themselves (both emotionally and psychologically) in their families, they may suffer more anxiety and guilt than men do when imprisonment separates them from their loved ones. The second would deny that the present familial exploitation of women is either inevitable or desirable and therefore approach with caution any proposal – like the 'community houses' one – which implied that it is desirable to reproduce uncritically contemporary 'family' conditions for women prisoners. The final section of this chapter outlines why the difficulties raised by these opposed positions should be ceaselessly confronted and worked on, but never suppressed.

WORKING ON THE CONTRADICTIONS

To conclude this polemic about the politics of women's imprisonment in Britain at the end of the twentieth century, a theoretical framework is offered which suggests some possible criteria for the assessment of future proposals for change in the social and penal response to women lawbreakers.

Recognition, Deconstruction and Denial

If campaigners are to make relevant and progressive policy interventions into the women's prison system, it is essential that they recognize the gender, race and class differences (as well as other) which shape individual women's experiences differently both in and out of prison. In other words, it is not only the different gender histories of men and women prisoners which need to be taken seriously, but also the differences between women themselves (including those between campaigners outside prison and women with first-hand experience of its cutting edge inside!). That acknowledged, it is none the less our contention that because official policy for the women's prison is often based either on stereotypes of *all* women, or on society-wide gender relationships which disempower (in varying degrees) *all* women, it is important to investigate and describe the ideological discourses and material conditions that result in women's imprisonment taking the form that it does, before *analyzing* it to explain *why* it does take that form.

Once the present forms of women's imprisonment have been broken down into their constituent parts, the relationships between carceral and extra-carceral social and ideological conditions can be specified. And their inevitability denied! By both recognizing present realities of women's imprisonment *and* denying that their existence preempts conceptions of utopian (and always unfinished) alternatives (Mathiesen, 1974), campaigners can facilitate the setting up of 'worst scenario' and 'best scenario' models against which changes in penal policy can be evaluated. Additionally, if answers to the three questions discussed below were to be sought in relation to every proposed reform of custodial arrangements for female prisoners, they might aid assessment of the contribution each new initiative might make to better or worsen conditions in women's prisons in the short term; and/or to increase or decrease the numbers of women jailed in the future.

Whom are Women's Prisons For? (A Question of Legitimacy)

Questions about the composition of the female prison population should not only concern the offending histories of women prisoners, but should also query the relationships between classes, racisms, genders and imprisonment. These latter are undoubtedly very complex, and extraordinarily difficult to investigate (see Daly, 1994), but, until the time comes when there is good reason to believe that lawbreaking is *not* evenly distributed between classes, prison campaigners *must* assume that prison populations composed of disproportionate numbers of poverty-stricken and/or black people are *illegitimate*. For too often, when women's imprisonment is discussed, the debate is framed solely in terms of evidence that the majority of jailed women have committed less serious offences than male prisoners and that, on the whole, they also have shorter and less violent criminal records.

Argument of this kind is of course important if it is assumed that the state's power to imprison is predicated upon the classic justification that punishment should fit the crime and that therefore only the most serious offenders merit imprisonment. Assumption of that kind is, however, unwarranted. Empirical analyses of prison populations suggest that in recent times no equivalence between crime-seriousness and severity of punishment has either been sought or achieved, and that female prison populations in Britain continue to contain disproportionate numbers of black British or foreign women as well as too many with sociobiographies characterized by multiple social disadvantage and deprivation. This being so, new initiatives for women's prisons should not be assessed only in the light of answers to questions about *whom* women's prisons are for. Bearing in mind the *class-skewed* nature of the female prison population, campaigners for social justice should also insistently ask the following question.

What Are Women's Prisons For? (A Question about Realities)
The drawback to arguing for a reduction in the women's prison population solely on the basis of what is known about women prisoners'
offending profiles stems from the impossibility of deducing from
statistical analyses alone exactly why any prison population takes the
form it does. In relation to female prison populations, it is also necessary
to consider what is known about judicial reasoning in cases when a
judge feels that he or she has a real choice as to whether or not to impose
a custodial sentence on a woman (Carlen, 1983; Kennedy, 1992). Given
that the judicial sentencing logic in such cases is likely to be shot
through with all kinds of discriminatory reasoning (even though the
Criminal Justice Act 1991, Section 95, made discrimination on the
grounds of gender illegal), a two-pronged attack on women's imprisonment is called for.

First there should be a routine monitoring of both women's prison
regimes and the population confined within them, and secondly a persistent denial of the legitimacy of locking up convicted women (and those on
remand) because of their failure to conform to prevailing stereotypes of
respectable daughter-mother-wife-hood. Working on the contradiction of
both appreciating the present realities of women's imprisonment without
conceding that they are inevitable and forever, involves also the uneasy
recognition that any reform undertaken in the justifiable hope that it will
empower women currently remanded in custody or serving jail terms may
also increase the likelihood of *certain* women being imprisoned more
frequently in the future.

For example: if the advent of 'community houses' were to result in
more women being allowed to have their children with them while
they were serving a custodial sentence, it is very likely that particular
reform might remove one inhibition (reluctance to separate a mother
from her child – see Carlen, 1992) from judges otherwise inclined
towards custodial sentences for women living independently of men and
on welfare. The lesson of these contradictions for 'women in prison'
campaigners is not that they should reject every initiative on the
grounds that it must inevitably be retrogressive in the long term; but
that in the short term they themselves should always be on the alert to
spot any increase in the female prison population which might be
attributable to recent and well-publicized reforms in the women's
gaols. For the time being, however, and while women's prisons
exist, the only ethical stance towards them is to work also on the
utopian contradiction that in reality they are, and must always be,
Otherwise.

How Can Criminal Justice for Women Be Otherwise? (A Question of Utopias)

In order for criminal justice for women to be other than it is, campaigners for its reform have constantly to acknowledge and understand all the extra-legal and extra-judicial (Other) conditions of women's existence which together shape the regulation of women under different political and economic regimes. In this chapter we have argued that in 1990s Britain there is a New Punitiveness that is, in large measure, directed first at young people in general, and secondly at young women. Additionally, it has to be recognized that the increasing wealth and income inequalities of the last two decades have fallen most heavily on women. Furthermore, women have become increasingly vulnerable to the continued welfare-policing of families, with resistance to this being met by the media pillory-ing of women seen to be challenging social orthodoxies about women's proper place (Byrne, 1987; Coote and Campbell, 1987; and Rose, 1989).[2]

Unless proposed reforms of criminal justice for women are contextual-ized within the Other arena of social inequities whose material force always and already make criminal justice impossible, custodial conditions for women are likely to worsen, their post-prison effects are likely to mul-tiply and become more deleterious, and the numbers of women jailed in the future will probably increase. That is why, as well as always being appraised of the current realities (both official and Other, both general and gender-wise) of women's imprisonment, prison justice campaigners should conceive of criminal justice as a long-term and always unfinished project necessarily involving the formal assumption that whatever is must be Otherwise;[3] and committed, also, to the social ethic that a fundamental prerequisite for a *legitimated* criminal justice must inhere in the criminal justice system's capacity to redress criminal harm without increasing still further class, racist and gender injustices.[4] It was as a result of a passionate belief that realistic campaigning must always be accompanied by utopian theorizing that Pat Carlen (1990) put forward a strategy for the abolition of women's imprisonment.

We believe that the arguments adduced then still hold, and that for an *experimental period of five years, imprisonment should be abolished as a 'normal' punishment for women and that a maximum of only a hundred places should be retained for female offenders convicted or accused of abnormally serious crimes.* During that time:

1. Women convicted or accused of abnormally serious crimes should only be imprisoned after their cases have been referred by the trial judge to a Sentencing Council who would make the final adjudication.

2. There would be close monitoring of the sentencing of all women and especially of those whose sentences ran counter to the usual tariff.

3. A fundamental and far-reaching examination of *all* sentencing should be undertaken as called for by Andrew Ashworth (1988).

And as for the prison buildings?
Pull them down.

Notes

1. The term anti-social control is used as Carlen (1995) defines it: a generic term for a variety of malign institutionalized practices which *either* set limits to individual action by favouring one set of citizens at the expense of another so as to subvert equal opportunities ideologies in relation to gender, race, and class (or other social groupings); *or* (in societies without equal opportunities ideologies) set limits to individual action in ways which are anti-social because they atrophy an individual's social contribution and do so on the grounds of either biological attributes or exploitative social relations.

2. Note the telling report of Coote and Campbell (1987: 280): 'The women of Greenham Common came in for a particularly nasty brand of misogynist reporting, which characterised them as dirty, violent scroungers who were probably in the pay of Moscow.'

3. The term 'Other' is being used here in at least two ways. First to refer to the present ordering of non-criminal matters which, though they remain in an asymmetrical relationship to the criminal justice system, none the less partly determine the form that it takes through the *coup de force* (see Derrida, 1992) which always has to be presented as other than it is ... i.e. legitimated. A *radical* politics of criminal justice both recognizes and denies the power of that *coup de force*. Secondly, it refers to a notion that at the moment of simultaneous recognition and denial of present realities, new, and presently utopian, visions of social and criminal justice become possible (see Carlen, 1994b).

4. There are other prerequisites, and, because the conditions for change change, there will always be. As Thomas Mathiesen has argued (1974: 13): 'The "finished alternative" is finished in a double sense of the word'.

References

Ashworth, A. (1988) 'The Road to Sentencing Reform', in *Prison Reform*, no. 5 (London: Prison Reform Trust).

Bull, D. and Wilding, P. (eds) (1983) *Thatcherism and The Poor* (London: Child Poverty Action Group).

Byrne, D. (1987) 'Rich and Poor: The Growing Divide', in A. Walker and C. Walker (eds), *The Growing Divide: A Social Audit 1979–1987* (London: Child Poverty Action Group).

Carlen, P. (1983) *Women's Imprisonment* (London: Routledge and Kegan Paul).

Carlen, P. (1988) *Women, Crime and Poverty* (Buckingham: Open University Press).

Carlen, P. (1990) *Alternatives to Women's Imprisonment* (Buckingham: Open University Press).

Carlen, P. (1992) 'Justice and Gender: The Need for Reform', in L. Samuelson and B. Schissel (eds), *Criminal Justice: Sentencing Issues and Reform* (Toronto: Garamond).

Carlen, P. (1994a) 'Why Study Women's Imprisonment? Or Anyone Else's?', in *British Journal of Criminology*, vol. 34, Special Issue.

Carlen, P. (1994b) 'Modernisms, Poststructuralisms and Miscarriages of Justice', paper presented at The 64th Annual Meeting of the American Society of Criminology in Miami, November.

Carlen, P. (1995) 'Virginia, Criminology and the Anti-Social Control of Women' in T. Blomberg and S. Cohen (eds), *Law, Punishment and Social Control* (New York: Aldine de Gruyter).

Clare, A. and Thompson, J. (1985) *Report on Visits Made to C1 Unit Holloway* (London: National Council for Civil Liberties).

Coote, A. and Campbell, B. (1987) *Sweet Freedom* (2nd edn) (Oxford: Basil Blackwell).

Daly, K. (1994) *Gender, Crime and Punishment* (New Haven and London: Yale University Press).

Derrida, J. (1992) 'Force of Law: "The Mystical Foundation of Authority"', in D. Cornell, M. Rosenfeld and D. Carlson (eds), *Deconstruction and the Possibility of Justice* (London: Routledge: 1–67).

Dobash, R.; Dobash, R.; and Gutteridge, S. (1986) *The Imprisonment of Women* (Cambridge: Polity).

Haln-Rafter, N. (1985) *Partial Justice* (Boston: Northwestern University Press).

Home Office (1982) *Prison Statistics for England and Wales, 1981*, Cmnd 9027 (London: HMSO).

Home Office (1985) *Report of the Holloway Project Committee* (London: Home Office).

Home Office (1988) *Punishment, Custody and the Community* Cmnd 424 (London: HMSO).

Home Office (1994) 'The Prison Population in 1993 and Long Term Projections to 2001', Home Office Statistical Bulletin 16/94 (June).

Howe, A. (1994) *Punish and Critique: Towards a Feminist Analysis of Penality* (London: Routledge).

Kennedy, H. (1992) *Eve Was Framed* (London: Chatto and Windus).

Lester, A. and Taylor, P. (1989) *'H' Wing, HM Prison Durham* (London: Women in Prison).

Liebling, A. (1992) *Suicides in Prison* (London: Routledge).

Mathiesen, T. (1974) *The Politics of Abolition*, Oxford, Martin Robertson

Messerschmidt, J. (1986) *Capitalism, Patriarchy and Crime* (Totowa, N.J.: Rowan and Littlefield).

Murray, C. (1990) *The Emerging British Underclass* (London: Institute of Economic Affairs).

NACRO (1991) *A Fresh Start for WOMEN Prisoners* (London).

O'Dwyer, J., Wilson, J. and Carlen, P. (1987) Women's Imprisonment in England, Wales and Scotland: recurring issues in P. Carlen and A. Worrall, *Gender, Crime and Justice* (Milton Keynes: Open University Press).

Player, E. (1994) 'Women's Prisons After Woolf', in E. Player and M. Jenkins (eds), *Prisons After Woolf* (London: Routledge).

Rose, N. (1989) *Governing the Soul* (London: Routledge).

Seear, N. and Player, E. (1986) *Women in the Penal System* (Howard League for Penal Reform).

Shaw, M. (1992) 'Issues of Power and Control: Women in Prison and Their Defenders', in *British Journal of Criminology*, vol. 32, no. 4.

Women's National Commission (1991) *Women in Prison* (Cabinet Office).

Woolf, Lord Justice (1991) *Prison Disturbances April 1990: Report of an Inquiry by the Rt Hon. Lord Justice Woolf (Parts I and II) and His Honour Judge Stephen Tumim (Part II),* Cmnd 1456 (London: HMSO).

11 The Russian Prison System: Past, Present and Future

Alexander S. Mikhlin and Roy D. King[1]

In this chapter we set out to do three things. First, to say something of the repressive history of the Russian prison system; secondly, to describe the system as it exists today, giving an indication both of its recent reforms and the problems it faces; and then to offer a glimpse of some likely future developments.

THE YEARS OF REPRESSION

In the early years after the October Revolution in Russia no system for the implementation of punishment in the true sense of the word actually existed. The first Code of Corrective-Labour Law of the Russian Soviet Federative Socialist Republic (RSFSR) was introduced in 1924 and this was superseded by another in 1933. However, the status of these Legal Codes was largely symbolic since repression outside the law was perpetrated on a major scale. By the mid-thirties any force the Code of Corrective-Labour Law might once have had was almost completely eroded, although it was not officially abolished. Instead, repressive organs of state power simply sidestepped the Code by issuing directives which, in practice, became the effective guidelines governing the bodies implementing punishment. So-called enemies of the people were summoned before 'special committees' or 'troikas' and dispatched without trial to special camps set up by the NKVD.[2]

The special committees or troikas were administrative bodies attached to the NKVD and were established in accordance with a resolution of the Central Executive Committee[3] which was adopted by the Council of People's Commissars[4] of the USSR on 5 November 1934. Special committees were set up in the provinces as well as the capital; although they were only authorized to issue sentences of imprisonment and internal exile, in practice they also issued sentences of execution (by shooting). As à rule their decisions were taken and acted upon secretly and were not subject to appeal. Death sentences were implemented without delay. Any reference to the rights of prisoners at that time would be quite meaningless, for none existed. In the camps the staff could do as they pleased: there were many instances of group shootings of prisoners by staff.

Reliable data on the deliberations of the courts and troikas and on the numbers sent to the camps or executed are hard to come by. On the other hand estimates are common, although, not surprisingly, they vary widely. It is not always clear to which time periods they refer, or to what causes the deaths are attributed, or where the camps of the GULag end and other forced mass movements of the *kulaks* and ethnic populations begin. Thus, at the 1992 Conference on Prison Reform in the Former Totalitarian Countries it was claimed 'that during the years of Soviet rule between 30 and 55 million people were executed, or died in labour camps, or while in exile, or during transit between camps'; and that 'between 27 and 45 million people currently living in Russia are former prisoners (at least one fourth of the adult population)'.[5] For the most part these figures are published without reference to sources and leave considerable room for argument and speculation, although Brzezinski (1990: 27) quotes figures of between 20 and 40 millions, who are loosely described as Stalin's victims, and cites Conquest (1968) as a historian who favours the upper part of that range as the best estimate.

Such broad brush estimates are not very useful for our purposes. Although it is hard to get more detailed figures some statistics have recently entered the public domain based partly upon the archives and partly upon estimates derived from the archives. According to Dugin (1991), for example, 9.5 million Soviet citizens passed through the GULag of whom 650 000 were shot. A large proportion of those persons never even appeared before a court. The same researcher reported that 3 777 380 persons were given sentences for so-called 'counter-revolutionary' crimes between 1921 and 1955, and of those 2.9 million were sentenced by the board of OGPU[6] and troikas and special committees of the NKVD (Dugin, 1991: 7). It is not immediately obvious how these data can be reconciled with those quoted at the Conference on Prison Reform in Former Totalitarian Countries.

Detkov (1992: 66) presents a table giving the numbers of prisoners deprived of their liberty, pre- and post-trial, as at 1 January of each year which is in turn based upon materials researched by V. Zemskov and D. Volkogonov.[7] We reproduce this table, for what it is worth, because it surely has limitations, below.

It is important to recognize that the figures in Table 11.1 will only be as reliable as the archives themselves. When presenting these data Detkov

Table 11.1   Population in prisons and camps under Stalin as at 1 January 1930–1953

1930	179 000	1938	996 367	1946	600 897
1931	212 000	1939	1 317 195	1947	808 839
1932	268 000	1940	1 334 408	1948	2 199 535
1933	334 300	1941	1 500 524	1949	2 550 275
1934	510 307	1942	1 415 596	1950	2 561 351
1935	725 483	1943	983 974	1953	2 561 351
1936	839 406	1944	663 594		
1937	820 881	1945	715 506		

himself points out that the following alternative figures, which sometimes differ widely from his own, had already appeared in the press for various years:[8] (1935) 965 742; (1940) 1 659 992; (1945) 2 468 524; (1946) 1 371 986; (1950) 1 460 677. At present, without a good deal of further research, there seems to be no good reason for preferring one set of figures to another. We have not had direct access to the archives ourselves for the purposes of writing this chapter. One thing is clear however, the numbers of prisoners for each of those terrible years in the history of the USSR were very large indeed and were measured in their many hundreds of thousands and often in their several millions.

It seems particularly likely that the figures quoted above will be subject to considerable margins of error for the key years of repression. The data for 1937 and 1938 seem particularly incomplete, bearing in mind that these years saw Stalin's purging by shooting of some 37 000 army and 3 000 navy officers – more than actually perished during the first two years of the Second World War (Brzezinski, 1990: 24). It may be that the archive figures simply omit certain categories. Conquest (1968), piecing together estimates from a variety of necessarily speculative sources concludes that during the great purge of 1937–8 there were perhaps between six and eight million arrests, of whom perhaps 10 per cent – some 700 000 or so persons – were executed. Moreover, the Stalin–Molotov Secret Instruction of 8 May 1933 referred to some 800 000 persons in places of detention, not counting those in labour camps and colonies. By the end of 1938 Conquest supposes that there were perhaps as many as eight million in camps, and that two million may have died there in the preceding two years. It seems that Conquest excludes 'criminals' as not being specifically victims of the purge. Disentangling 'political repression' from 'criminal justice' for these years is likely to remain a difficult process.

Nevertheless, taking Detkov's figures in conjunction with what might reasonably be supposed in the light of other known historical events, there appears to be two major periods when the use of the camps was at its most extensive: first, the years immediately prior to the war and at its outset (1937–42) and the post-war period (1948–53). The strong probability is that the peak years were 1937 and 1938. During the war there was a big drop in numbers because prisoners were allowed to volunteer for the army: if they were wounded in action they did not have to return to complete their sentences. At the end of the war there was an amnesty which appears to have substantially reduced numbers in custody, although there are no official figures available as to how many prisoners were released in this way. The repression of the post-war period, which ranged from incarcerating those who returned to the USSR after having been prisoners of war for 'betraying their homeland', through the hunting out of 'enemies of the people', to the arrests before and after the 'Doctors' Plot', was interrupted by the death of Stalin at the beginning of 1953. There is little doubt that but for that event the number of victims would have been even larger.

The conditions in which prisoners were held in the years immediately prior to the war, and during the war itself, were very bad indeed. In the Butyrka prison in Moscow a prisoner reported in 1933 that his cell which was intended for 24 prisoners actually housed 72: but in 1937 it contained 140 (Ivanov-Ruzumnick, 1965: 209), and the cell once occupied by Pugachev alone, before his execution under Catherine the Great, now held 65 prisoners (Lipper, 1951: 57). Butyrka was built in 1771 and probably had a design capacity of up to 3500 prisoners with about 2.5 square metres of space per prisoner. During the Great Purge it held about 30 000 prisoners (Lipper, 1959: 7). Kharkov, a prison which was built for about 800 prisoners, held about 12 000 in the autumn of 1937 (cited in Conquest, 1968: 290). In the first months of the war, according to some estimates, as many as 750 000 prisoners were evacuated from camps and prisons in the European part of the USSR. In the new premises to which the prisoners were relocated there was less than one square metre per prisoner (Ivanov and Yemelin 1991). Mortality rates rose sharply as a result of poor food, overcrowding, and the consequent spread of disease; still other prisoners fell victim to the stresses associated with separation from relatives, many of whom died at the front. According to Zemskov (1989), 100 997 prisoners died in the camps during 1941, while in 1942 the figure was 248 877, and 1943 accounted for a further 166 967: during the war years (1941–45) the GULag buried 621 637 prisoners, and over the period 1934 to 1947, the total was 963 766 dead. Once again, it should be noted that these figures are much lower than those adduced by Conquest and others.

It is perhaps worth pointing out that during those years most of the Soviet population lived in very difficult material conditions and suffered great privations. The situation in the camps, however, was made worse by the callous treatment of the prisoners by many prison staff. Between 1941 and 1944 a number of decrees were issued by the Ministry of the Interior proposing that food and accommodation for prisoners should be improved. Some authors, for example Smirnov, hold that this led to a certain improvement in conditions in the camps. However, the main reason for the overcrowding in the camps – the confinement of enormous numbers of innocent people – had not been touched. Therefore, there would appear to be little justification for Smirnov (1948: 22) referring to these improvements as constituting any 'fundamental change'. Quite apart from anything else, when large tracts of the country lay in ruins, the actual prerequisites for such fundamental change were simply not available (see, for example, Detkov, 1992: 72).

THE TENTATIVE RE-EMERGENCE OF LEGALITY

In the middle of the 1950s legality began gradually to be reinstated. The special committees, troikas, and other bodies which had been responsible for implementing the earlier repression were disbanded. The process of rehabilitating innocent people who had been victims of the purges and who had been kept in the camps began on a wide scale. It is less clear what happened to camp staff who had participated in atrocities. If prisoners had been beaten or shot in accordance with orders from above, then it seems unlikely that the camp staff, or perhaps anyone else, would have borne the consequences. In situations where they were held to be acting outside their authority or otherwise infringing 'socialist legality' then they might have been dismissed, or convicted and sentenced for criminal activities. In some cases they too may have been shot, for the death penalty could also be used as a punishment for staff, although there are no figures available on any of these matters.

In December 1958 the Council of Ministers of the USSR ratified a new Statute concerning Corrective-Labour Colonies and Prisons of the Interior Ministry of the USSR. This Statute defined the main tasks for penal establishments; specified the nature of the system of corrective labour colonies as a whole; established criteria for classifying colonies into different types with different regimes and conditions for different types of prisoners; and set out the admissible means for bringing influence to bear on prisoners that would correct their behaviour or deter them from committing further crimes. It was, perhaps, a small beginning. Nevertheless, one of the leading scholars of the period – Professor B. S. Utevskii – wrote that this Statute prepared the ground for the transition from a corrective-labour system organized according to administrative decrees issued by the organs of executive power to one governed by corrective-labour legislation.[9] Thus the new statute specified the level of restrictions that applied in colonies of different types with regard to the number of parcels which could be delivered to prisoners by hand or by post, the number of visits they might receive, and the opportunities they could have for buying additional food and other items on sale in prison and colony shops. After the unbridled tyranny of the past, when prisoners could be held incommunicado unable even to correspond with their families, these modest new rights for those serving sentences in colonies and prisons were regarded as a major achievement.

On 9 September 1961 the new Statute concerning corrective-labour colonies and prisons of the Interior Ministry of the RSFSR was duly ratified by a Decree of the Presidium of the Supreme Soviet of the RSFSR. Shortly afterwards, in 1963, a new type of colony was set up – the settlement colony – in which prisoners lived and worked without guards but under supervision, and were entitled, if they so wished, to have their families living with them and to wear their own clothes.

In the first half of the 1960s a start was made on the preparation of new corrective-labour legislation, and in 1969 the Fundamental Principles for Corrective-Labour Legislation of the USSR and Union Republics were adopted. Then, in 1970–71, the Republican Corrective-Labour Codes were introduced and still operate today, albeit with numerous modifications. Although the protection these offered to the rights of prisoners remained limited, in comparison with what had gone before the new Codes represented a further step forward. However, by the beginning of the 1960s the prison population, which had declined substantially after the death of Stalin, had once again begun to rise.

The sharp fall in the numbers in prison after 1953 was accounted for, in part, by the release through amnesty and subsequent rehabilitation of persons who had been victims of illegal repression and who were not replaced by newly defined 'enemies of the people'. It was also partly a product of the fact that criminal prisoners were, at first, dealt with less harshly by the courts even without actual changes in the law. The same discretion which allowed the courts to sentence more leniently for a particular offence also allowed them to sentence more severely in response to 'directives from above', and by 1966 the suppression of 'hooliganism' under Brezhnev led to a sharp rise in the use of punishment involving deprivation of liberty and growth in the prison population. According to Detkov, in 1961 the total number of prisoners in colonies and prisons had fallen to 395 600 yet, by 1966 it had risen again to 583 600. In the years that followed, that figure continued to rise: 1970 – 816 700; 1975 – 896 500; 1979 – 937 200; 1985 – 1 525 600. It was only after 1985, with the introduction of *perestroika*, that a change made itself felt. The number of prisoners began to fall again: in 1986 there were 1 461 800 prisoners; in 1987 – 1 139 400; in 1988 – 860 200; and in 1989 – 761 900.

Changes in the size of the population in custody in Russia as elsewhere are a product of complex changes in the numbers of offenders coming before the courts, the proportion of those who receive custodial sentences, and the length of time they can expect to spend in custody. It is not possible on the basis of currently available data to offer a full analysis, but it is clear that over the last thirty years or so, since legal statistics were first published in 1962, there has been a major proportionate decline in the use of immediate custody. Deprivation of liberty in prisons or corrective labour colonies remains the most widely used form of punishment, but whereas in 1970 it accounted for almost two-thirds of court disposals, in 1992 that had been reduced to a little over one-third. The remaining two-thirds of offenders were given suspended sentences or else were sentenced to corrective labour without the deprivation of liberty, or were given fines or other forms of punishment which do not involve isolation from society. The details of these changes in sentencing outcomes are given in Table 11.2.

In Table 11.2, as so often with Russian statistics, the data are presented in percentage terms without giving an indication of actual numbers. However, in 1992 in Russia the 34.2 per cent who were sentenced to deprivation of liberty involved some 225 900 new admissions to the prisons and colonies.

THE PRISON SYSTEM TODAY

In a recent paper (King, 1994), one of the authors of this chapter has discussed the developments in the Russian system of corrective labour since *perestroika*, especially in the light of reforms introduced on 21 October 1991 and 12 June 1992. However, there have been further changes in the year since that was written, and so it is necessary to update that here.

Table 11.2   Percentage distribution of court disposals 1962–92

Year	Depriv. Liberty	Correct. Labour	Suspend Dep. Lib.	Deferred Sentence	Suspend S. or Lab.	Fine	Other
USSR							
1962	57.3	20.7	9.4	–	–	11.0	1.6
1965	57.6	21.9	13.2	–	–	6.2	1.1
1970	63.7	17.9	7.5	–	4.3	5.9	0.7
1975	58.0	17.9	7.4	–	10.0	6.1	0.6
1980	57.0	16.0	8.7	–	13.1	3.6	1.6
1985	45.2	21.8	3.8	9.3	8.5	9.7	1.7
1990	36.2	22.0	7.7	13.8	7.4	12.4	0.5
RUSSIA							
1990	37.8	21.8	8.4	13.4	6.6	11.6	0.4
1991	34.9	21.8	10.1	14.1	6.7	12.2	0.2
1992	34.2	18.3	11.2	14.4	5.9	9.5	6.5*

*Includes 6.3 per cent released under amnesty: previously, amnestied prisoners were excluded.

Remand or Isolation Prisons

Persons awaiting trial or sentence are held in cellular *remand* or *isolation prisons* which may also hold a small number of sentenced prisoners, either on a temporary basis while awaiting transfer to a colony or more permanently as cleaners or food service workers or in some other capacity. Often the cells in remand prisons are more like wards or dormitories; today the 160 remand prisons are grossly overcrowded with more than 200 000 prisoners. The Butyrka prison in Moscow, for example, currently houses over 5 000 prisoners – some in crowded cells with less than a square metre of living space per prisoner. Prisoners may spend many months, and sometimes several years, before trial, during which time visits are at the discretion of the investigating magistrate and are rarely permitted until the investigation is completed.

Corrective Labour Colonies

The vast majority of persons sentenced to deprivation of liberty serve their sentences in corrective labour colonies while a small proportion are held in more conventional cellular prisons. Colonies can be divided into three categories: *open*, *semi-closed* and *closed*. The first category comprises the *settlement colonies* which were introduced in 1963. There are presently 158 of these, catering for 39 300 prisoners who have committed less serious crimes, or who have already served part of their sentence in semi-closed colonies where their behaviour has been deemed to have indicated their intention to reform.

Prisoners in settlement colonies are not under guard although they are subject to supervision. Under no circumstances are they allowed to go beyond the confines of the district, region or republic in which they are held. However, they may move freely around the colony during the day, and with the permission of staff they can go outside to visit local shops, canteens and other buildings. If the necessary accommodation is available, prisoners can be given permission to live with their families, to acquire a house and to cultivate a small plot of land. No limits are laid down for the number of parcels such prisoners are allowed to receive by post or by hand, the number of visits they may receive, or to the amount of cash or valuables they are allowed to keep with them. They are also allowed to wear their own clothes. Clearly such establishments involve less than a full deprivation of liberty, although it must be remembered that most of these colonies are in the more remote Forest Zones, and prisoners may be a considerable distance from their homes.

There are presently 511 *general* and *strict regime colonies*, which might best be described as semi-closed establishments, in which some 506 600 prisoners live in hostels or barrack-style accommodation. The hostels are not locked, although the colonies are surrounded by barbed wire fences and the perimeter guards are armed. The rooms in the hostels vary considerably in size: some house 4–6 prisoners while others hold 50–100 prisoners. The prisoners are not confined to their hostels during the day, and most will go to work in a separate compound. The colonies have sports halls and recreation rooms where meetings are held and films are shown. Prisoners are organized into detachments for work and other purposes. Each detachment of between 70 and 100 prisoners has a special room used for educational work ranging from lectures to individual and group discussions between prisoners and their Detachment Head – an officer who is roughly equivalent to a Borstal house-master or an American case manager. Prisoners can also spend their leisure time there, watching television, writing letters or reading newspapers and books.

The differences between strict regime colonies which are intended for recidivists and general regime colonies for first offenders are primarily to be found in the levels of prisoners' entitlements: the number of parcels delivered by hand or post (4 or 6 a year respectively), the number of visits

(5 or 7), the amount of money a prisoner is allowed to spend (25 per cent or 30 per cent of the minimum monthly wage as laid down by law – 14 620 roubles in April 1994[10]).

After serving one-third of the sentence originally imposed by the courts, and providing a prisoner has carried out his work assignments conscientiously (if he has any), and not committed any serious infringements of prison discipline, he is given additional privileges: parcels once a month, 10–12 visits a year and the right to spend twice as much money as before. In addition, a general-regime prisoner can be given the right to spend his annual leave outside the colony after serving a third of his sentence, but a strict regime prisoner is not eligible for this privilege until he has served two-thirds of his sentence.

Until recently there were also colonies with what was called a *reinforced regime* for more serious first offenders. These occupied an intermediate position between general regime and strict regime. In 1993 these were amalgamated with general-regime colonies. There were two reasons for this. First, the expansion of non-custodial penalties and the introduction of settlement colonies creamed off many of the more minor offenders in custody so that the remaining differences among first offenders no longer justified two separate regimes. Secondly, the amalgamation of these colonies meant that first offenders could be held closer to their homes than previously had been possible. In several regions of the country there had not been a complete range of colonies, which meant that prisoners sometimes had to be transferred from one region to another to serve their sentence.

Since 1970 it has been theoretically important that prisoners should serve their sentence in the region where they were registered as living before arrest in order to facilitate contacts with their families. Recent improvements in visiting entitlements often served only to highlight the difficulties of taking advantage of the new arrangements. Amalgamation of general and reinforced regime colonies should have reduced these problems. The same logic has led researchers and penal reformers to argue that general and strict regime colonies should also be amalgamated, and such a proposal has been incorporated into the draft for a new Penal Code for Russia.

The closed colonies comprise some 50 establishments with a *special regime* and contain 32 500 prisoners described as particularly dangerous recidivists. The conditions in which these prisoners are held are significantly tougher than in the other colonies. Even so, rather more than half the special regime prisoners are housed in dormitories, albeit with restricted freedom of movement inside the colony. Only those prisoners who have committed the most serious crimes, currently about 45 per cent of the total, and prisoners on disciplinary segregation are held in locked cells, that is in conditions similar to those which can be experienced in prisons.

Young offenders aged between 18 and 20 are held in 59 educational labour colonies with either a general or a reinforced regime. The total number of such prisoners is currently 19 200. They are entitled to considerably more parcels, delivered by post and hand, and also to more visits.

Prisons

Cellular prisons, of course, constitute a more conventional variety of closed institution but they account for rather less than 1 per cent of the sentenced population. Only just over a fifth (22 per cent) of the population in cellular prisons have been directed by the courts to serve their sentences in prisons on the basis of their original crimes – as distinct from receiving a sentence of corrective labour with deprivation of liberty in the colonies. The other 78 per cent have been transferred from the colonies to prison after a serious violation of discipline in the colonies. All colonies have some limited accommodation for housing prisoners who have committed offences against discipline, and in recent years some eight special colonies have been developed with special cellular accommodation to which repeated offenders against discipline in the colonies may be transferred by administrative decision. However, the decision to transfer to prison is always taken by the courts. It follows that those who are held in prisons are generally regarded as the most dangerous criminals and the most difficult prisoners.

To speak of prisons as cellular should not convey the impression that they are necessarily intended to isolate prisoners in individual cells. The Russian prison system, like most others today, is overcrowded: but even if it were not, the normal situation would be to have several prisoners to each cell which are often, though not always, larger than cells in British prisons. Prisoners can be transferred to solitary cells to ensure an individual's own safety or to prevent him causing harm to others on the decision of the prison governor, which has to be approved by the local Procurator. Prisoners may appeal against such transfers and against other decisions to various authorities under Article 54 of Part II of the Corrective Labour Code.

Prisons provide two categories of regime conditions – *general* and *strict*. All prisoners who are sentenced to deprivation of liberty in prison, as opposed to colonies, for the first time are entitled to general regime conditions. Prisoners may also be transferred from strict regime to general regime conditions after a period of good behaviour. General regime prisoners are entitled to one hour of exercise a day and four visits and four parcels a year. They are also allowed to spend up to 20 per cent of the minimum monthly wage on extra food products and other essential items in prison shops.

Prisoners who have previously served sentences in prisons, persons who have been sentenced by the courts to terms in prison for crimes committed in institutions or who have been transferred from colonies to serve part of their sentence in prison for breaches of discipline, and prisoners who have violated prison discipline while on general regime, are all confined under strict regime conditions where they have fewer rights. Prisoners can be held under strict-regime conditions for periods of between two and six months.

CURRENT PROBLEMS AND THE IMPACT OF RECENT REFORMS

Work and Education

The dominant features of the old GULag were that political repression and Soviet needs for industrial and other developments dictated the nature, size and distribution of the population in custody. Indeed these constituted its dual *raison d'être*. The system had precious little to do with criminal justice. With the emergence of a more conventional prison system the legacy of corrective labour means that the position of work remains controversial. Ironically, some penal reformers in Russia are opposed to the law which stipulates that those sentenced to deprivation of liberty have to work in accordance with their capacities and, where possible, their skills. In practice in recent years it has often been difficult to provide work in accordance with prisoners' skills because of the limited range of work available, although prisoners can now be given the opportunity to engage in the manufacture of small articles for their own financial gain. As unemployment has struck the Russian economy as a whole, moreover, so it has become increasingly difficult to find work for prisoners. By the middle of 1993 approximately 100 000 prisoners were not provided with work. The absence of employment is likely to destabilize the system, both from the point of view of large numbers of prisoners remaining idle and because of the contribution of prison work to the funding of the system.

Conditions of work for prisoners, levels of remuneration and safety regulations are the same as for those in similar jobs outside. The only exceptions are that prisoners work six eight-hour days a week instead of the normal five, and their annual leave is shorter – 12 working days – regardless of whether that leave is spent inside the colony or outside it. Young offenders are obliged to complete their secondary education while serving their sentences, just as those who have not completed any vocational training before being sentenced are required to do so while serving their sentences.

Food and Health Care

In each corrective labour colony there is a sick-bay complete with beds for in-patients where prisoners can consult doctors and receive treatment for minor conditions. Within the penal system there are also a number of hospitals as well as some colonies specifically for the custody and treatment of prisoners suffering from infectious diseases, primarily tuberculosis. Medical care in all such establishments is free of charge.

Some of the most important reforms in recent years have been directed towards health care. A special census of the prison population carried out in early 1989 revealed that prisoners' health deteriorated the longer they stayed in prison. While only 2.9 per cent of prisoners serving sentences of less than a year were Category I, II or III invalids[11], the equivalent figures for those who had been in prison for 1–2 years was 3.3 per cent, for 2–3 years – 4.1 per cent, 3–5 years – 5.6 per cent, 5–8 years – 6.5 per cent, 8–10 years – 7.7 per cent, and for those in custody for more than 10 years the figure was 11.3 per cent. The incidence of tuberculosis (TB) in the colonies is also far higher than among the population as a whole. According to 1990 figures made available by the Procurator's Department of the USSR, every eighth prisoner was suffering from some degree of tuberculosis: thus the incidence of TB was 17 times higher than for the USSR population as a whole.[12]

As on many other matters controversy surrounds the prevalence of tuberculosis in prisons. In the past poor diet and poor conditions in the colonies can have done little to promote the health of prisoners, and over-crowding especially in the remand prisons made it difficult to prevent the spread of infection. However, it also has to be said that an important factor which may help to account for the difference between tuberculosis rates inside and outside prisons has to do with how effectively TB is detected. All prisoners now have to be tested for TB, which means that virtually all cases are picked up. This does not apply in the community outside. In addition, it is probable that the prison population is drawn primarily from that section of the community whose living conditions and lifestyles are such that they already have a higher incidence of TB than the general population. It is said that many prisoners diagnosed as suffering from TB, particularly in the early stages of the disease, refuse to be treated. At the same time, however, doctors consider that the low quality of food and poor living quarters for offenders undermine their health as did, until recently, the fact that they worked without holidays and often in harsh and unfamiliar climatic conditions. Prisoners are now entitled to 12 days' leave from work each year, and some categories of prisoner are granted home leave.

Prisoners have access to three sources of food: what is served to them in their canteens, what they buy in their colony shop and what they receive in parcels delivered by hand or by post. In recent years food rations for several groups of prisoners have been increased, although in an over-crowded system operating on meagre resources prison governors often express anxiety as to how they are going to be able to feed their prisoners. Nevertheless, the use of reduced rations for those in punishment cells or solitary confinement was abolished in 1988. The law introduced on 12 June 1992 significantly increased the sum of money prisoners could spend on additional food or essential items in the colony shop; this applied in particular to pregnant women, women whose children were being cared for in their colony's children's home, the disabled, elderly and sick. The same law also introduced changes in regard to food parcels. Formerly, prisoners had been entitled to receive these only after they had served half their sentence. Now they may receive parcels immediately upon reception, the permitted weight has been raised from 5 to 8 kilograms, and the number which can be received each year has also risen considerably.

Family Contacts

Another important area of reform has involved measures designed to facilitate contacts for prisoners with their families, in the hope of preserving family ties and helping prisoners adapt more easily to life in normal society after their release. A prisoner who no longer has a family to which to return is likely to be bereft of both material and moral support during this crucial period. Research has shown that 31.7 per cent of men's families and 50.8 per cent of women's break up while they are serving their sentences in Russian prisons or colonies. When a prisoner's family breaks up this makes his or her eventual return to society that much harder. Unless a prisoner actually owns his house or flat he may have nowhere to live on discharge because the Residence Code dictates that anyone not using their state provided accommodation for more than 6 months loses the right to that living space. He can only return to his former flat or house if all adult members of his family are prepared for him to do so. If he had been living alone his flat or room will be reallocated. A recently released prisoner with nowhere to live can buy or rent accommodation if he has the money to do so: otherwise he may be given a hostel place or a flat from the local housing committee when his turn on the waiting list comes round.

Under the law of June 12 1992 restrictions on correspondence were lifted, the frequency of visits – some of which can involve members of the family staying overnight with the prisoner in special accommodation – was increased, and some categories of prisoner were granted the possibility of home-leave. In cases where it was not possible for relatives to visit, prisoners could be allowed to telephone home. Also under the regulations of 12 June 1992, pregnant women and women with children under three years of age, have been allowed to have their sentences deferred. If it is established that a woman is pregnant while she is serving her sentence she will be released at the beginning of her maternity leave and be able to live at home and care for her child. When the child reaches the age of three, the local department of the Interior Ministry where she is registered for residence will submit a report to the court. This report will cover her behaviour, how well she has cared for her child, the nature and seriousness of her crime, how much of her sentence she had already served and how much is left to serve. On the basis of this report the court decides whether the rest of her sentence should be waived, replaced by a lesser punishment, or whether she should be sent back to a corrective-labour establishment for all or part of her remaining term. If a woman is not released to give birth and care for her child, then the child can remain in a children's home inside the colony where she is serving her sentence until it reaches the age of three or four years.

Freedom of Religion

Until recently ministers of religion were not allowed access to colonies. Prisoners were not permitted to have crosses, rosaries or other religious objects in their possession. Religious literature was banned. These prohibitions were gradually dismantled in the mid-eighties, and from 12 June 1992 more permissive regulations concerning such matters were introduced into the Corrective-Labour Code. In every colony there is now a special room or rooms where ministers of religion can meet prisoners and hold services, including baptisms and marriage ceremonies, and hear confessions. Churches have even been built in certain colonies. There is now a flood of evangelical literature which pervades even remote colonies.

Inspection

The responsibility for inspection to ensure that laws are observed within the institutions of the penal system rests with the Procurator's Office. People's Deputies and representatives of public organizations are also entitled to inspect the work of corrective-labour establishments. They are entitled to visit institutions and to talk to prisoners and staff. However, the role of such bodies is by no means confined to inspection, and may extend to executive decision-making. Thus, the approval of the committee of inspectors or the board responsible for juvenile affairs is an essential prerequisite for the granting of parole. The rights of these committees, as of the groups of representatives from other public organizations associated with specific corrective-labour institutions, such as boards of visitors working in educational-labour colonies and volunteers working to rehabilitate young offenders, are laid down in articles 110–15 of the Corrective-Labour Code.

Unfortunately, despite the inspection procedures and the strict punishments meted out to offenders, breaches of legality among prison staff are far from rare. For such acts, and also for other breaches of the law (including drunkenness, absence without leave, various forms of domestic disputes with, and assaults upon, family members or neighbours, hooliganism, motoring accidents, and so on), over 1500 prison staff are annually dismissed from the service. Breaches of discipline are committed by almost one in ten members of the prison service each year. It has to be said that in many colonies the living conditions for staff are very poor and it is not easy to recruit. Nevertheless, a great deal still needs to be done in order to get rid of confrontational relations between staff and prisoners in a situation where professional standards often fall a long way short of those in British prisons.

A LOOK AT THE FUTURE

Although the Law of 12 June 1992 achieved a good deal for prisoners there are still many questions which need to be resolved. One matter currently under consideration, for example, is whether prisoners should be entitled to receive their pensions like all other citizens of pensionable age (Mikhlin, 1993). Of course, one might wonder, given that crime is generally a young man's game, how many persons this will or should affect. Nevertheless, a restoration of pension rights would better enable such prisoners to support their families, pay compensation for loss or damage caused by their crimes, and to save towards their release.

Some of the new regulations have defined *rights* for prisoners, such as the increased number of parcels and visits, which cannot be removed even as a punishment for offences against prison discipline. Others, such as home leave and some of the special arrangements introduced for the benefit of pregnant women and nursing mothers, are contingent upon good behaviour in custody or assessments of risks to the community. They are thus regarded as *privileges* which may serve to encourage good behaviour in custody and perhaps also upon release. It is not known how far these new rights and privileges are actually taken up by prisoners nor to what extent the system of inspection ensures that new norms are implemented. At the time of writing it is expected that a new census to be conducted among prisoners may reveal the answers to these and other questions. Meanwhile, it seems likely that there may be pressures both for the transfer of more privileges into the domain of rights and for the development of more effective and independent systems of inspection. Much may depend, however, upon developments in the state of crime, and upon the public reaction to those developments.

Prison reform is never likely to be a subject that captures the public imagination for long. There are signs that the sympathy felt for persons held in harsh conditions in the colonies has evaporated with the release of the last political prisoners from Perm Colony 35: such sympathy is not being transferred to the conditions for 'ordinary criminals', especially in a situation of rising crime rates and a flagging economy. The prison population is currently rising, sometimes by as much as a thousand a week, although the effect is moderated by periodic amnesties, the most recent of which, at the time of writing, was on 23 February 1994. It would be rash, indeed, to attempt any kind of prediction as to what will happen to the Russian prison population in the future. A glance at what has happened elsewhere, however, makes it clear that these pressures will not be easily abated. In California the prison population quadrupled in a decade (Zimring and Hawkins, 1994) and in Italy it doubled in just two years (Pavarini, 1994). The sudden turnaround from a declining to an increasing prison population in England and Wales in 1993 and 1994 serves also to show how volatile such matters can be. Perhaps the best that can be hoped for is that over the next couple of years, during which time well over 100 000 prisoners might have been added to the Russian system, the situation could begin to stabilize, and perhaps then to decline once again. It is unlikely to be a smooth growth curve because the probability is that there would be further amnesties to relieve the pressures as there have been in the past.

It seems likely that there will be significant changes in the nature and quality of the prison population as a result of social and economic change.

Although economic and commercial crime and tax evasion will continue to burgeon as a market economy develops, these are unlikely to have much impact upon rates of imprisonment. Unlike economic crimes under the Soviet system which resulted in custodial sentences, new economic crimes will more likely attract fines and other penalties which do not involve deprivation of liberty. But if the widespread concern about racketeering backed by organized 'protection', the increase in armed robberies and drug-related crimes, and the high levels of violence including murder is translated into convictions, then it will change the quality of the prison population which presently includes substantial numbers of minor property offenders who in England and Wales would currently not expect custodial sentences. In the present climate in Russia the continuing commitment to the death penalty is unlikely to change, but in December 1992 life sentences were somewhat hastily introduced for persons whose death sentences had been commuted to deprivation of liberty. The number of life sentence prisoners seems destined to increase, and there remain many questions pertaining to the conditions of their confinement which have yet to be resolved.

One result of the imprisonment of a more violent and more organized criminal fraternity may be that rates of crime in penal institutions may increase. There were 2934 crimes committed in penal institutions in 1992, including 167 premeditated murders, increases of 6.7 per cent and 5.7 per cent respectively over the preceding year. Although these rates of increase were much lower than the 27 per cent growth in officially recorded crime and the 41.7 per cent growth in the murder rate outside prisons, the image of a violent prison system within a violent society is not likely to win easy converts to the cause of further humanizing what remains one of the harshest prison systems in the world. There is a major public education programme to be carried out to show that many of those presently deprived of their liberty in corrective labour colonies could as effectively be dealt with in non-custodial ways. Nevertheless, the best hope for reducing the size of the prison population in the face of increasing numbers coming before the courts must remain the acceleration of the proportionate trend away from custody and towards other measures that was shown in Table 11.2.

Meanwhile, how well will Russia be able to cope with an increased prison population in a system that in parts is already intolerably overcrowded? Two conflicting pressures will have a bearing on the outcome. On the one hand, Russia is increasingly aware of the need to strive to meet accepted international standards. On the other, it seeks to meet those standards at a time when the economy is spiralling downwards and when the historic means of funding the corrective labour colonies through the productive capacities of prisoners has been severely eroded and is likely to deteriorate still further. For the foreseeable future the balance is likely to be struck in a manner that takes account both of specific cultural features of Russian society and the position of ordinary Russian citizens in the international league tables on a variety of other socio-economic indicators.

The present legal norms regarding living space specify two square metres per prisoner in colonies and 2.5 square metres each for those serving their sentences in educational labour colonies or in prisons. These compare unfavourably with the newly published British operating standards, which specify 5.5 square metres for refurbished cells in single occupancy and 3.575 square metres per prisoner for those in double occupancy;[13] and with the American Correctional Association Standard of 3.25 square metres per person of unencumbered space.[14] The Russian standards are recognized as blatantly inadequate, but even so they are regularly breached: as we have noted some prisoners in Burtyrka and Kresty, for example, the large urban remand prisons in Moscow and St Petersburg, have less than one square metre of space each and have to sleep in shifts. There is no prospect that this situation will be swiftly turned around. The prison system is now financed directly by the Government, and two priorities have been established: to build more remand establishments or otherwise provide more remand places in centres of urban populations, and to build colonies in the central parts of European Russia so that prisoners may spend their sentences closer to home. Two new colonies for life sentence prisoners are currently under construction. But it is not easy to vote funds for prison building when there remain shortages of domestic accommodation for ordinary citizens and also for prison staff.

The United Nations Standard Minimum Rules stop short of specifying a space standard measured in square metres, but link conditions to the meeting of health requirements. However, it is hard to see how the United Nations expressed preference for accommodation in single cells or rooms could find much favour as the norm in Russia when few people will have been brought up in circumstances where there was a separate room for each member of the family. It seems likely that many Russian prisoners would actually prefer to share accommodation, albeit not in such numbers or in such close proximity as they do at present. Plans being drawn up for new colonies, and for converting existing colonies, are on the basis of smaller rooms accommodating between five and ten prisoners rather than the large barrack-like buildings presently housing groups of 50 to 100 prisoners.

As one contemplates the enormity of the task that lies ahead in further humanizing the Russian system of corrective labour, it is hard to be optimistic. However, it should be remembered that Russia is far from being alone in violating either international or its own standards in the prisons field. It is also important to acknowledge that considerable steps have already been taken. The task now is to consolidate these reforms, at a time when rising crime rates and falling economic production figures could so easily put them in jeopardy, and then to generate mechanisms for ratcheting up the conditions throughout the system. Perhaps the most important safeguards to reform lie in the spotlight of international publicity and the impetus that can give to the development of a well-informed and vigilant public on the one hand and an effective system of monitoring and independent inspection on the other.

Notes

1. We are grateful to our interpreter and translator, Kathy Judelson, for smoothing the difficulties of communication in the preparation of this paper.

2. NKVD stood for the People's Commissariat for Internal Affairs, which after 1946 became the Ministry of Internal Affairs. Until 1946 all Ministriesd were known as People's Commissariats.

3. The supreme organ of power prior to the adoption of the Constitution of the USSR in 1936.

4. The name used for the Government until 1946 after which it was known as the Council of Ministers.

5. The quotations are from the inside cover of *Prison Reform in the Former Totalitarian Countries, Conference Report,* Issue II, Moscow Centre for Prison Reform, October 1993.

6. United State Political Administration – predecessor of the KGB.

7. Detkov's sources were as follows: Zemskov V., "The GULag Archipelago" – through the eyes of a writer and statistician, in: Arguments and Facts, 1989, No. 45; Zemskov V., Documents of a Tragic Time: the Archives Reveal their Secrets, in *Arguments and Facts,* 1990, No. 35; and Volkogonov D., *Triumph and Tragedy,* Book I, Part 2, Moscow, 1989.

8. In Dugin's article 'GULag – The Heresy of Arithmetic ('Koshchunstvo Arifmetiki'), in *Chronicle of Crime,* Issue 7, 1991: 7.

9. See: Problems in the Development of Soviet Corrective-Labour Legislation, Saratov, 1961, p. 12.

10. At the time of the first draft in September 1993 it was 7000 roubles, and at the second draft in November 1993 it was 8000 roubles. Such is the rate of inflation.

11. Categories of invalidity are determined on the basis of the degree to which the person concerned is incapacitated for purposes of work: a Category I invalid requires constant care and is unable to do any kind of work; a Category II invalid is not fully able to work in the accepted sense, but can carry out some types of work activity, which are not physically taxing; a

Category III invalid is able to work but cannot carry out all types of physical work. By law work is not compulsory for Category I and II invalids, or for men over 60 and women over 55.

12. See *Arguments and Facts,* 1990, Issue no. 25.
13. The British standards (Prison Service 1994, Standards H1 and H2), which were finally published in April 1994, were lower than those contained in the July 1993 draft standards: the draft standard for double occupancy was 4.125 square metres. The published British standards also stopped short of specifying the minimum space requirement for all types of accommodation which had been in the July 1993 draft.
14. ACA (1990) Standard 3-4128 specifies 35 square feet of unencumbered space per prisoner. When prisoners are confined for more than 10 hours a day there should be 80 square feet (7.432 square metres) of total floor space per occupant.

References

ACA (1990) *Standards for Adult Correctional Institutions,* 3rd edn, American Correctional Association in cooperation with the Commission on Accreditation for Corrections, Maryland.
Brzezinski, Z. (1990) *The Grand Failure: The Birth and Death of Communism in the Twentieth Century* (New York).
Conquest, R. (1968) *The Great Terror: Stalin's Purge of the Thirties* (London).
Detkov, M. G. (1992) *The Content of the Penal Policy of the Soviet State and Its Implementation Through Punishments Involving Deprivation of Liberty in the 1930s, 1940s and 1950s* (Domodyedovo).
Dugin, A. (1991) 'GULag – The Heresy of Arithmetic' ('Koshchunstvo Arifmetiki'), in *Chronicle of Crime,* Issue 7.
Ivanov, L. and Yemelin, A. (1991) 'The GULag: 1941–1945', *Education, Law and Order,* Issue 8: 41–3.
Ivanov-Razumnik, R. V. (1965) *The Memoirs of Ivanov-Razumnik* (English edn) (London).
King, Roy D. (1994) 'Russian Prisons after Perestroika: End of the Gulag?', in *British Journal of Criminology,* 34, Special Issue (January): 62–81.
Lipper, E. (1951) *Eleven Years in Soviet Prison Camps* (London).
Mikhlin, A. S. (1993) 'Pensions for Prisoners', in *Crime and Punishment,* nos 8–9.
Pavarini, M. (1994) 'The New Penology and Politics in Crisis: The Italian Case', in *British Journal of Criminology,* 34, Special Issue (January): 49–61.
Prison Service (1994) *HM Prison Service: Operating Standards* (London).
Smirnov, A. (1948) *The GULag of the Interior Ministry of the USSR: Its Organisational Structure and Objectives* Moscow.
Zemskov, V. (1989) 'The GULag Archipelago – Through the Eyes of a Writer and Statistician', in *Arguments and Facts,* no. 45.
Zimring, F. E. and Hawkins, G. (1994) 'The Growth of Imprisonment in California', in *British Journal of Criminology,* 34, Special Issue (January): 83–96.

12 Prison Privatization: An International Perspective
Kristel Beyens and Sonja Snacken

WHY PRIVATIZE PRISONS?

It should be noted at the outset that private prisons are not a new phenomena. Throughout the nineteenth and early twentieth centuries, contract and lease agreements between prison authorities and private entrepreneurs were common, either for the use of inmate labour, or for transportation. Public awareness of abuses, demands for better standards, objections from trade unions that jobs were taken up by prison workers and the adoption of rehabilitation as a major goal of punishment were the impetus for a change to a more centralized public system (McConville, 1987; DiIulio, 1990; Feeley, 1991; Moyle, 1993; Borna, 1986; Ryan and Ward, 1989a, 1989b).

The most controversial issue in the privatization of corrections today is the handing over of the entire management of prisons to the private sector. Contracting out specific services, such as food, laundry, health care and work for prisoners, to the private sector is widespread and generally accepted (see Camp and Camp, 1984, 1985). It has also to be remembered that voluntary, non-profit or religious organizations have a long tradition of involvement in the running and organization of prisons (Chan, 1992).

The most common reason given for privatization is the massive growth of the prison population since the 1980s. Prison overcrowding and deteriorating prison conditions have encouraged governments to expand their prison capacity. At the same time, governments struggling with budget deficits find themselves under increasing pressure to cut costs and save taxes. Consequently, they have resorted to the private sector in order to reduce costs. This policy is also related to the current trend to privatize public facilities and services. Privatization has become an important issue on the political agenda of Conservative governments. The Thatcher and Major administrations in the United Kingdom and Reagan and Bush administrations in the United States have been heralded as the forerunners of this development. During the 1980s and 1990s privatization has been presented as a panacea for a variety of financial and managerial problems.

Limiting the power of the trade unions has also been an important aspect of privatization in a number of different countries (Ryan and Ward,

1989; Harding, 1991). It was also claimed that privatization would stimulate innovation. Finally, the development of privatization in the area of corrections has been linked to the abandonment of the rehabilitative ideal and the growing emphasis upon incapacitation as a justification for punishment. As a result the 'warehousing' of the rising prison population by the private sector has become more acceptable.

PRISON PRIVATIZATION: INTERNATIONAL EXPERIENCES

The involvement of the private sector in corrections varies between different countries. This chapter deals with the typical characteristics and pressures leading to privatization in the US, Australia and some European countries. Special attention will be paid to the difference between Anglo-Saxon countries such as the United States, Australia and Britain, as well as some continental European countries, since the Anglo-Saxon countries are more likely to involve the private sector in the management of the prison than other European countries.

The United States of America

In the United States, the move towards the re-privatization of prisons started in the mid-1980s. By the end of 1991, private companies operated approximately 60 secure adult facilities in 12 out of the 50 states, housing about 20 000 local, state and federal prisoners (Lilly and Knepper, 1992: 176). Privatization is most widely accepted in the southern States with Texas having the highest number of private facilities. However, still less than 2 per cent of the total American prison population (more than one million prisoners) is housed in prisons owned or managed by private companies.

Some major characteristics are relevant for the explanation of the privatization movement. A decentralized authority system and a great number of different institutions enhance the possibilities for private sector involvement. During the 1980s, many states were placed under court order as a result of litigation directly or indirectly related to overcrowding (Bernat, 1991). The financial aspect of the building of new prisons turned out to be of particular importance. Projects involving large capital investments such as new prisons have to be financed by raising funds on the open market by bond issues, which usually require voter approval as well as various tax and debt limitations (Mullen, 1985; Ryan and Ward, 1989a; Press, 1990; McDonald, 1990c; Leonard, 1990; Logan, 1990: Chan, 1992).

Alternatives like leasing or 'creative financing' are used by governments to avoid voter (dis)approval in bond referenda, even if these 'solutions' are much more expensive in the long run due to higher interest rates.

The private sector involvement in running prisons began in 1979 with detention centres under the authority of the US Immigration and Nationalization Service. Subsequently juvenile and the less difficult minimum – medium facilities were targeted. More recently, private contractors have expanded to take over the management of (closed) jails and high-security prisons. Speculative prison building is developing in Texas, Oklahoma, Minnesota and Georgia. Money is raised from investors and the prison is built prior to the establishment of a contract. Once the prison is built and set up governments are approached for business (Mason, 1993).

The privatization movement started in the US and was then exported to Australia and England and Wales mainly through the lobbying by some large international companies. Corrections Corporation of America (CCA) and the Wackenhut Corrections Corporation are two American private companies which aimed at international expansion. The Corrections Corporation of America, based in Nashville, Tennessee, is considered to be the world market leader in private sector corrections management. Having started the whole business in the United States in 1983, this company ran 21 facilities in 1991 in 6 states of the United States, Australia and the United Kingdom. It achieved notoriety by its attempt to take over the entire Tennessee prison system in 1985 with a 99-year lease from the state (Lilly and Knepper, 1993; McDonald, 1994).

In sum, privatization has been stimulated in the United States by a decentralized authority, overcrowded prisons, a pro-privatization political climate, a great number of different institutions, an extremely fragmented correctional system, as well as a number of financial problems.

Australia

Currently, there are three private facilities in Australia, which house about 8 per cent of the total prison population. The first minimum – medium security private prison (Borallon, 240 places) opened in Queensland on 1 January, 1990. The operational contract was given to the Corrections Corporation of Australia, a third of which is owned by the American company CCA. In July 1991, while operating at full capacity, the classification was changed to a full medium-security prison.

In October 1991, following the breakdown with the State Services Union (prison officers branch) on revised work practices, the management of the Arthur Gorrie Correctional Centre (380 places) in Brisbane was also contracted to the private sector (Harding, 1992a; Moyle, 1994a). Arthur Gorrie performs a remand and reception function and holds 380 prisoners from all security classifications (Moyle, 1994d). It is operated by the Australasian Correctional Management (ACM), which is 50/50 controlled by the American Wackenhut Corrections Corporation and the Australian security company ADT.

Junee in New South Wales, which is the biggest private prison (600 inmates), opened in March 1993. It is both built and managed by ACM, the same company that operates the Arthur Gorrie Correctional Centre in Queensland. Consequently there is American involvement in all three Australian projects. Moreover, key management posts are usually taken up by Americans who import American methods of management.

Following the introduction of the Contract Management Act in December 1993, the state Government of Victoria called for expression of interest for the finance, design, construction and management of three prisons (Moyle, 1994d). The government of New Zealand did the same for a 350-bed regional minimum/medium-security prison and a 250-bed remand facility (Moyle, 1993b). With the election of the Liberal Party in South Australia and Western Australia, Moyle (1994d) expects that both states will follow the example of Queensland. It should also be noted that in July 1991 the Northern Territory Government called for a tender to design, construct and manage a new prison in Alice Springs. This prison should house all levels of security for sentenced offenders, remand facilities and a section for women inmates. Finally, the public system was awarded the contract (Harding, 1992a; 1992b).

The impetus for privatization in Queensland and in New South Wales came from two reports. In Queensland, the Kennedy Report (1988) carried out a general review of the prison system. Privatization was recommended in the context of the substantial reform of corrective services. Remarkably, in the interim report private contract management was rejected. Due to discussions with some major companies with an interest in participating in correctional operations, full privatization of Borallon was explicitly recommended some months later in the final report (Moyle, 1994b).

Some advantages of privatization were listed in the report: it would solve the problems of finding adequate staff; it would add flexibility; it would create a competitive market for corrective institutions ; it would provide an opportunity for correctional staff to improve their status: it would also serve to improve the working conditions of staff. In general, it was suggested that privatization would open up career prospects for correctional officers and managers, while providing a real measure against which to test the performance and costs of the existing public corrective services (Harding, 1992b; Moyle, 1993).

Although the private contract management of Borallon was only a part of a larger reform process, it dominated the parliamentary debates at the time and resulted in the passing of the Corrective Services Act 1988, which authorized the delegation of 'powers, authorities, functions or duties ... upon a general manager of a prison'. The Labour opposition at that time wanted the part of the Bill which allowed the privatization of prisons to be deleted but after being elected to government in December 1989, they confirmed the contract for Borallon with the CCA.

In New South Wales the Kleinworth Benson Report was released in 1989. Unlike the Kennedy Report, this study offered a narrow, merely pragmatic and financial approach which explicitly recommended privatization. Consequently, in 1990 the Prisons (Contract Management) Amendment Act (NSW) modified the Prisons Act 1952 (NSW) to allow privatization. Although both reports provided a justification for involving the private sector in the prison system, neither dealt with more fundamental criminal justice policy options.

In general, the main reasons for privatization in Australia were prison overcrowding (especially in New South Wales) and excessive costs of the public system. A 'quasi-militaristic' attitude of some of the old guard prison officers was seen to hamper progressive reform in prisoner programmes in Queensland and privatization offered a strategy for changing the existing system of industrial relations.

Europe

The United Kingdom

What happens in the United States today, happens in the United Kingdom tomorrow. The emergence of privatization in England and Wales was influenced by the pro-privatization influence of the Adam Smith Institute. Their views found support from the Home Affairs Committee after its visits to American private prisons (Ryan and Ward, 1989). In March 1987, a report from the Government Home Affairs Select Committee recommended an experiment with the private construction and management of custodial institutions. This attitude towards privatization was further encouraged by the political pressure from the Conservative party, representatives from the business sector and the dramatic increase in the UK prison population. The Home Office Green Paper of 1988 provided a legal basis for experimenting with private sector involvement in the remand system and escort service. Protest from the Prison Officers Association

(POA), from some Labour MPs and from estab
Prison Reform Trust, the Howard League and the N
the Care and Resettlement of Offenders (NACRO
privatization movement.

The lobby from the private prison industry was str
During a conference on privatization in the Netherla
Director of UK Detention Services (UKDS), Mr Hopkins

> It took us two or three years to finally convince the government that
> this was indeed the right course of action ... Prisons were not working
> and there was a viable alternative ... UKDS was very much involved in
> bringing forward the arguments in favour of the case. It was a time
> when privatization was the watchword of the Conservative government.
> (Hopkins, 1993: 2)

In August 1991 Section 84 of the Criminal Justice Act authorized the
contracting out of new remand prisons. Group 4 Remand Services
Ltd received a five-year contract for managing the Wolds remand prison
(320 beds), starting on 5 April 1992.

Two months later, in July, the Act was amended to allow the contracting out of all new prisons, for remand as well as for convicted prisoners.
The five-year management contract for Blakenhurst prison, a local prison
in Redditch was awarded to UK Detention Services (UKDS) in December
1992. It started operating in May 1993. UK Detention Services is a joint
venture between the American CCA and two British construction companies, John Mowlem and Co, and Sir Robert McAlpine and Son.
Blakenhurst provides 649 places for medium-security prisoners, and
houses both remand and convicted prisoners.

In February 1993, the Criminal Justice Act was further amended to
permit existing and new prisons to have their management contracted
out. In 1993 the Home Office also decided to call for tender for the
operation of (the public) Strangeways prison. It was the first time that
the Prison Service was allowed to bid against the private companies. The
contract was awarded to the Prison Service although it was not the lowest
bid (Nathan, 1993b). In the same year the Government also announced
plans to privatize secure units for disturbed and dangerous children
(Nathan, 1993).

A third privately-run prison at Doncaster opened in April 1994. The
five-year, £66 million contract to manage this big newly-built multi-
purpose prison (771 prisoners) was awarded to Premier Prisons, a
consortium with the American security firm Wackenhut (Nathan, 1994).
Moreover, the government is planning to expand the prison capacity with

privately built and financed prisons and to call for tender for the
ration of up to seven existing prisons. Furthermore, the Scottish Office
is intending to introduce competition from the private sector for five new
prisons to be built in Scotland (Hopkins, 1993).

The United Kingdom, and England and Wales in particular, have taken
a leading position within Europe with regards to private sector involvement in the prison system. Since the Green Paper of 1988, the concept of
privately managed prisons has become increasingly accepted and the
government intends the private sector eventually to manage around ten per
cent of all prisons (Hopkins, 1993; Nathan, 1993b).

From the beginning, Group 4 has been openly criticized in the press.
A report by the Prison Reform Trust (1993) was positive about the general
physical conditions in the Wolds prison. Prisoners were for instance
allowed to spend 14 hours out of their cell. No activities were however
organized in communal areas, resulting in prisoners just 'hanging around',
feeling bored or bullying fellow inmates or staff. Apart from some
'teething problems', the Prison Reform Trust expressed its concern about
inadequate staffing levels, the widespread availability of drugs, the level of
incidents and disturbances and the high incidence of stress and sickness
among the staff. The level of incidents and disturbances at the Wolds is
higher than the national average and within the first month of its contract
there were two escapes. Group 4 rejected the criticisms directed at them
by reform groups, the POA and the press, and claimed that they were
misleading. To improve the public image of the company, Stephen Twinn,
who was the former Director of the Wolds prison was made Director of
Communications. In order to evaluate the functioning of the Wolds, the
Home Office commissioned the Wolds Remand Prison Research Project,
undertaken by Hull University.

To summarize, a rising prison population, overcrowding and bad prison
conditions, lobbying from the international private prisons industry and
the influence of right-wing views have been successful in promoting the
privatization of prisons. The presumed positive effects of competition has
been the main justification put forward by the Conservative government to
foster privatization.

The European Continent

Although American companies have attempted to expand their activities to
the European continent, there has been considerable resistance to privatization, particularly in the form of taking over the management of specific
prisons. These developments are evident in a number of European
countries including the Netherlands, France and Belgium.

An enormous extension of the prison capacity in the Netherlands (a doubling of the number of prison cells in ten years) during the 1980s and 1990s followed in the wake of considerable organizational and financial problems. Although a number of services (for example, catering, laundry, education) and the design and construction of new prisons had already been privatized to a large degree, the Dutch government remained convinced that the management of the prison system remained a core function of the state and thus could not be contracted out. On the other hand, there is an openness to privatize maintenance functions, escort services as well as 'specific security tasks' (Greven, 1994).

Research in the Netherlands on privatization of other public services such as the railways has shown that, in the long run, privatization is often more expensive. As part of an efficiency operation, the Dutch government decided to give the prison system executive agency status (so called *'interne beheersverzelfstandiging'*) (Beyens, Snacken and Eliaerts, 1992). Through this reorganization, local prison governors were given more autonomy in the daily prison management, while the Minister of Justice is to be held accountable for overall prison policy and management.

In 1987, due to the continuously rising prison population, the French government decided to expand its prison capacity by 13 000 cells nationally (25 prisons). One of the main reasons given for involving the private sector was the urgency of the prison building programme. And indeed, the prisons were designed and built by four private companies in about two years. They are all owned now, however, by the French government.

It is interesting to note that while the building programme was being carried out, the emphasis on privatization changed. In the beginning, total privatization was proposed. That is, the privatization of the construction as well as of the management of the prisons. But under pressure from both the penitentiary administration and parliament, as well as a change of government in 1988, the private management of prisons was abandoned and this role was retained by the Service Public Pénitentiaire. The other operating functions, the so-called 'hotel functions' – education, prison labour and technical assistance – have been contracted out in one package to the same private companies which built the prisons. These prisons are now referred to as 'mixed prisons' or 'prisons *sémi-privées*'.

Proper evaluations of these institutions are not yet available. However, some newspaper articles mention less profit for the private companies than expected, due to the limited privatization of the operation functions (Logeart, 1991). The private companies hoped to make most of the profit on the operational functions and plans were developed accordingly.

However, these functions were withdrawn in a later phase. Also, the co-operation between a public prison governor and prison guards and private persons working in the same setting is reported to be strained.

However what happens in Paris today, happens in Brussels tomorrow. Representatives from the Belgian government visited the French semi-private prisons. Although the Belgian prisons have been seriously over-crowded since the mid-1980s, these problems were neglected for a long time by politicians. Budget problems hindered the renovation of the nineteenth-century institutions (mainly the instalment of sanitary facili-ties) and caused a shortage of prison guards. As a result the existing capacity is still not fully operational.

The decision to expand the capacity of the Belgian prison system was taken in the wake of a number of highly publicized and politicized incidents including the escape of some 'dangerous' prisoners who had taken hostages. In the summer of 1993, the Minister of Justice announced, without further explanation or discussion, that the next prison to be built in Belgium (Andenne) would be 'alternatively financed'. In short, the inten-tion was to follow the French example of a semi-private prison. This would mean that the entire building process and all operating functions would be contracted out, except from the operation and guarding func-tions. In November 1993 the private companies were invited to tender and the prison in Andenne is planned to open by the end of 1996. It will provide 400 additional places for long-term convicted prisoners. Following heated discussions in Parliament on early release of short-term prisoners to relieve prison overcrowding, the Minister of Justice announced in March 1994 another 'alternatively financed', (semi-private) prison to be built in Saint-Hubert.

As for the prison in Andenne, the decision was taken under serious political stress and in the context of a growing dissatisfaction about poor living conditions in overcrowded institutions. The key question is where the government will get the money from to finance the construction and operation of these two new prisons. Semi-private prisons may be cheaper and quicker to build but they still need to be staffed and staff costs constitute the major part of the overall costs.

Put briefly, full privatization has until now been avoided in the contin-ental European countries discussed. Nevertheless, the private sector con-tinues to lobby. The aversion of governments to privatize the management of prisons has, however, allowed them to resist the offers put forward by the private sector. Without doubt, private companies have gained import-ance in relation to a number of prison activities. The evolution may be called semi-privatization (France), alternative financing (Belgium) or internal managerial autonomy (The Netherlands) but the overall involvement of the private sector in these forms appears to be increasing.

From this survey of the developments in continental Europe two questions arise. First, will governments continue to resist the full privatization of prisons? Secondly, and maybe more importantly, what will the effect of the privatization debate with its emphasis on cost reduction and efficiency be on penal policy in general? These questions will be addressed in the following sections.

THE PRIVATIZATION DEBATE

The privatization debate raises a number of pragmatic, economic, political, moral, legal and criminological issues. The international overview above shows that privatization in relation to prisons is not a unitary phenomenon. Since private management of prisons is the most controversial issue, the debate tends to focus mainly on this relatively extreme form of privatization.

Arguments in favour of privatization are usually propounded by people connected to the (private) prison industry and by right-wing, conservative politicians. Proponents (Hutto, 1990; Logan, 1990; Fulton, 1989) claim that privatization is the best way to decrease costs and construct new, better designed prisons more quickly. By introducing the element of competition and new management techniques, better quality for less money can be achieved. It is stated that private correctional services can operate more efficiently, because of less bureaucratic 'red tape' and a higher motivation to control costs.

Prisoners' rights organizations, in response, focus mainly on the constitutional aspects and the propriety of private prisons. Reactions of the trade unions are influenced by a fear of loss of jobs and the undercutting of wages. The left-wing penal lobby in most countries emphasizes the disadvantages of privatization. Due to this unavoidable ideological dimension, even academic research tends to take a definite stance on this issue.

Comparative Studies and Evaluations of Performance

Although economic arguments have been the main motives for privatization, comparative evaluations are difficult and inconclusive (Mullen, 1985; Borna, 1986; Donahue, 1988; Leonard, 1990; Logan and McGriff, 1989; Logan, 1987b, 1990, 1992; McDonald, 1990b; Keating, 1990; Matthews, 1989; Harding, 1992; Sellers, 1993; Moyle, 1993, 1994). Most existing studies start from a very narrow quantitative approach. Consequently the results are mostly distorted by hidden costs and deflated by excluding overheads and monitoring costs. Facilities vary widely, implying that simple comparisons of per diem rates are not very meaningful. Inconsistent results are also caused by a lack of established methodology for measuring or comparing the quality of prison services.

In relation to the UK, Hopkins (1993) reports a 29 per cent difference in the weekly cost per prisoner, in favour of the private Blakenhurst prison compared to a local prison. In the United States there are two recent, rather extensive quantitative studies, which have attempted to compare costs and quality of confinement in public and private prisons.

Logan (1992) compared three women's prisons in New Mexico and West Virginia. One was a private prison, one a state prison and the other a federal institution. The quality of confinement was measured along eight dimensions: security, safety, order, care, activity, justice, conditions and management. In total 333 indicators were used, derived from institutional records and surveys of inmates and staff. No inmates were surveyed at the federal prison.

The results are summarized in a comparative Prison Quality Index. Logan mentions that, in absolute terms, quality was high at all three prisons. Generally, the private prison performed better than the state and federal prison, except for the dimensions 'care' (health care, counselling, staffing for programmes and services) and 'justice' (staff fairness, use of force, grievances, discipline). It is interesting to note that staff and inmates had very different perceptions and perspectives on many indicators relating to the quality of confinement. Inmates moderately favoured the state prison on every dimension, except activity (work, education and training programmes). The inmates' displeasure with the private prison related mainly to the more prison-like atmosphere and tighter administrative regime in comparison to their former conditions at the state prison. They tended to complain of an overemphasis on security. When based only on the staff surveys, the quality index scores of the private prison exceeded those of the state prison. Logan (1992: 593) concluded that 'the stricter governance of inmates at the private prison may have been a factor behind both the more positive evaluations from staff, as well as the more negative evaluations from inmates'. The staff's preference for the private prison was much stronger than the inmates' preference for the state prison. It is important to remember, however, that this study relates only to women's prisons.

A more limited study carried out by Sellers (1993) compares costs and programmes of three privately operated correctional facilities and three public correctional facilities in the United States. Based on inmate per diem costs, the three privately-operated correctional centres proved to be operated more cost-efficiently than their publicly operated counterparts, which Sellers attributed to better control of resources, the more flexible use of manpower, better financial control, less bureaucracy and less union problems.

In Australia, capital savings appear to have been made for the Junee prison. The annual contract management fee for ACM for operating the newly constructed Arthur Gorrie Centre is expected to be $11.5 million as opposed to an estimated $18 million if it were run by the public sector (Harding, 1992a).

An extensive comparison of the Australian private Borallon prison with the very similar public Lotus Glen Correctional Centre showed that the public facility was more cost-efficient and more open to the public. Even with a more diverse range of inmates and a wider variety of functions to perform, the net daily cost per offender at Lotus Glen was lower ($101.54) than at Borallon ($104.69). Moyle (1992) points out that, in order to prove the cost-efficiency of Borallon, initial figures were changed by adding the cost of administrative overheads (computer databases for prisoner's files) to Lotus Glen and not to Borallon, which artificially increased the unit cost per offender for Lotus Glen.

The evaluation of correctional facilities should, however, contain more than purely quantitative and financial comparisons. Moyle's (1994b) field research at Borallon provides a unique example of a well-elaborated qualitative study of the functioning of a private prison. A semi-structured interview methodology was used to collect data from 56 individuals including 25 inmates as well as a range of employees. Also transcripts, research diary notes and published and unpublished information were analyzed. Moyle has examined industrial and work issues, the prisoner's experience of the correctional environment, including their impressions of the discipline, training opportunities, prison management and officers' attitudes, accountability, monitoring and performance of the prison.

His study showed that employees of CCA and Wormald Security were in a weak bargaining position. Costs were cut by reducing the overall number of custodial staff giving a ratio of approximately 2 staff to 80 inmates. There was also a high ratio of casual labour. Consequently, custodial staff reported a lack of job security. Staff-inmate relations were evaluated positively. The environment was experienced as humane and inmates felt less threatened than in older public prisons. Interestingly, similar experiences were reported by inmates and staff at the public Lotus

Glen Correctional Centre. Several progressive trends such as an open campus style and the establishment of an 'Inmates Need Committee' promoted direct communications between inmates and staff at Borallon. However the Inmates Need Committee was also asked to decide whether they were prepared to pay for overtime costs for visits on Christmas Day. A member of the committee said: 'all [inmates] wanted to see their families on that day. It cost us $1,500 for the officers salaries, but what choice have you got. I'd pay anything. I had to see my family on Christmas Day' (Moyle, 1994d: 28). This way inmates were obliged to pay for a service which normally is provided by the centre. Moyle also reports a conflict between a profit motive and the provision of more costly industrial apprenticeships and training programmes. Unskilled contract work was promoted because it provided higher financial rewards for the CCA.

One feature which is apparent in a number of studies is the limited access to financial and contractual information. Borallon, for example, was found to be sensitive about its financial and policy operations; and in the United Kingdom, details of the profit level or of payments made by Group 4 is declared to be subject to commercial confidentiality and cannot therefore be made public (Prison Reform Trust, 1993). It is obvious that this hinders objective comparisons and evaluations.

As labour costs constitute approximately 80 per cent of the total operating costs (Logan, 1990: 81; Matthews, 1990; Donahue, 1988), it is evident that any savings will be achieved by reducing labour costs. Private companies hire fewer and less qualified staff who are generally inexperienced. They are mostly non-unionized and tend to be less well paid and employed on a more flexible (temporary) basis (Moyle, 1993a, 1994b; Sellers, 1993). The conditions of employment and the level of wages have been the main concern of the trade unions. The Prison Reform Trust's evaluation of England's Wolds prison reports that pay rates in the Wolds are lower than in the public Prison Service. The same is true for Blakenhurst (UK), where pay and conditions compare unfavourably with the Prison Service (Nathan, 1993).

Prison officers are partly replaced by electronic surveillance equipment such as cameras. It has been suggested that this depersonalizes and dehumanizes prison life, for both the inmates as well as for the prison officers. Moreover, reduced personal contacts between prison staff and inmates is known to affect security and control in prison. Critics argue that private prison operating costs may be lower in the short run, but might increase in the long run to the same level or even higher than public sector operations. They also point to the phenomenon of initial 'lowballing' by private companies, in order to enter the market and win contracts.

National and International Legal Issues

Legal considerations are an important element in the process of privatizating correctional services. In the United Kingdom legal issues were discussed in the Green Paper (1988) and by the Criminal Justice Act (1991, 1992). In Queensland, Australia, the Corrective Services Act was introduced in 1988 and France provided a legal basis for the semi privatized prisons with the 'Loi no 87–432 relative au service public pénitentiaire' (22 June 1987). In Belgium the proposed form of semi-privatization is possible within the existing legal framework.

Due to the decentralized and differentiated prison system in the United States legal requirements differ from state to state. State constitutions provide no clear legal ban on the private delegation by correctional authorities. In Pennsylvania, the Private Prison Moratorium and Study Act was passed in late 1986, which explicitly forbade private involvement in the prison sector (Sellers, 1993). But in the absence of explicit prohibitions, state governments may, according to prevailing doctrine, take any action whatsoever as long as it does not contravene the United States' Constitution. To clarify this, several states have passed laws authorizing the delegation of correctional authority to the private sector (McDonald, 1990c).

The relevant international norms are examined in a study of the Economic and Social Council of the United Nations. The study concludes that all rules indicate that prisons must be operated by public officials. It also expresses the principle that human rights are to be ensured by the State and where they are restricted, this must be done by the State through its governmental organs (Palley, 1993).

Examination of the Universal Declaration of Human Rights shows that privatization of prisons by way of contracting out management and custody is not in accordance with international human rights law. Following a complex argument, starting from Art. 21 (the will of the people is the basis of the authority of government) and Art. 7 (all persons are equal before the law and entitled to equal protection of the law), Palley (1993: 31–2) concludes that 'the responsibility of the State does not permit it to sub-delegate the power of giving effect to restrictions on personal liberty, including having custody of prisoners'. Rule 46 (3) of the Standard Minimum Rules for the Treatment of Prisoners, adopted by the First United Nations Congress on the Prevention of Crime and the Treatment of Offenders (Geneva, 1955) and approved by the Economic and Social Council (1977) expressly provides that prison administration personnel shall be professional prison officers and have civil service status with security of tenure.

Principle 2 of the Body of Principles for the Protection of All Persons under Any Form of Detention or Imprisonment provides that 'Arrest, detention or imprisonment shall only be carried out strictly in accordance with the provisions of the law and by competent officials or persons authorized for that purpose'. Palley (1993) points out that the structure of the Body of Principles as a whole shows that the numerous references to 'authorities' and 'law enforcement officials' relate to state officials.

It is also implicit in the Code of Conduct for Law Enforcement Officials that persons exercising police powers and responsible for detention are 'law enforcement officials' and that private citizens acting in terms of contract were not contemplated as forming part of the criminal justice system. Moreover rule 54 (2) of the Council of Europe's Standard Minimum Rules for the Treatment of Prisoners (as amended in 1987) provides that 'Personnel shall normally be appointed on a permanent basis as professional prison staff and have civil service status ...' The word 'normally' underscores that non-civil servants can only exceptionally be members of the prison staff. This exception is not enough to cover contracting out of the whole prison administration or particular prisons, but only allows a continuation of long-standing practices, such as appointing certain external professional persons, like doctors and chaplains (who do not have civil service status), to perform limited services for the prison (Palley, 1993). Although these rules are not legally binding, they are considered to represent the basic norms of human dignity governments should attempt to achieve.

The Boundaries of Privatization

A key issue in the privatization debate is the propriety of private prisons and the changing role of the state (Robbins, 1987; DiIulio, 1988, 1990; Field, 1988; Ryan and Ward, 1989; Weiss, 1989; Porter, 1990). The debate on this issue is often clouded by competing ideologies. Arguments against private prisons focus on the acceptability and propriety of the privatization of punishment. Opponents consider punishment as a core function of the modern state. A major argument against privatization is that it will undermine the very essence of a liberal democratic state. Prison sentences are executed in the name of the State and it is thereby considered improper to delegate this function to a private agency.

Incarceration relies directly upon the use of organized force and delegating the use of deadly force is especially considered as being improper. 'Symbolically, only the state should have the power to administer justice and to execute it by coercion, because only then will justice have legitimacy in the eyes of those subjected to it' (Palley, 1993: 30).

Proponents such as Logan (1990) argue that it is not the civil status of the actor that determines whether any particular use of force is legitimate. It is the law that specifies who is authorized to use force in particular situations. Sparks (1994) rightly points to the fact that advocates of private initiatives draw a sharp division between the allocation of punishment by the state and the delivery of penal services by a private agency. Proponents argue that private contract management does not involve the allocation of punishment, but only the administration of punishment within statutory limits. Further arguments on the propriety of private prisons are irrelevant to them.

Such a separation seems slightly artificial however, for the execution of a prison sentence is intimately linked with the punishment. Employees in private contract management are directly involved in disciplinary decisions, such as the imposition of solitary confinement and the awarding of privileges. Parole or remission decisions rely on the advice of private custodial and administrative staff. The privatization of the Arthur Gorrie Correctional Centre in Australia implies that the classification procedure, which influences the way inmates move through the correctional system, is also handed over to the private sector (Moyle, 1994b).

In an attempt to explain the divergences in the degree of privatization between countries, some authors stress the importance of broader differences in political and legal culture (McConville, 1987, 1990). In Common Law countries such as the United States, the United Kingdom and Australia, the state is considered as a mediator, while in the political and legal culture of Civil Law countries, the state fulfils a supreme role. Christie (1993) argues that 'Europeans to a larger extent regard both national states and national cultures as something that has always existed, something given, while this for Americans, to a somewhat larger extent, is something created by them as individuals'.

The presence of a centralized or decentralized authority system is another factor of importance. Compared to other countries, a broader general deregulation has also occurred in the United States and the United Kingdom. Considering these elements, it is not surprising that full privatization is more widely spread in the United Kingdom, the United States and Australia and that continental European governments remain more sceptical. However, the existence of a dynamic and complex relationship between the state and the penal system cannot be denied. The distinction between what can be considered as public and as private can be susceptible to redefinition. Ryan and Ward (1992) point out that radical opponents are now less likely than they once were to view the state as a monolithic structure exerting power in a simple, downwards direction. They stress the need to develop a more adequate conception of the role of the state in a modern, complex society. Consequently, they argue 'for sharpening our awareness of the complexity and ambivalence of the relations between different agencies which exercise power, and between those agencies and their targets or opponents' (Ryan and Ward, 1992: 332).

Liability

Directly related to the delegation of the power of the administration of punishment is the issue of liability in problems such as responsibility in cases of suicide, abuses by the prison staff, and in the event of prison disturbances. Sceptics have argued that privatisation can be used by governments to avoid liability for maltreatment of prisoners or for the provision of bad living conditions.

In the United States, the Civil Rights Act 42 U.S.C. Section 1983 permits suits against the state for violations of constitutional rights. The federal courts have declared private operators of detention centres as acting 'under the color of state law'; they are thus liable for any deprivation of life and liberty prohibited by the U.S. Constitution (Robbins, 1987; Kay, 1987). Therefore, both private prisons and their contracting units of government can be sued under the provisions of Section 1983. Although other countries do not have such legislation, it is generally acknowledged that the ultimate responsibility for all prisons, independent of whether there is public or private management, lies and should lie with the government. Proponents of private prison operators find the political issue of whether democracy is circumvented by contracting out the operation of a prison meaningless (Sellers, 1993) or spurious (Hopkins, 1993). For them it is evident that governments retain ultimate responsibility. However, the question arises who will be liable for damages if an incident such as suicide or a riot happens due to the company's negligence. It is also unclear who will pay additional services such as police tactical response and emergency services such as the fire brigade in case of a major riot (Moyle, 1994d). In this regard it is important to know the contract specifications.

Political Accountability and Public Control

Prisons carry out public policies, and therefore their management must be open to political accountability and public control. Mechanisms for public scrutiny are thus necessary. An important element is the provision of accurate information. As pointed out above, however, financial information and staffing details in private prisons are sometimes considered to be 'commercially confidential'. This hinders public scrutiny and democratic control.

In April 1993 the British Home Secretary announced, in a Framework Document, that the British Prison Service would become an 'executive agency'. In order to find new ways of improving the quality of service he suggested more autonomy of the prison service is necessary with the freedom to develop new and imaginative ideas. Although the Home Secretary continues to be accountable to Parliament for the Prison Service, he will no longer be involved in day-to-day managerial issues, but will expect to be consulted on the handling of operational matters which could give rise to grave public or parliamentary concerns.

Monitoring

Prisons in different countries are submitted to different forms of internal and external control (for example, boards of visitors, prison inspectors, grievance commissions, political bodies). These regulatory mechanisms should also apply to private prisons, allowing unlimited entrance and visiting. Control over private prisons however also entails monitoring of the contract specifications. The range of detail varies between countries and even between prisons: contracts may define all aspects of regime, staffing, living standards, etc. To monitor such a contract, a full disclosure of its financial aspects, including staffing requirements, costs and profits is needed. A monitor or ombudsman appointed by the government is often entrusted with the task of obtaining this disclosure (e.g. Wolds Prison, United Kingdom). His position may be a difficult one. Keating (1990) does not expect 'magic' in the use of a full-time monitor, who may be seduced by the contractor's 'overt corruption or subtle cooption'. Sichor (1993) points also to the 'revolving door' syndrome. In this respect he mentions an example of a state official who monitors a private institution, but who already has a job waiting for him at the corporation upon his retirement.

In Queensland, the initially full-time presence of a monitor was reduced to twice weekly visits by an auditor once operations were considered no longer to need constant supervision (Palley, 1993). According to Moyle (1992, 1994) the monitor of Borallon spends less than one hour a week actually auditing CCA's performance. The remaining time is filled with administrative tasks and the monitoring of four other prisons. The performance criteria and evaluation methods of the Queensland Corrective Services Commission (QCSC), which is responsible for auditing the prisons, are also extremely vague.

Internationalization, Commercialization and Overlapping Interests

The evidence found from different countries indicates that the prison sector can be regarded as a large international market in expansion. Lilly and Knepper (1992) contend that this market is closely linked to the security industry and various sections of the international military industries, resulting in an international 'corrections-commercial complex'. Another study by Lilly and Deflem (1993) gives empirical evidence for the United States on the intertwining business interests of corrections and non-corrections industries, the internationalization and strive for expansion and the huge amount of capital invested.

Lilly and Knepper (1992, 1993) also point to the often neglected extensive overlap of business, political and private interests and the influence of the private firms on the development of criminal justice policy. In this respect, the concept of 'sub governmental policy making' is introduced, referring to the merging alliance between government and private enterprise. For the United States, Lilly and Knepper describe the interrelationships between the different participants in the corrections sub-governments: private concerns, federal agencies (e.g. the National Institute of Justice [NIJ]) and professional organizations (e.g. the American Bar Association [ABA] and the American Correctional Association [ACA]). Although these sub-governmental organizations are not a legally recognized forms of regulation, they often exert greater influence over public policy than formal structures of government.

The overlapping of commercial and political interests has also been mentioned in relation to the United Kingdom. Recent newspaper articles have provided details of the intertwining political and commercial activities of Mowlem and McApline, two companies involved in a consortium with UK Detention Services, who were awarded the Blakenhurst prison contract. Both companies have contributed to Conservative party funds and Lord McAlpine is a former Conservative party treasurer.

Lobbying by private organizations also raises questions about the increasing power of the industry and its potential influence on criminal justice policy. Critics are concerned that commercial advertisements may manipulate government officials and public opinion. Experiences with electronic monitoring in the United States seem to corroborate these concerns (Christie, 1993).

SUMMARY AND DISCUSSION

Regime Innovations and Profitmaking

The ultimate objective of private companies is to make profit. Their criteria of success is cutting costs. But what will the consequences of applying these criteria be on the operation of prisons and the daily life and work of the prison officers and inmates? The need for innovation in prison programmes are increasingly stressed by governments as a reason for privatization. Consequently, these objective have also become part of the discourse of the private sector. The question is whether these proposed changes will correspond to the overall objectives of incarceration. Research studies have generally acknowledged that imprisonment should entail more than the pure warehousing of inmates. But the increased involvement of private security firms in the private operation of prisons indicates a general trend towards security and control.

To what extent will private companies be concerned with rehabilitation of offenders? Elements of rehabilitation may be incorporated into the contract, but are likely to be subordinated by the profit motive in day-to-day practice. This tendency is well illustrated by the Wolds prison in the United Kingdom in which prisoners are allowed 14 hours a day out of their cell, but no activities are provided. At Borallon in Australia the CCA tends to engage inmates in relatively low-skilled and repetitive work rather than engaging in more expensive forms of training so they could undertake more skilled work (Moyle, 1994a, 1994b).

Since contracting and auditing of performance requires a detailed translation of the goals (Harding, 1992b), the main benefit of privatization could be that the government is encouraged to specify more clearly the purposes of imprisonment (Logan, 1990). Most of the reported discussions, however, seem to focus on organizational matters such as efficiency and effectiveness of management, rather than on the interpretation of purposes of punishment.

In the attempt to cut costs, privatization encourages investment in extensive electronic control (cameras, tagging) to replace personnel. Private prisons are designed to minimize the number of staff required. In the long run, a decrease of human control and personal contacts will have negative consequences on the general atmosphere in the prison and on security. This has been confirmed by practitioners working in the prison system and by inmates.

Consequences of Commercialization

The move towards prison privatization is linked to a need from private industries to transfer activities to 'new' market sectors. For these companies the prison sector is regarded as a stable, long-term investment deserving the outlay of considerable marketing.

Prison management is not a culturally neutral activity (Harding, 1992c). American companies such as the CCA and Wackenhut have clearly tried to expand their international activities. They now have interests in both Australia and the United Kingdom. There is also a significant interest from American companies to gain a foothold in the European continent. These entrepreneurs appear to be relatively insensitive to differences in legal and penal culture between countries and certainly between continents.

Apart from the question whether private prisons are better, cheaper, more hygienic or more efficiently operated, some important criminological considerations relating to criminal justice policy need to be addressed. In most countries prison privatization has been introduced as a *deus ex machina* to cope with rising prison populations and overcrowding problems. It is a convenient way to provide an immediate and flexible answer to a persistent penal problem. It is suggested that major prison problems can be solved by a better and more efficient management. The presentation of private prisons as a panacea for all kind of penal problems does not, however, touch the essence of the current penal crisis. The overall increase in remand and long-term prisoners, the war on drugs, the shift towards incapacitation and, the introduction of more severe penal policies are not questioned (Tubex and Snacken, 1993).

Moreover, another level is added to the already existing two-tier prison system. First, a bifurcation in sentencing and early-release policy resulted in a growing difference between short-term and long-term prisoners (King and Morgan, 1980; Beyens, Snacken and Eliaerts, 1993). Short-term prisoners are seen as less problematic and less dangerous, still susceptible to rehabilitation, while long-term prisoners (from more than five years up to life imprisonment) are increasingly regarded as 'dangerous' and difficult. Several governments seem less prepared to invest in regime activities and rehabilitation programmes for this group.

The introduction of private prisons creates another level of bifurcation: in living standards. Modern, hygienic private prisons exist alongside decayed, overcrowded public prisons. Paradoxically, while overcrowding is the main argument for privatization, it seems that the public sector will still have to cope with the peaks of rising prison populations, while the private prisons, by way of contract specifications, will be able to escape the worst overcrowding. An even more important mechanism in this two-tier system is the phenomenon of 'creaming off' by the private sector: the selection, through contract specifications, of the easiest, most tractable, least expensive prisoners. The public system is left to cope with the remaining, least desired, most difficult or expensive inmates. This is witnessed in Queensland, Australia (Harding; 1992; Moyle, 1992, 1994a), where the contract with Borallon provides the highest number of exclusions of any correctional centre in Queensland.

These dual standards of course also hamper a genuine comparison and evaluation of the private and the public system. The combination of incorrect comparisons, detrimental to the public prisons, with the general process of rationalization and competition, can have a negative effect on penal policies in the long run. Fear of privatization or market testing compels public prisons to adopt a more 'business-like' approach, to perform budget cuts or to reduce prison staff. This so-called confrontationalist approach is experienced in the UK and in Australia where the state-run Lotus Glen prison has been threatened with privatization on several occasions when it failed to comply with budgetary and staffing requirements (Moyle, 1992, 1994b, 1994c).

It would be an overstatement to suggest that privatization drives current penal policy, but the lobbying and marketing activities of the private sector clearly increases the pressure towards increasing prison capacity. Thus privatization encourages expansionism and provides a distraction away from the more fundamental issues of penal policy. The privatization option also reinforces the erroneous assumption that incarceration rates are primarily influenced by external factors such as crime rates. Research on changing prison populations shows, however, that the level of incarceration is also a function of particular criminal justice policies (Beyens, Snacken and Eliaerts, 1993; Snacken and Beyens, 1994). Consequently, overcrowding should be regarded as a problem which can also be tackled from within the criminal justice system.

Without challenging the legitimacy of the prison system as such or addressing current criminal justice policy, privatization will at best only bring temporary relief to prison overcrowding. More fundamental decisions need to be taken by governments and prison administrators. Decarceration and reductionism may be difficult political options in the current punitive climate in which a 'get tough' policy towards criminals has become very politically attractive in many countries. Nevertheless, in relation to the search for reductionist measures, the contracting out of the management of prisons is ultimately a counterproductive strategy.

References

Beyens, K., Snacken, S. and Eliaerts, C. (1992) *Privatizing van Gevangenissen*, (Brussels: VUB Press).
Beyens, K., Snacken, S. and Eliaerts, C. (1993) *Barstende Muren. Overbevolkte Gevangenissen: Omvang, Oorzaken en Mogelijke Oplossingen*, IRCS, n. 26 (Antwerp: Kluwer; Arnhem: Gouda Quint).
Borna, S. (1986) 'Free Enterprise Goes to Prison', *British Journal of Criminology*, 26, 4: 321–34.
Boulan, F. (ed.) (1987) 'Les prisons dites "privées". Une solution a la crise pénitentiare?' Actes du colloque organisé a Aix-en-Provence le 23 et 24 janvier, (Presses Universitaires d'Aix–Marseille: Economica).
Camp, C. and Camp, G. (1984) *Private Sector Involvement in Prison Services and Operations* (Washington, D.C.: NIJ).
Camp, C. and Camp, G. (1985) 'Correctional Privatization in Perspective', *Prison Journal*, 65, 2: 14–31.
Chan, J. B. L. (1992) 'The Privatisation of Punishment: A Review of the Key Issues', *Australian Journal of Social Issues*, 27, 4: 223–47.
Chemin, A. (1992) 'Prisons surpeuplées', *Le Monde* (12 February).
Christie, N. (1993) *Crime Control as Industry. Towards GULAGS, Western Style?* (London and New York: Routledge).
DiIulio, J. J., Jr. (1988) 'What's Wrong with Private Prisons', *Public Interest*, 92: 66–83.
DiIulio, J. J., Jr. (1990) 'The Duty to Govern: A Critical Perspective on the Private Management of Prisons and Jails, in D. McDonald (ed.), *Private Prisons and the Public Interest* (New Brunswick and London: Rutgers University Press): 155–78.
Donahue, J. D. (1988) *Prisons for Profit: Public Justice, Private Interests* (Washington, D.C.: Economic Policy Institute).
Durham III, A. M. (1988) 'Evaluating Privatized Correctional Institutions: Obstacles to Effective Assessment', *Federal Probation*, 52, 2: 65–71.
Feeley, M. M. (1991) 'The Privatization of Punishment in Historical perspective, in W. T. GORMLEY, Jr. (ed.), *Privatization and Its Alternatives* (University of Wisconsin Press: 199–225.
Field, J. E. (1987) Making Prisons Private: An Improper Delegation of a Government Power, *Hofstra Law Review*, 15: 649–75.
Greven, H. B. (1994) 'Privatisering van het gevangeniswezen in Nederland?', *Sancties*, 1: 21–8.
Harding, R. W. (1991) 'Unfit Things and Degrees of Unfitness: Public and Private Corrections', paper presented at the annual conference of the Law and Society Association, The Netherlands, 26–9 June.
Harding, R. W. (1992a) 'Private prisons in Australia', *Trends and Issues in Crime and Criminal Justice*, no. 36 (May) (Canberra: Australian Institute of Criminology).
Harding, R. W. (1992b) 'Prison Privatisation in Australia: A Glimpse of the Future', *Current Issues in Criminal Justice*, vol. 4, 1 (July): 9–27 (Sydney University Institute of Criminology).
Harding, R. W. (1992c) 'Privatising Prisons: Principle and Practice', paper presented at the New Zealand Conference, on Criminology.

Home Office, (1988) *Private Sector Involvement in the Remand System*, Green Paper, Cmnd 433 (London: HMSO).

Hopkins, R. D. N. (1993) 'The formation of UK Detention Services', paper presented at 'Private gevangenissen in Nederland' seminar, Utrecht, The Netherlands, 1 December.

Hutto, T. D. (1990) 'The Privatization of Prisons', in J. W. Murphy and J. E. Dison (eds), *Are Prisons any Better? Twenty Years of Correctional Reform*, Sage Criminal Justice System Annuals (Newbury Park and London: Sage): 111–28.

Kay, S. L. (1987) 'The Implication of Prison Privatization on the Conduct of Prisoner Litigation Under 42 U. S. C. Section 1983', *Vanderbilt Law Review*, no. 4: 867–88.

King, R. D. and Morgan, R. (1980) *The Future of the Prison System* (Westmead: Gower).

Keating, J. M., Jr. (1990) 'Public over Private: Monitoring the Performance of Privately Operated Prisons and Jails', in D. D. McDonald (ed.), *Private Prisons and the Public Interest* (New Brunswick and London: Rutgers University Press): 130–54.

Leonard, H. B. (1990) 'Private Time: The Political Economy of Private Prison Finance', in D. McDonald (ed.), *Private Prisons and the Public Interest* (New Brunswick and London: Rutgers University Press): 66–85.

Lilly, J. R. and Deflem, M. (1993) 'Penologie en profijt. Een exploratief onderzoek naar de bestraffingsindustrie, *Delikt en Delinkwent*, 23, 6: 511–27.

Lilly, J. R. and Knepper, P. (1992) 'An International Perspective on the Privatisation of Corrections', *The Howard Journal*, 31, 3: 174–91.

Lilly, J. R. and Knepper, P. (1993) 'The corrections-commercial complex', *Crime and Delinquency*, 39, 2: 150–66.

Logan, C. H. (1987a) *Privatising Prisons – The Moral Case 'Enlightenment'*, (London: Adam Smith Institute).

Logan, C. H. (1987b) 'The Propriety of Proprietary Prisons', *Federal Probation*, 3 (Sept.): 35–40.

Logan, C. H. (1990) *Private Prisons: Cons and Pros* (New York: Oxford University Press).

Logan, C. L. (1992) 'Well Kept: Comparing Quality of Confinement in Private and Public Prisons', *The Journal of Criminal Law and Criminology*, 83, 3: 577–613.

Logan, C. H. and McGriff, B. W. (1989) 'Comparing Costs of Public Private Prisons: A Case Study', *N.I.J. Reports*, no. 216.

Logeart, A. (1991) 'Prisons hybrides', *Le Monde* (24 October).

McConville, S. (1987) 'Aid from Industry? Private Corrections and Prison Crowding', in S. D. Gottfredson and S. McConville, *America's Correctional Crisis* (New York: Greenwood Press): 221–42.

McConville, S. (1990) 'La privatisation des services pénitentiaires', in Council of Europe, *Privatisation du contrôle de la criminalité* rapports présentés à la 18e Conférence de recherches criminologiques, 1988, Etudes relatives á la recherche criminologique, vol. xxvii (Strasbourg): 83–114.

McDonald, D. C. (ed.) (1990a) *Private Prisons and the Public Interest* (New Brunswick and London: Rutgers University Press): 1–18.

McDonald, D. C. (1990b) 'The Costs of Operating Public and Private Correctional Facilities', in D. McDonald (ed.), *Private Prisons and the Public Interest* (New Brunswick and London: Rutgers University Press): 86–106.

McDonald, D. (1990c) 'When Government Fails: Going Private as a Last Resort', in D. McDonald (ed.), *Private Prisons and the Public Interest* (New Brunswick and London: Rutgers University Press): 179–200.

McDonald, D. C. (1994) 'Public Imprisonment by Private Means: The Re-emergence of Private Prisons and Jails in the United States, the United Kingdom, and Australia', *British Journal of Criminology*, vol. 43: 29–48.

Mason, T. (1993) 'For Profit Jails: A Risky Business', in G. W. Bowman, S. Hakim, and P. Seidenstat (eds) *Privatising Correctional Institutions* (New Brunswick: Transaction Books).

Matthews, R. (1989) 'Privatization in Perspective', in, Matthews, R. (ed.), *Privatizing Criminal Justice* (London: Sage): 1–23.

Matthews, R. (1990) 'New Directions in the Privatisation Debate?', *Probation Journal*, 37, (June): 50–9.

Ministère de la Justice (1991) *Programme 13 000 Places: I. Présentation générale, II. Evolution Historique et Contenu, III. Marches de Conception. Construction, IV. Marches de Fonctionnement*, Direction de l'Administration Pénitentiaire, Paris.

Moyle, P. (1992) 'Privatising Prisons. The Underlying Issues', *Alternative Law Journal*, vol. 17, 3 (June): 114–19.

Moyle, P. (1993a) 'Privatisation of Prisons in New South Wales and Queensland: A Review of Some Key Developments in Australia, *The Howard Journal*, 32, 3: 231–50.

Moyle, P. (1993b) 'Private sector involvement in criminal justice: explorations of recent developments', *Socio-Legal Bulletin*, Autumn, 9: 41–2.

Moyle, P. (1993c) 'Privatizing Correctional Institutions', paper presented to the American Society of Criminology, Phoenix, Arizona, 27–30 October: 1–15.

Moyle, P. (1994a) 'Private adult custodial corrections in Queensland and the First Wave: A Critical Reflection on the First Three years – Reform or regression?', D. Biles, D. and J. Vernon (eds), *Australian Institute of Criminology. Conference Proceedings on Private Sector and Community Involvement in the Criminal Justice System*, no. 23 (Canberra: AIC): 49–69.

Moyle, P. (1994b) 'Private Prison Research in Queensland, Australia: A Case Study of Borallon Correctional Centre, 1991', *British Journal of Criminology* (forthcoming).

Moyle, P. (1994c) 'Private Contract Management of Corrections. Some Pressing Issues That Will Challenge Victorian Policy Makers', in P. Moyle (ed.), *Private Prisons and Police: Recent Australian and New Zealand Trends* (London: Pluto Press) (forthcoming).

Moyle, P. (1994d) 'Contracting for Private Prisons in Queensland, Australia. Lessons for Penal Policy', *Socio-Legal Bulletin*, Autumn, 12: 16–22.

Mullen, J. (1985a) *Corrections and the Private Sector*, N.I.J. Reports, May, (Washington, D.C.: U.S. National Institute of Justice/NCJRS).

Mullen, J. (1985b) 'Corrections and the private sector', *Prison Journal*, 65, 2: 1–13.

Nathan, S. (1993a) 'Privatisation. Factfile 2', *Prison Report*, Issue 23, Summer: 12–13.

Nathan, S. (1993b) 'Privatisation. Factfile 3', *Prison Report*, Issue 24, Autumn: 13–16.

Nathan, S. (1994) 'Privatisation. Factfile 5', *Prison Report*, Issue 26, Spring: 13–16.

Palley, C. (1993) *The Possible Utility, Scope and Structure of a Special Study on the Issue of Privatization of Prisons*, United Nations, Economic and Social Council, Commission on Human Rights, Sub-Commission on Prevention of Discrimination and Protection of Minorities, 45th session.

Porter, R. G. (1990) 'The Privatisation of Prisons in the United States: A Policy That Britain Should Not Emulate', *The Howard Journal*, 29, 2: 65–81.

Press, A. (1990) 'The Good, the Bad and the Ugly: Private Prisons in the 1980's', in D. McDonald (ed), *Private Prisons and the Public Interest* (New Brunswick and London: Rutgers University Press): 19–41.

Prison Reform Trust (1993) *Wolds Remand Prison. Contracting-Out: A First Year Report* (London: Prison Reform Trust).

Prison Reform Trust (1994) *Privatisation and Market Testing in the Prison Service* (London: Prison Reform Trust).

Robbins, I. P. (1987) 'Privatization of Corrections: Defining the Issues', *Vanderbilt Law Review*, 4: 813–28.

Robert, P. (1988) 'The Privatization of Social', in R. Hood (ed.) *Crime and Criminal Policy in Europe*, proceedings of a European Colloquium, Centre for Criminology Research, University of Oxford: 104–20.

Ryan, M. and Ward, T. (1989a) *Privatization and the Penal System. The American Experience and the Debate in Britain* (Milton Keynes: Open University Press).

Ryan, M. and Ward, T. (1989b) 'Privatization and Penal Politics', in R. Matthews, (ed), *Privatizing Criminal Justice* (London: Sage): 52–73.

Ryan, M. and Ward, T. (1992) 'From Positivism to Postmodernism: Some Theoretical and Strategic Reflections on the Evolution of the Penal Lobby in Britain', *International Journal of the Sociology of Law*, vol. 20: 321–35.

Sellers, M. P. (1989) 'Private and Public Prisons: A Comparison of Costs, Programs and Facilities', *International Journal of Offender Therapy and Comparative Criminology*, 3: 241–56.

Sellers, M. P. (1993) *The History and Politics of Private Prison. A Comparative Analysis* (Cranbury, England; Canada: Associated University Press).

Sichor, D. (1993) 'The Corporate Context of Private Prisons', *Crime, Law and Social Change*, vol. 20: 113–38.

Snacken, S. and Beyens, K. (1994) 'Sentencing and prison overcrowding', *European Journal of Criminal Justice and Research*, vol. 2, 1: 84–99.

Sparks, R. (1994) 'Can Prisons Be Legitimate? Penal Politics, Privatization and the Timeliness of An Old Idea', *British Journal of Criminology*, vol. 43, 14–28.

Tubex, H. and Snacken, S. (1995) 'L'évolution des longues peines ... Aperçu international et analyse des causes', paper presented at the 10th International Congress on Criminology, Budapest, August, *Déviance et Société*, no. 2.

Weiss, R. P. (1989) 'Private Prisons and the State', in R. Matthews (ed.), *Privatizing Criminal Justice* (London: Sage): 24–51.

Index